Edward Campbell

D1825027

The Theater of
Yuri Lyubimov

The Theater of Yuri Lyubimov

Art and Politics at the Taganka Theater in Moscow

ALEXANDER GERSHKOVICH

TRANSLATED BY

Michael Yurieff

PARAGON HOUSE

New York

First English translation, 1989

Published in the United States by

Paragon House Publishers
90 Fifth Avenue
New York, NY 10011

Copyright © 1989 by Paragon House Publishers

All rights reserved. No part of this book may be
reproduced, in any form, without written permission
from the publishers, unless by a reviewer who wishes
to quote brief passages.

Originally published in Russian under the title
Teatr na Taganke, 1964—1984 by Chalidze Publishers. Copyright © 1986
by Alexander Gershkovich.

Library of Congress Cataloging-in-Publication Data

Gershkovich, Aleksandr Abramovich.
[Teatr na Taganke, 1964–1984. English]
The theater of Yuri Lyubimov : art and politics at the Taganka
Theater in Moscow / by Alexander Gershkovich ;
translated by Michael Yurieff. — 1st English language ed.
    p.   cm.
  Translation of: Teatr na Taganke, 1964–1984.
  Bibliography: p.
  Includes index.
  ISBN 1-55778-060-9
  1. Moskovskii teatr dramy i komedii na Taganke.   2. Liubimov, IU,
I. Title.
PN2726.M62M85313   1988
792'.0947'312—dc19   88-10233
                                                              CIP

Manufactured in the United States of America

Form is the more expressive way of saying the truth; it is the maximum sharpness of an idea, capable of breaking through the armor of indifference.

—*Yuri Lyubimov*

Contents

Preface   ix
Foreword   xi

THE TAGANKA IN SOVIET LIFE
One Day at the Taganka Theater   3
Morning: Rehearsal   8
Afternoon: A Conversation with the Director   18
Evening: Master and Margarita in Performance   24

LYUBIMOV AND HIS TIME: Before the Taganka   33

THE STAGE AND THE AUDIENCE
How the Taganka Began   51
Ten Days That Shook the World   57
The Fallen and the Living   67
Rush Hour   74
The Dawns Are Quiet Here   79
Wooden Horses   84
Crime and Punishment   92
The Three Sisters   100

VLADIMIR VYSOTSKY: ACTOR AND POET
The Last Role   109
The Banned Vysotsky   114
The Phenomenon of Vysotsky   127

CONTENTS

THE END OF THE TAGANKA
Pushkin's Boris Godunov—Banned   137
Lyubimov's Revolt   145
At the Bottom   155

LYUBIMOV AND HIS TIME: After the Taganka   167

Epilogue: Lyubimov and Efros   179
Repertoire of the Taganka Theater (1964–1984)   191
Notes   196
Suggested Reading   201
Appendix: Words and Images from the
         Modern Scene   202
Index   221

All of the poems and songs cited in this book have been translated by Michael Yurieff.

Preface

I started writing this book while still in Moscow, and I finished it in America. The Taganka Theater was perhaps the most colorful event in the theatrical life of my generation. One would wonder: What can a handful of enthusiastic actors accomplish in huge, gloomy Moscow? Meanwhile, in the small, cramped Taganka auditorium people drew strength so as not to completely lose heart from the banal lies and despondency of official art.

It is possible that two views on the avant-garde theater of Soviet Russia in the 1960s and 1970s intersected in this book: from inside, through the viewpoint of a Soviet critic, and from outside, through the eyes of an émigré writer who can willfully say what he thinks. I did not consider it right to smooth out the seams; the reader, I hope, will figure out for himself what was written in a conditional tongue and what was written as an open text.

Prominent Soviet critics wrote about the Taganka in its early period—their testimony has not lost its documentary and esthetic value (some of them are included in the book). However, the Taganka's final, more dramatic phase, when the authorities placed a taboo on the theater, forcing its founder and permanent director, Yuri Lyubimov, into exile, was left completely unilluminated.

This book is the first attempt to systematize the material, telling about the theater's more outstanding productions and delineating the particular atmosphere surrounding the theater in Moscow. As has happened many times in Russia, as with the theater of Meyerhold, for example, critics will write about the Taganka when it has already finished its journey. Today, while the theater is still breathing, I want to preserve and convey those emotions, feelings,

PREFACE

and thoughts that the bold and pointed art of the Taganka awakened in us, its contemporaries.

It is my pleasure to thank the Harvard University Russian Research Center for giving me the opportunity to work in their friendly atmosphere.

ALEXANDER GERSHKOVICH

Foreword

When Yuri Lyubimov was named director of the Moscow Theater of Drama and Comedy in 1964, the Taganka Theater was born. It died, or at the very least passed on into another life, when he was deposed in 1984. (Shortly thereafter Lyubimov was deprived of his Soviet citizenship.) The twenty intervening years represent one of the most important and fascinating artistic stories in the history of Russian culture. Several years before the events of 1984, Alexander Gershkovich recognized the role the Taganka had come to play in Russian society and he began collecting material for a book on it. *The Theater of Yuri Lyubimov* is the result of his efforts.

Reading this book produces an effect akin to that of a documentary film montage. Gershkovich, who tells us his primary task is to reconstruct for posterity the atmosphere at the Taganka, utilizes various styles of reporting including interviews, chronologics, memoiristic notes, and stenographs of repartee between Lyubimov and his actors during rehearsals. His account, then, has a personal feel and as a result succeeds eminently in conveying the dynamism of life at the theater.

Lyubimov, as the soul of the Taganka, is at the center of Gershkovich's account, but he never could have realized his dream without the collaboration of numerous other talented artists. The patronage of his good friend, the playwright Nikolai Erdman, the artistic vision of the set designer, David Borovsky, and perhaps most of all the enormous talent of the Taganka's leading actor, Vladimir Vysotsky, provided inspiration and raw material from which Lyubimov fashioned his finished artistic product. The Taganka was the epitome of what a repertory theater should be—a thoroughly collaborative enterprise—and Gershkovich gives us a glimpse into the inner workings of the special and complex relationships that existed at the Taganka.

One should not, however, confuse Lyubimov's reliance on the artistic intuition of trusted colleagues with a lack of a strong, personal vision. Lyubimov's uniqueness, his individuality, his innovativeness, and not coincidentally, his stubbornness, are legendary among those who know him. Rebellion and iconoclasm would appear to be the key elements in at least his artistic, if not his personal, nature.

Like Vsevolod Meyerhold, Lyubimov became a director by rebelling against what he perceived to be a stagnant, primarily Stanislavskian, theater. In his memoirs, *The Sacred Fire (Le feu sacré: Souvenirs d'une vie de théâtre.* Paris: Fayard, 1985), he flatly proclaimed his aversion to the theater of imitation. Indeed, the theater's essence, he noted, is the antithesis of verisimilitude, while the common ground for all great art is the primacy of imagination and metaphor.

Lyubimov's interests in specific aspects of the arts of dramaturgy, prose writing, filmmaking and stage direction tell us a great deal about his own creative work. For example, he sees in the creations of Meyerhold, Eisenstein, and Shakespeare the common techniques of montage, brevity of scenes, and intensity of shock imagery. Shakespeare's imagination, invention, and fantasy are, he says, "three sorcerers without which the theater cannot exist." His attraction to Dostoevsky "is in the text of the work itself; in its density and visual intensity," and he goes on to draw special attention to the "turbulence, states of trance and phantasmagorical characters" which make that novelist's works so theatrical.

As for the role of the actor, Lyubimov believes that the theatrical product is a collaborative effort. "Like Molière," he says, seemingly without excessive bravura, "I have lived a life in the theater as both an actor and the head of a theater." This experience has led him to respect a proper division of labor. "It would be naive," he says, "to think that [the director and actor] occupy the same place in the creative process, [although] I do not make a distinction of hierarchy." He does admit, however, to being an authoritarian and he notes the necessity of "battling" with actors because the good director is an expert in the actor's art just as he is an expert in the art of lighting, sound, decoration costuming and all the other aspects of the stage. At its best, as in his staging of *Lulu*, the opera by Alban Berg at the Chicago Lyric Opera in 1987, Lyubimov's style of directing brings actors, singers, and artistic works themselves to new heights.

Over the years, Lyubimov has expanded the notions of drama and theater beyond their canonical limitations. In doing so, he takes his cue primarily from the tradition that was rediscovered for Russian theater by Meyerhold. Like him, Lyubimov often imparts a carnivalistic atmosphere to his productions, and like Meyerhold, he does not merely reproduce the classics but reinvents them. But where Meyerhold's theater was often "poetic," Lyubimov's theater frequently becomes *a poet's theater*. Thus, traditional dramatic texts play only a small role in his work (though this is naturally less true of his operatic productions). He staged just eight traditional dramatic texts between 1964 and 1982, while for approximately the same period he created twenty-three adaptations from novels, poetry, and popular song. Between 1970 and 1980 he created an additional five productions, or "montages," only two of which originated from dramatic literature. His stagings of journalism by John Reed (Ten Days That Shook the World), novels by Mikhail Bulgakov *(The Master and Margarita)* and Yuri Trifonov *(The House on the Embankment)*, and dramatic adaptations of poetry by Vladimir Mayakovsky, Sergei Esenin, Yevgeny Yevtushenko, Andrei Voznesensky, and Bulat Okudzhava, among others, formed the heart of his output at the Taganka. Clearly, we have here a new idea about what constitutes a "play," or a "theater piece." For Lyubimov, who claims to have been a "bad poet" in his youth, the director is no less a creator than is the writer. And, in fact, Nikolai Erdman once noted that in the absence of an in-house playwright at the Taganka, Lyubimov had taken on that role itself.

Lyubimov's abandonment, as it were, of traditional dramatic texts occurred, coincidentally or not, at roughly the same time as similar experiments were being conducted by such directors as Jerzy Grotowksi and Robert Wilson, and at such theaters as the Julian Beck, Judith Malina's Living Theater, and Joseph Chaikin's Open Theater. While there can be no real consideration of mutual influence, it is intriguing to contemplate the notion that at various corners of the world talented artists were working out similar ideas colored and shaped by the unique circumstances of their different (and sometimes not so different) cultures and social climates. Lyubimov's emergence into prominence outside the Soviet Union at a time when the idea of the *auteur* director has reached its peak is both fitting and timely.

Lyubimov's unique notions of theater are brought to life onstage in part through his bold use of plastic images, elemental techniques of gesture, and the unusual application of lighting and music. In this his work bears a striking resemblance to the new theater of Robert Wilson. Wilson, whose custom it is to completely resolve problems of blocking and structure for his works before he even considers problems of dialogue, would probably understand very well why Lyubimov insists on having a precise mental picture of every element of the work before he takes it to the actors. What Lyubimov's stagings all have in common is their attempt to transmit to the viewer the explosion of inspiration the director has experienced when taking on the raw stuff of someone else's work. Lyubimov seems to go beyond Meyerhold, who had no compunction about drastically altering a work in order to strike closer to its essence; he actively creates new works for the stage rather than seeking to rediscover in a printed text a preexisting work.

Non-dramatic works would appear to provide for Lyubimov both the creative freedom to devise a whole new theatrical structure for a work not originally intended for the stage and the opportunity to tap into themes that are close to his heart. His politically oriented stagings were—and are—almost always a mix of journalism, social observation, moral commentary, drama, and theatrical art. One primary reason for the Taganka's importance as a social phenomenon was that it addressed not only the audience's aesthetic interests, but also its moral concerns: "You don't need me if all you want are glorious voices and nice costumes," Lyubimov has said.

Lyubimov's fascination with the moral or spiritual content of his works is at all times, of course, an integral element of his overall artistic vision, and is not, to borrow a phrase from Peter Brook, a civic-minded weapon to be used for "keeping children good." The spirituality, the sacredness of Lyubimov's theater is essentially the same as that of Brook's "holy theater," or Grotowski's "poor theater." As different as they may be in the way they are realized onstage, they all attempt to transcend the trivial, the temporal, and the superficial and to tap into the universal and eternal elements of the human condition.

When spectators walked past two bloody corpses to take their seats at Lyubimov's 1987 production of *Crime and Punishment* at the

Arena Stage in Washington, DC, an actress carrying a flashlight silently examined their feet for blood stains. The delight of the imaginative playfulness and the solemnity that the play-acting implied were inextricable from one another and immediately tangible to the audience. This is a trademark of a Lyubimov production. When Lyubimov repeats Nikolai Gogal's exhortation that "one should do one's job as if it were an order from God," one senses that his intensity and his sense of his work as a mission are of one and the same source. His dedication and sense of purpose is something he strives, by means of his creations, to bring to all of his audiences, no matter what country they may call home. "It is very important that the theme I choose indeed concerns spectators today," he has said. "If it turns out an enormous number of people need it, if they see it 'as their own,' it means we have made a correct choice." His concern with reaching his spectator's needs accounts for his popularity with audiences all over the world, as well as his former theater's endless clashes with the Soviet government.

Not all of Lyubimov's clashes, however, have been political, for as the critic Alma Law has noted, Lyubimov's creative juices have always thrived on crisis. Indeed, his first production after having been stripped of his Soviet citizenship in 1984 was a scandalous staging of *Rigoletto* at the Teatro Comunale in Florence, Italy, where singers and conductors alike were unable to work peaceably with him. Many of them abandoned the production before it opened. When the opening night audience expressed its displeasure with the staging by booing, Lyubimov himself responded with some antagonistic gestures of his own aimed at the unhappy audience. His unorthodox style caused the soprano Gabriela Benackova to back out of a production of Janáček's *Jenufa* at London's Covent Garden in 1986, and the following year the eagerly awaited American premiere of his legendary staging of *The Master and Margarita* was cancelled on short notice at the American Repertory Theatre in Cambridge, Massachusetts, after a series of charges and counter charges between Lyubimov and Robert Brustein, the ART's Artistic Director. Such confrontations, however, ultimately must be seen as the occasional inevitable consequences of strong artistic visions and egos clashing. Far more often, the sparks that fly are those of artistic inspiration and creativity.

As of this writing, there has been somewhat of a rapprochement between Lyubimov, who now resides in Israel, and the powers that be in the Soviet Union. After meeting in April 1988 with members of his Taganka, who were on tour in Spain, Lyubimov agreed to return to Moscow for a limited time in order to oversee the staging of his version of *Boris Godunov*, which had been banned by the censor in 1982. Whether or not the reunion turns out to be an isolated event, Lyubimov's reputation in Russian theater is already of a stature equal to that of Meyerhold and Stanislavsky, and in time his worldwide reputation will certainly assume a place of privilege alongside the most praised names of twentieth century theater. His impact on British and American theater has already been felt: Arthur Miller said the Taganka had "renewed his faith in theater," Peter Sellars called the Taganka "the most important theater I have seen in my life," and the British critic Martin Esslin called Lyubimov "one of the greatest directors of our time."

The Theater of Yuri Lyubimov is valuable as a chronicle of the theater which, until 1984, was the workshop for nearly all of Lyubimov's greatest achievements. As a contemporary account, it will always be a source of information about one of Soviet Russia's most important cultural phenomena.

JOHN FREEDMAN
Boston, Massachusetts

The Taganka in
Soviet Life

One Day at the Taganka Theater

ON THE MORNING OF MAY 29, 1977, THE ACTORS OF THE Taganka came for rehearsal as usual. At the service entrance—"the watch" in theater slang—news awaited them.

"Did you read it?" asked the "watchman" pointing at the opened newspaper, *Pravda*.

For the first time in many years, the chief organ of the Central Committee of the Communist Party of the Soviet Union broke the silence concerning the country's most popular theater, bursting out in a bitter denunciation of it. In a newspaper article under the bold headline "Black Magic Performance at the Taganka,"[1] the semi-official critic N. Potapov cast upon the theater and its chief director a barrage of accusations and directives. Analyzing the première performance of Lyubimov's adaptation of Mikhail Bulgakov's *Master and Margarita*, the party organ, in the spirit of Stalinist times, charged the Taganka with "lacking the semblance of a specific historical method," "sopping up the impoverishment of the spectator," "petty bourgeoisie narrow-mindedness," and even with the propagation of sex.

The Taganka actors were used to controversy surrounding the theater. They did not enjoy any particular affection from the authorities. Neither Ekaterina Furtseva nor her successor the Minister of Culture, Pyotr Demichev, concealed their hostility. The actors recalled the big scandal over the banned production, *The Life of Fyodor Kuzkin* (*Alive*), based on B. Mozhaev's novel about a contemporary Soviet village. At the time rumors spread that Lyubimov's theater was living out its last days. The theater, however, had not yet known so categorical and public a verdict as that put out by the main party newspaper in 1977. From past experience, all expected the theater to be closed down—if not today, then tomorrow.

Pravda was particularly indignant that in the sixtieth year of the Great October Revolution, when "the whole country was, with dignity, getting ready to welcome the anniversary and the theaters competed in productions on revolutionary themes," Lyubimov, the Taganka's director, dared to stage Bulgakov's *Master and Margarita*,

3

presenting Satan as the main hero. Moreover, in *Pravda*'s words, Satan was presented "righteous as always: a hope for people's spiritual and moral revival, and the deliverance of their centuries-old lust for vile passions, is futile."

"No!" passionately exclaimed the reviewer. "Where Bulgakov's Satan 'hosts the ball,' there is no sign of real history." The explosive verdict concluded: "The director's magic is powerless here." To translate from the Soviet language into Russian, *Pravda* announced the bankruptcy of the Taganka's director, who was not worth talking to. It was a signal for the obstruction of the theater.

For a long time afterward it was forbidden to write about Lyubimov's theater. They were punished by silence, passed by. An attempt was made at creating a vacuum around the theater. Leafing through the thick, comprehensive reference books *Chronicle of Newspaper Articles* and *Chronicle of Magazine Articles* for the years 1978–82 reveals not even a mention of the Taganka, as if no such theater existed on Soviet soil. The Taganka is not usually named in *Pravda*'s announcement section "Today at the Theaters." People went to the Taganka, fought for tickets, and discussed and debated about the theater, but nothing was written on it; rather, nothing was published on it.

It was then that I was seized with an unquenchable desire to tell of Yuri Lyubimov's theater's place in the lives of the Soviet people. Every night except Tuesday, the theater's night off, I frequented the Taganka. I saw their entire repertoire, attended rehearsals, and talked with the actors, the crew, and the spectators, trying to retain everything, to thoroughly investigate the theater, to understand it.

In the theater's atmosphere, in its pulse, in the rhythm that created its best productions, I felt, of late, a familiar condition of the soul: still living in an accustomed dimension, I was yet in a new relationship to it, freeing myself from the crammed, bitter taste of convention, though still obligated to take convention into account and wait for some kind of change. Indeed, the Taganka Theater is, on one hand, completely legal, subject to censorship, and within the jurisdiction of the Ministry of Culture of the RSFSR; on the other hand it is somehow hard to manage because it violates the even flow of Soviet art, stubbornly calling firestorms upon itself. Does not "partisan" art in the spirit of this transitional period— when supposedly something can be said, but not yet fully said— embody this theater? The attentive spectator, finding himself among the lucky ones who have gained access to the productions, cannot help but notice that the theater's small stage, always open to the back brickwork, is *already* not yesterday's Soviet theater, although it may not *yet* be tomorrow's either.

I thought in those days, the Taganka Theater is needed the way it is—with its innovations, simultaneously serious and sarcastic, lyric and garish, unexpected and never indifferent; with the portraits of the dissimilar directors Stanislavsky and Meyerhold next to each other on the wall; with bold metaphors and innuendos; with transparent allegories; and, with the obligatory concessions to the censors and the authorities. It would not have survived on Moscow soil otherwise, and its contemporaries would hardly have understood it.

The Taganka is ahead of its spectators by only one step, not more, giving its art a particularly infectious quality. It appears, in one fine moment, that anyone can make that step right after exiting the theater auditorium onto Upper Radishchev Street. He for whom the steep street is named suggested we look around, "wound our souls," and understand "that the poverty of a person frequently happens only because he gazes evasively at surrounding things."[2] At the Taganka Theater's productions one involuntarily remembers Radishchev. His call "to rise from despondency" in order "to resist delusion" appears quite topical.

"To resist delusion" is the destiny of all leading Russian culture and the source of its strength. The Taganka Theater continues this Radishchevian tradition quite consciously; and is inspired by it in the cycle of its productions on Russian history from Yesenin's *Pugachev* through Chernyshevsky's *What Is to Be Done?*, Reed's *Ten Days That Shook the World*, and Trifonov's *The House on the Embankment*, right up to the last première, Pushkin's *Boris Godunov*, in December 1982.

Today, in the freedom the West takes for granted, Westerners are skeptically surprised at the possibility of a non-conformist theater surviving under Soviet conditions, and they usually judge it by Western standards. Nonconformity in the West and in Eastern Europe is not at all the same. In Russia its character is not so much of political opposition but of moral opposition. Also, the forms are different; in the framework of Western democracy theater acts upon an open text, but within the blinders of socialist democracy, the codes are understood between the lines only by those who wear

5

the blinders. In Western theater a villain in a leather jacket is just a character, but in Soviet theater this indicates a dangerous sedition, even if the "Cheka" uniform is worn by the smooth-tongued courtier of False Demetrius's time.[3] If, in addition, he has a wedge-shaped beard, then the whole epoch of "iron Felix"[4] rises up as if alive before the Soviet spectator.

The more carefully the government controls art, the more refined its language becomes. Russian culture, alas, has a vast and bitter experience in this . . . .

In Soviet Russia, the tradition of moral opposition in art accompanied the history of the theater in all its periods, including the evil years of "Zhdanovism."[5] For example, the opposition of the brilliant Meyerhold to the government's taming of the arts, the levelling of its talents, and to the apathetic atmosphere is well known. This frenzied innovator, who found diverse and subtle forms of theatrical nonconformity even when he turned to the classics (Gogol's *The Inspector General* and Ostrovsky's *The Forest*) or to the writing samples of socialism (*How Steel Hardens*), never surrendered his esthetic positions.

The politics of "twisting arms" in art was also resisted in many ways, though not with identical success, by Tairov, Mikhoels, Diky, Okhlopkov, Akimov, and others. Looking back, we see that there was not a period in the Soviet theater when their resistance ceased. All of them, however, were only daring individual artists until the birth of the Taganka, a collective of like-minded people. It was the half-forbidden, half-allowed fruit of the tormented, quieted, but still alive and unbreakable tree of Russian theater.

Arising in 1964, the sunset of Khrushchev's era, out of a studio in the Shchukin Theatre Institute at the Vakhtangov Theater, the Taganka Theater wasted no time. While still at the studio it established its principles and quickly gathered up its energy. Starting with Brecht's *The Good Woman of Setzuan* the theater created with daring, youthful, sincere enthusiasm productions that became social events, not just theatrical ones: *Ten Days That Shook the World; Galileo, What Is to Be Done?; Hamlet Comrade, Believe; Mayakovsky; Mother; Tartuffe; Pugachev* . . . . What was not a production, however, was the moral and esthetic program: "Rise from despondency! Feel enough strength within yourself!"

Artistically, Lyubimov strives for a theater synthesis in which the theatrical means of expression are not limited by words but include other forms of art such as music, pantomime, song, and even film. The actors of the Taganka must be able to do everything: move, sing, recite poetry, play the guitar, perform pantomime and shadow theater. Through the years, the Taganka created a whole system of theatrical means to convey ideas to the spectator, at times without words. "Theater is not for the blind," said Lyubimov at the beginning, "it is an art that is not only aural, but visual."[6]

In contrast to the painter or poet, the art of the actor lives for the moment, disappearing with the emptying of the stage. Theater is chained to its day, and if its art is not fixed in our memory it will pass without a trace. He who gave the command not to write about the Taganka knew what he was doing. But witnesses live to tell of its triumph. They will preserve the memory of this disobedient theater, attest to its courage and talent, and tell the story of its kind and angry art.

Morning: Rehearsal

THE TAGANKA THEATER IS STAGING THE PRODUCTION *THE House on the Embankment* by Yuri Trifonov. The last few rehearsals are taking place. The theater shops are working a full load.

The stage opening is completely enclosed by glass in metallic frames. As if in a giant aquarium, the mysterious life of the large house, reflected in glass, is inaccessible to people on the street. The elevator door, clanging with a lock, is the only break tying this strange house with the outside world, but is guarded by vigilant watchmen. In the dim light of the electric bulbs, burly guys with indistinguishable faces speak hoarsely and intimately: "To whom?" and "Not allowed."

The small stage of the Taganka, belonging to the pre-revolutionary movie theater Vulcan, is cut mercilessly. The actors are crowded, as the director wants it, forced to play on a narrow strip of the proscenium where two people cannot pass one another. All of the space is taken up by the "aquarium," as the glass and concrete house is now called.

It is hard for the actors to work under such conditions. They have to force their way onto the stage from between the aisles, brushing by spectators in the last row. They have to act in the aisles of the orchestra. From this artificial narrowness and discomfort an almost physical hostility toward *The House on the Embankment*—with its absurd shopwindow sweep for those who live in it, and lordly contempt for those left outside its walls—arises in the hall. In this way, atmosphere is created.

The working through of scenes and the lighting arrangement, and the first complete run-through is taking place. Yuri Lyubimov is in the aisle of the seventh row behind his director's stand. In front of him is a microphone, a small shaded light, and a working copy of the play. Next to him, reclining in a chair, is the author— the quiet and attentive Yuri Trifonov in horn-rimmed glasses with thick lenses. From time to time, in undertones, they exchange responses.

Lyubimov turns on the lamp: "Let's have this scene, and then from the beginning. Did David leave?" He refers to the designer, David Borovsky.

Give me the transition, Veniamin! [This is to the actor, Smekhov, who plays the main role in turn with Zolotukhin.] The transition has to be done more precisely, without any mud. Yesterday I saw *Master*. What happens? The transition from one scene to another is given carelessly. How much time and energy is spent in order to work everything out as it should be, and then you yourselves pull it apart. It gets muddy. From this comes carelessness, disrespect for yourself and the audience. The performers begin "smearing," then the lighting people "smear," then the sound effects people. So, I ask you to make better transitions. Our production is made up of pieces. If we don't put them together as we're supposed to, nothing will come of it. Let's go.

"Veniamin! Listen, try to play the indignation. You have to be- have in such a way as to become offensive." Lyubimov jumps up and goes up to the stage already "in the role." He demonstrates convincingly, sharply.

" 'What did I do to you that was bad? Well, what? Why do you hate me so much?' You play this too lightly. And you should do this as if you were worn out, as if you took validol. Well, try it."

"Again, no reaction. Somehow it comes out literary with you. We don't need literature, more from within."

The actor Aleksandr Sabinin plays the old, lonely, dogmatic pro- fessor.

Very superficial, Sasha. Very superficial. You know, you're going to play the finale in five minutes. And you're lying physically. This is his swan song. A lonely old man. This is just before his death. . . . You're going to the store with empty milk bottles. With empty ones, do you understand, with empty ones! And you say that, after all, Aleksey Maksimovich Gorky wasn't right about something, and you own up to the rightness of Fyodor Mikhailovich Dostoevsky, for whom—before—you wouldn't have given the time of day. For you this is a tragedy of insight. Now, if it was the opposite, then you wouldn't be going to the store with empty bottles, you'd have milk at home. And because at the end of your life you show a preference for Dostoevsky, then God himself ordered you to be without milk.

"Yes, you are absent-minded," he continues. "But what is absent- mindedness in our situation? It is a higher form of concentration. Well, let's go."

9

And so on, without end.

The actor Sabinin, who plays Professor Ganchuk, again enters the proscenium from the stairwell with a cane and empty, jingling milk bottles in a shopping bag. In a revelation, he speaks the thought that has tormented him for so long: "Aleksey Maksimovich is wrong. A new understanding is needed. Everything is allowed, if you have nothing but a dark room with spiders. It exists till now."[7]

Sabinin is significantly better. Strangely, the further an actor progresses in his role and the closer he comes to its essence, the more the director demands from him. On this occasion, Trifonov helps the actor find the necessary psychological frame of mind. "Ganchuk came to this seditious thought about the rightness of Dostoevsky recently, with great difficulty side-stepping his previous convictions. Here, strictly speaking, for the first time he expresses his thoughts out loud. He searches for words. They aren't ready yet, he finds them in our eyes. The quest for a word is needed. . . ."

Lyubimov, catching the author's remarks, realizes them in action, feeling for the intonation. He tries a few variations and, turning to the auditorium, says with an old man's intonation, as if finding himself in the role of Ganchuk:

> It has to be more concentrated. It can't be so quick. It has to be that you yourself felt the meaning of these words. Then, we will also feel them, but if you chatter, then it doesn't reach us. Let's go.

He says this in the rhythm of the character. From the director's fleeting remark not only the sense but the emotional character is acquired.

Sabinin once again returns to the initial boundary at the elevator doors and once again, but differently, very close to what Lyubimov just said, plays the complex and important episode. He is not interrupted now; the actor, with an old man's heavy walk approaches the left portal with particular expressiveness and converses with himself, rather, with his shadow thrown up on the brick wall by the lantern.

But Lyubimov does not stop. It appears that he particularly values this moment when the actor is progressing in his role, entering into that zone of inspiration and change, revealing newer and newer facets. A minute before no one thought of them or even suspected—including the director. Then, the director delivers his favorite phrase, the highest sign of approval and creative achievement: "Well done! The bewitchment begins."

The main difficulty the director, actors, and author fight is the presentation of the modern anti-hero Glebov as the key figure. How did this common conformist, who is ready to agree with notorious but plausible lies, arise in a country of "advanced revolutionary traditions"? Is his conscience clean? Yes, of course; he did not denounce anybody. However, in remembering the past Glebov, with the help of his "double," who comments upon his actions as if "from the author," transfers himself to childhood.[8] A respectable man in a fashionable raincoat and hat clumsily ties a red tie, wiping himself with it as if it were a handkerchief. Our "hero" recalls how in school he betrayed his friends Manyunya and Slava, who pulled a prank on Shelep, the son of the high-ranking Cheka officer Shelepnikov (acted by Dzhabrailov). Pulling at the Pioneer tie that was literally choking him, Glebov recalls how Shelepnikov, threatening in spite of his dwarfish size, interrogated him. Glebov recalls a shaft of bright light being directed into his eyes, and that his boyish stomach rumbled disgracefully. Our "hero" confesses his weakness: "It was so unexpectedly shameful."

"Right there, finally take off your red tie!" Lyubimov jumps up from his place. "Childhood has ended! You are an adult person!"

During rehearsals, Lyubimov's temperamental outbursts alternate with restrained, weary, almost entreating remarks. Any minor faults in the work of the lighting or sound effects crew bring out extreme irritation. "Volodya," he yells, "well, why isn't it coming out with you today? Give me 'the rumbling stomach.' Why can't you? We had a recording of 'water'. Well, find it!" He withdraws in a minute, however, when it is necessary to enlarge and more narrowly focus the anti-hero. Gentle and ingratiating, not at all the "director-despot," he convinces the actor Smekhov:

> Forgive me, Veniamin, but you have to take the main attention upon yourself. You're doing neither this nor that, right now. It's coming out dull, I want to yawn. It needs to be abrupt, varied—then it will be interesting. Well, let's try it again!

After a break an episode is rehearsed that, unfortunately, is not to be included in the upcoming production: the termination and victory of World War II. I cannot recall the Soviet theater ever

11

trying to show it in the unexpected way I saw it at Lyubimov's rehearsal. Why did he refuse to include this scene? It is understandable, but a pity nevertheless.

From the glass of the vestibule, someone is tearing off strips of paper, crosswise, that were glued onto the windows as a bomb shield. At the same time, from somewhere in the distance, an accordion plays and a lonely, hoarse voice reaches us:

> Hey, you, daddy, don't listen to your mom,
> Hurry up and come home.
> It's okay, daddy, that you're a cripple,
> It's okay, daddy, that you're lame.

And that's all.

Even those actors who have seen a few things in their lives could not control themselves or continue working after this naive song. Even Lyubimov took a break. It was so unexpected, truthful, and frightening to hear the voice of victory without fanfare on Red Square, to hear it accompanied by the three-tiered accordion of a war invalid without legs. You could picture him rolling on castors in the carriage of a suburban electric train with his hat on the stumps of his maimed limbs.

Yes, victories are senseless sacrifices as well. Who is to answer for them? Who is to remember them, if not the theater?

Lyubimov stops the rehearsal and keeps silent, thinking about something.

"It's somehow too sentimental," he says, as if to himself.

I probably was not the only one in the rehearsal hall who wanted to object: Leave it, Yuri Petrovich, it works beautifully! However, the overall plan is clearer to the director; he doesn't want tears to cloud common sense. Lyubimov, answering higher considerations, pitilessly removed this touching scene.

Lyubimov always imparts music in a Taganka production with significant shades of meaning. In *The House on the Embankment* the numerous musical interludes beat out the rhythm of the scenes, often as a counterpoint to the mood of the era. Each period had its own music. During the pre-war years it was, of course, the jubilant Dunaevsky: "Oh, how good it is to live in the Soviet land. . . ." During the war, it was Aleksandrov: "Rise up, enormous country. . . ." In the post-war years, Soviet ears were charmed by the ingratiating voice of Leonid Utyosov. The more the country's problems piled up and the more difficult it became to breathe, the more joyously, almost mockingly, sang the Leonid and Edit Utyosov duet: "All's very well, you, you wonderful Marquess, and very well are things with us. . . . Not one, not even one sorrowful surprise. . . ." During the production's most pointed moments, the theater's radio thundered out Utyosov's hit song: "What to say to you in parting, Muscovites, good night, Muscovites, good night. . . ." When Lyubimov uses these hit songs in his production, he well defines his position. He unambiguously shows how art can serve not only truth but lies as well, and in our time, primarily lies.

The scene of the "Zhdanovist" destruction of art, with the party putting out the "fire of cosmopolitanism" and fighting the "antipatriotic critics," was accompanied by the happy, Utyosov motif about "The Fireman" as performed by the carefree Edit. The rehearsal hall fills with her little voice: "He is ready to put out all of the fires, but he wants not to put out my own. . . ."

Lyubimov is constructing a strange *mise en scène*: a small group of people with faces distorted by evil, in uncomfortable poses, crowded into an elevator entrance, with the main "unmasker" sitting in a wheelchair and foaming at the mouth in the direction of the audience because the one who is being unmasked is standing among us in the aisle.

The administration demands that Glebov accuse his academic advisor of cosmopolitanism. But our anti-hero's conscience, which has not completely dozed off, meekly protests, looking for a ruse. Glebov, at the crossroads, recalls how it happened. Lyubimov is willing to spend time to find the right intonation for the beginning of this scene. He approaches the edge of the stage and many times he himself tries to articulate one single thought—"I'm remembering!"—infusing it with many emotional shades of meaning.

The unmaskers are already giving thunderous speeches. The man in the military jacket is particularly savage; his wheelchair is pushed up to the open elevator door. He is a living ruin, but he is full of malice, ready to flood the whole world with it. In a fit of rage he rises from his wheelchair, forgetting his ailment, and curses cosmopolitanism, anti-patriotism, formalism, and constructivism, together with individualism. For a second the paralytic turns into an epileptic and, having exhausted his supply of venom, pale and wrung out, lifelessly falls back into the chair. (Later, in the actual

13

production, he and his wheelchair will be lowered by hand into the orchestra and wheeled through the narrow aisle, forcing those spectators sitting on folding chairs to shy away from him as if he were the plague.)

The "unmasking of the cosmopolitans" is one of the most powerful scenes in the production, but Lyubimov is unsatisfied with it. Again and again, he clarifies his conception to the performers, accompanying his comments with short demonstrations:

> You do not have to explain what cosmopolitanism is. In the few minutes you're given, you won't be able to explain it anyway. Not even in a few hours. It's not even our goal. You make appearances at the meetings and articulate your speeches, throw out slogans and hang labels: "Strike them!" "Put an end to it!" "Eradicate!" "Wipe them off the face of the earth!" "Vermin!" "Secret agent," "He has no passport!," "He has no homeland!"—that is your entire lexicon.

With a low, quiet voice Lyubimov sits down behind his stand and says his singular "Let's go, try it again." Everything starts from the beginning and the actors harness themselves again with inspiration following gradually. Volodya, the sound man, turns the loudspeaker on full power and plays Utyosov's hit song "What to Say to You, Muscovites, in Parting" . . . that concludes the scene.

At one rehearsal, Valery Zolotukhin tries the role of the main character. This is a completely different Glebov—smoothed out, pale, wearing metal-rimmed eyeglasses through which his pupils shine keenly. He has thin, nervously expressive hands that seem to be inquiring about something all the time. Where is this careful man taking us? Why is he so familiar in his frank cynicism with which he makes his career? What kind of social type is he?

Lyubimov interferes significantly less with Glebov-Zolotukhin's monologue than with that of Glebov-Smekhov. He makes only one general comment to Zolotukhin:

> There needs to be a connection with the auditorium in everything that you do, Valery. Understand that Glebov is a *bogatyr* at the crossroads.[9] We substantiate this on stage with the "aquarium" and in the auditorium with the spectator. Start the monologue by addressing the stage, then gradually turn to the auditorium and address us. It'll serve as a connection. Let's try it again!

14

At first everything goes smoothly, in complete accordance with the director's orders, but suddenly there is an outburst. It started with a seeming trifle—a passing scene played by the other actors. That is just the point. Nothing happens by chance in the theater. Everything is tied in a single knot, every detail working for the whole.

Smekhov, Zolotukhin, and others participating in the production sit in the rehearsal hall and look at the stage, commenting on their friends' performances and on the director's remarks. The grandmother episode is being rehearsed. She is played by the character actress Vlasova. Her grandmother is touching: small, hunched, but very lively. The little finger of her hand is fussily tied up and held in front of her, like a church candle.

Lyubimov asks her to play sparingly, getting rid of what he considers to be excess psychologizing and the pauses, and not to "sprawl" all over the role, but just to give the essence. "It's not necessary to decorate this part of the role, get on with it, otherwise we get this 'abscess,' a lyric digression and we lose the tempo, we scatter the attention," he tells her, getting up to show her how the sickly grandmother should be played. Right away Lyubimov's shoulders disappear, he shrinks to half his size, his arms become unnaturally short, and his eyes become empty, faded . . . Lyubimov's transformation provokes an unexpected rebuff by the actress—his image was too convincing. Hurt, Vlasova vents her irritation: "Yuri Petrovich, let me play it at least once without cutting me off, for Christ's sake. . . ." Controlling himself, Lyubimov gently but not without reproach answers her: "I let you play it ten times already, and it's all the same. . . ." She responds: "Maybe it's not coming out to such an extent that it'll never come out." The old actress flares up and leaves the auditorium.

"What's with you today," says the director calmly, without moving, looking at the stage, but clearly having the idle actors sitting behind him in mind. "Our visitors will think God knows what about our relations with one another. Get a grip on yourselves. Let's go."

Here the main argument begins. Zolotukhin objects to Smekhov's interpretation of Glebov as a notorious "slug"; he is against any open judgment of his character. Zolotukhin intends to justify Glebov's conduct and expose his inner duality. Glebov, according to Zolotukhin, is more a victim than an active bearer of evil.

"In essence he didn't do anything evil," announces the aroused actor, stepping through the entrance.

"Didn't do anything?" objects Lyubimov, still sitting and looking at the stage where the actors are guardedly frozen, listening to the heated argument developing.

"His grandmother died," continued Zolotukhin. "His state of being can be understood."

"It's not important."

"Not important? It's very important. Glebov is also a man, he experiences the death of his grandmother, this should be shown."

"Those are your stories," objects Lyubimov, noticeably raising his voice as if calling his opponent out for discussion. "Those are your personal stories!" he repeats. "You thought it all up, so do it like that, but he—" Lyubimov indicates the other performer, "will do it a different way."

"Glebov is his own judge." Zolotukhin flies into a rage, not addressing Lyubimov but Glebov's "double," unwittingly usurping the director's role. "All you do is walk during the whole production and make suggestions as to how he should live."

Lyubimov objects: "Nothing of the kind. He's arguing with us, like we argue with him."

Zolotukhin doesn't give in. "This double is unnecessary. Through acting it has to be conveyed what Glebov is as a phenomenon, without any prompting from the side."

Lyubimov, quick-tempered, counters: "That's the actor's egoism speaking in you. Not everyone is Glebov in life and not every Glebov understands what kind of a social phenomenon he is."

"That's just why the one who plays Glebov should convey this psychologically. He has to play it himself without any double."

Lyubimov, himself a former actor, explodes: "We're not playing psychological drama, we're playing historical memory. That's all your egocentricity as an actor. The endless, 'I, I, I'. . . ."

Zolotukhin argues: "Glebov speaks ironically about himself, this is what should be played."

Lyubimov yells: "Not true!" The auditorium has quieted down, attentive to the argument over creativity. "Not true! It's Hamlet who believes in his father's ghost, but Glebov, if he was in his place, wouldn't believe in it. Glebov is a soulless person, he only believes in the reality of his circumstances. That this needs to be justified psychologically is something else altogether, but to play a psychological drama is not our goal. . . . Let's go."

Zolotukhin, standing in a patch of light in the aisle between the stage and the first row, begins his monologue; we see how everything in the scene begins to play, brightens, and gains meaning and significance.

In front of us the contours of the production are finally beginning to be drawn—the post-war theater chronicle of our lives cut out of a montage of scenes from short pieces not always connected by outer action. They form an organic whole as yet only in the imagination of one person who knows exactly what he wants and what he is searching for.

Afternoon: A Conversation with the Director

LYUBIMOV THE DIRECTOR LITTLE RESEMBLES A RESPECTED MASTER, notwithstanding his worldwide fame. He presents himself as the prevalent European type of contemporary intellectual, more a "physicist" than a "lyricist." In a thin sweater or checked shirt with an open collar (he never wears a tie, not even at diplomatic receptions at the Hungarian Embassy where he often appeared after marrying a Hungarian woman), Lyubimov at first glance charms one with his "Russianness" and slightly bulging cornflower blue eyes. Everyone calls him "Yuri Petrovich," while those close to him simply "Yuri," even though he is as old as the October Revolution.

Before becoming a director Lyubimov usually acted the role of the first lover; he has preserved his soul's freshness and radiant eyes. It seems as if he could still successfully play Romeo or Friday in the film *Robinson Crusoe*, with which he started his career. He has worked in art as a day laborer for almost forty years. He *works*, he does not serve. Meyerhold—one of his mentors and idols—did not like the word "work" applied to the actor's labors. "People work in the garden, but they *serve* in the theater" was how the master usually put it. Time compromised this word. Continuing Meyerhold's principles, Yuri Lyubimov corrects his teacher's conviction: People serve in ministries and various organizations, but in theater they *work*. One of his last poetic productions at the Taganka was called *Work Is Work*.

It is three o'clock in the afternoon on a day at the end of May 1980. Rehearsal has just concluded. Lyubimov lingers in the auditorium for a few minutes, giving out final instructions. He speaks a little with one of the actors, ascends the wide foyer staircase, and passes through the theater's refreshment bar into his room on the second floor accompanied by a staffmember.

He passes through a narrow corridor lined with cells containing the leading actors' bathrooms. There is his old guard, as if on review: Vysotsky, Zolotukhin, Smekhov, Demidova, Slavina, Zhukova, Shatskaya, Shapovalov, Gubenko, Khmelnitsky, Dzhabrailov, Sabinin, Roninson, Shcherbakov. In this congestion and in the ascetism of the decor—only a small make-up table, hard chair, and mirror—there is a close brotherhood without which the lively labors of this actors' artel are inconceivable.

The managing secretary, Elizaveta Innokentievna, hung a sign on the door of Lyubimov's study: "I ask that there be NO SMOKING at Yuri Petrovich's. It is forbidden by the doctors." The rest hour between rehearsals and the evening performance is the best time for an unhurried conversation with Lyubimov. He sits down at his big desk covered with manuscripts and books, on which stands a grotesque bust of Meyerhold made from colored porcelain. While Yuri Petrovich acquaints himself with my questions I look at the walls, covered with autographs of famous people who had been there: cosmonaut Yuri Gagarin, Fidel Castro, Brecht's "comrade-in-arms," Helene Weigel, Japanese film director Kurosawa, Laurence Olivier, and Jean-Louis Barrault, Heinrich Boell, Arthur Miller. People with different views and esthetic tastes gathered in recognition of the Taganka Theater's innovation. An especially expressive review was left by Arthur Miller: "My faith in theater has been renewed." It would be difficult for one professional to receive higher praise from another. Lyubimov values these walls, covered with autographs in a variety of languages, because they help him feel strong and independent.

"Perhaps we should begin," says Lyubimov, sipping hot tea with lemon brought us by the thoughtful Elizaveta Innokentievna. "You ask which date I regard as the true beginning of my theater—while at the studio or with the move to the Taganka? The beginning is here—at the Taganka, but with the production, which was prepared there, *The Good Woman of Setzuan*."

A. G.: *Yuri Petrovich, your theater is still considered young, even though it's been working a long time. Contrary to the predictions of the skeptics, the theater today is, perhaps, stronger than before. Many well-known productions have been put up and preserved in the repertory. Which of them appear to you as turning points, including those that didn't make it?*

YU. L.: We need to be more precise. Sixteen years for a theater is already maturity, it's even a critical age. It wasn't by accident that the "Sovremennik" fell apart in its fifteenth year after Yefremov left and Tabakov retired. Now, concerning "turning point" productions, here things are also far more complicated. The life of each production is a particular one. You grow cold toward some very quickly and then suddenly you start to value them again. For example, long ago, we wanted to close down the production based on Pushkin, *Comrade, Believe*, but we waited, revived it, and it went on again successfully. On the other hand, the production of Boris Mozhaev's *From the Life of Fyodor Kuzkin*, which we liked a great deal, we aren't able to play to this day. [As was mentioned earlier, the production based on the tales of B. Mozhaev was prohibited by the censors.] There are, of course, major productions—of them the main one is *Good Woman*. Everything started with it. Further, there's a divergence in the love shown for a production by the director, audience, and actors. For example, we prepared *Benefit Performance*— a montage from A. Ostrovsky's plays. The actors liked it, but I felt that the work didn't come off the way I wanted it to and I didn't release it. Every production has its own fate. They live and change like people. Vakhtangov's production, *Turandot*, was excellent, but the present-day one is already completely different. The spectator is also important and he tends to be different. Once I was watching *Twelve Angry Men* with Henry Fonda—an outstanding picture. The esthetes were sitting in the auditorium bored, but a simple old woman was watching, hardly breathing, and enthusiastically kept repeating: "How they're judging, how well they're judging."

A. G.: *Your passion for adaptations has become a given. Is this explained by the absence of your "own" playwright or by other circumstances, the nature of the Taganka for example?*

Yu. L.: You see, any composition demands its own solution. If there's a suitable play for us, we put it up. Right now F. Abramov and Yu. Trifonov are playing . . . . We don't have one single playwright who is our own. But we do have a circle of authors, composers and artists—in general we have our own circle . . . . And it's not a closed one.

A. G.: *How would you characterize the style of the Taganka actor?*

Yu. L.: We give preference to the synthetic actor, we strive toward a mastery of music and rhythm, we strive toward being professional in everything. Of course, none of this is an end in itself, but everything else depends on it.

A. G.: *Of late you have been working a great deal in Hungary. Your production of* Crime and Punishment *at the Vigszinhaz Theater in Budapest, according to the Hungarian masters, gave them a great deal. But what meaning did it have for you?*

Yu. L.: Working with actors of other countries helps me to check myself one more time. I won't say that in some way I worked differently over there; I worked in Budapest the same as I do here at home—which I can't say about the opera in Milan, where the conditions were different than the ones we have here in Moscow. In Hungary, I worked as if at home, even though the deadlines were more rigid and everything was scheduled to the hour—even the day of the première was designated at the very beginning of the work, as if no one had any doubts that the production would turn out and that it would be accepted, solved . . . We often don't know this until the last minute at our own theater. Of course, we had our own difficulties there. In Hungary, as in many other countries, there exists an inclination toward the supremacy of the actor. The actors there observe the Table of Ranks far too much. For example, understudies are lit less brightly and the main performers, the "stars," disdain working on the mock-up set: not according to our calling! I deeply regret that I wasn't able to work with the wonderful actor Zoltan Latinovich, who was then no longer among the living. I saw him in the movies and it seems that we would have worked together splendidly.

A. G.: *Why did you choose this particular theater?*

Yu. L.: I didn't choose it. Those who want to work with me are those with whom I work. [Our conversation is interrupted by a telephone call that Lyubimov was apparently waiting for. Jumping up from behind the table, he clung to the receiver and broke into a smile in response to the voice on the other end. He hung up the phone regretfully, and with eyes beaming he triumphantly announced: "My son has his first tooth!" He continued, smiling, "What I like most about him is his complete benevolence and openness. Where does it disappear to later, in man? Coming up to his bed,

21

you say 'Petya'—and he'll smile at you in such a way, he'll roll up his little legs as if saying, 'I'm well.' Yes, you have to be healthy in this life."]

A. G.: *There exists the opinion that you are the type of director who suppresses the actor. But, at rehearsals, I was persuaded that, at times, you are satisfied with the palliative. How is this explained—by faith in the actor, that he will mature in the production, or the understanding, as the French say, that one beauty cannot give more than she possesses?*

YU. L.: Do you know what Stalin answered when for some reason he was presented with this saying? "We'll force your French woman to give it to us twice." So, returning to our subject of the director-despot, I can "talmud" for a long time, but then I see: he doesn't take to it and that's it . . . It becomes necessary to be content with the possible. Or change the performer. But I'm worried that a production, in time, begins to fall apart. Who's responsible? The actors, who are the production part, but the main culprit is the whole school, the actor's school. This is explained in the poor teaching of the actor's craft; actors are not taught the profession in the way musicians are taught to read and write notes. It's impossible to imagine a musician who cannot read notes in an orchestra, but an actor who doesn't know how to do something in his profession is commonplace. It's mainly because of this that a production falls apart.

A. G.: *Was the "playing with shadows"* mise en scène, *the conversation of the professor with himself, found in the production by chance or not? In general, what role does chance or improvisation play in your work?*

YU. L.: A huge one! The role of the subconscious and intuition in stage art is, in truth, enormous. It has not yet been thoroughly studied.

A. G.: The House on the Embankment *fills the emptiness in theater's reflections of the difficult history of Soviet reality. In my understanding, through this production a chain is constructed:* Ten Days, The Master and Margarita, The House on the Embankment *represent 1917, the twenties, the thirties, and the forties, respectively. Is this so?*

22

YU. L.: If you've noticed this, it's necessary to go further. The cut goes from *What to Do?*, then *Mother*, and later the three productions that you named. Historical moments showing the turning points in the life of our society for the last hundred years. *The Dawns Are Quiet Here*—isn't this a reflection of our war years in theatrical language? And *Wooden Horses*? What is it, if it's not a tale of the fate of our post-war villages? There is something else concerning *The House on the Embankment*. I want to look at Glebov as a social type. How, through what means and thanks to what, did this human species come about?

A. G.: *Your theater, it seems, is allowed a lot?*

YU. L.: Not more than others. I would even say less. *The Thirteenth Chairman* was allowed the Vakhtangovites—but us—hardly. There are also people who are trying to get our theater building demolished as soon as possible. I am fighting for us for three years already.

A. G.: *But they're constructing an excellent building for you! Incidentally, when will you open it?*

YU. L.: I don't know. Ask Duppak.[10] He's fighting for it. But I still don't know what will come of all this stylishness. With great difficulty I got them to put some hard chairs in the auditorium. They wanted velvet ones, soft ones—so that it'd be more comfortable to sleep. The acoustics are repulsive. The secret of theatrical acoustics is lost, it seems. No one remembers anything.

A. G.: *Do you find that you and the actors in your theater feel somewhat tired and dissatisfied that the energy which you give your work brings only an esthetic effect in the best circumstances?*

YU. L.: I didn't quite understand the question, but I'll answer it like this: time will show what influence our theater has had.

Evening: Master and Margarita in Performance

THE PEOPLE WHO LIVE NEAR THE THEATER ARE USED TO GROUPS of people, both young and old, surrounding them on the platforms and escalators at the subway station Taganka and at the exit to the square between six and seven o'clock, all asking the same question: "Do you have an extra ticket?"

The old auditorium of the Taganka Theater had slightly more than 600 seats (477 with folding chairs in the orchestra and 136 in a narrow balcony), but there were hundreds more spectators wanting to get in, especially for the most sensational productions. *Master and Margarita*, severely criticized by the party press, was such a production.

When Bulgakov's novel was released to the world in 1966—thanks to a miracle in the politics of Soviet publishing—it caused a cultural shock. Its most striking feature is the unusual narrative form: tying into one knot such unconnected themes as myth and reality, Biblical past and the everyday world, and contemporary man. Every reader uncovered his own meaning: some found evangelical truths; others, mysticism; still others, the naturalism of real Moscow. All readers found a forgotten feeling for genuine art in which nothing is impossible, no theme, ideological direction, or narrow esthetic norm is forbidden or imposed from outside.

This did not mean, however, that everyone understood the underlying philosophical motives of the novel right away. The literature of "socialist realism" (with a moral), expressed in the style of terse telegrams, noticeably dulled the Soviet reader's sensitivity to indirect expressions in art and to the free play of fantasy.

The grotesque narrative of Moscow during the New Economic Policy (NEP), with old and new mixed together in freakish forms of everyday life and consciousness, connected with difficulty to the parallel plot of distant and vague Biblical times. So Bulgakov's novel remained an artistic puzzle for many Soviet readers.

Nevertheless, the novel appeared on the stage of the Taganka with another focus and approach, as if its presentation was figured out for the first time. Two heterogeneous planes combined. The production sparkled like a precious stone polished by a skillful engraver. Biblical motifs and current everyday life, philosophical thoughts and vulgar daily occurrences—the top and bottom of man's existence—interlaced and complemented one another, creating a sense of mixed character and full-bloodedness in life, and a carnival-like atmosphere.

A huge pendulum—a gigantic clock with a strange Roman dial—serves to substantiate the production's concept. Lowered into the middle of the proscenium, it hangs over the auditorium threateningly, as if counting out rebellious time's flight, suddenly dying down in moments of confusion. This theatrical metaphor was first found in *Hamlet*, another of Lyubimov's productions. Lyubimov repeats the device in *Master and Margarita*, turning it into an important generalization of the whole action. The same applies to the "brightening up" effect: During the performance the director periodically turns on the auditorium lights, underlining the particular actuality of one thought or another. *Master and Margarita* is a condensed encyclopedia of the theater's artistic devices, worked out in Lyubimov's studio over many years. These devices, by no means devoid of outrageous acts or even, if you like, theatrical "hooliganism," are intended to knock the spectator out of his drowsiness, activate his thoughts and fantasy, and show him that he came to the theater, not a boring lecture.

Because of the cramped playing space the narrow vertical portals at the ends of the stage are used, forming a sort of frame for the production. On the left is a corner of a life-size brick house in Moscow bearing the number 302B; on the right, in contrast, is a wide window pierced by the scorching sun, with a model of Pontius Pilate's Yerushalim courtyard. Two historical realias, very distant from one another, help us to go easily from one time to another during this three-hour production. Past is constantly linked with present.

Lyubimov's production consists of a few artistic layers. It is a montage: a variety of scenes, unbalanced in continuity and meaning, but each complete in itself. Individually the scenes reveal a new quality; every episode solves its own problem, suddenly becoming dependent on the whole and bringing us closer to the central point.

I saw this production three times and each time I discovered, surprisingly, new and deeper levels. At first the production's spectacularity, especially the epic Biblical scenes, startles one with its

25

theatricality. In his approach to this material Lyubimov has virtually no predecessors on the Soviet stage. He stylizes the evangelical parable, painting in bold strokes without lingering for details. The eternal duel between good and evil, falseness and truth, spiritual freedom and crude pragmatism is presented in the conflict between truth-loving Yeshua and his antagonist, the mighty Roman procurator Pilate. It turns out that Bulgakov's Pilate is not so simple. Like many mortals he suffers not only from headaches but from his conscience as well—something not everyone has. It was not only his will to say one thing and think another; his times were also to blame. It is somehow easier for us to understand him than the unyielding disciplinarian Yeshua. Why? What relationship does the conflict between Yeshua and Pilate have to our everyday life in Moscow?

Theater does not hurriedly form conclusions. Before leading spectators to an answer it entertains us with juicy, genre scenes of late Moscow. We are witness to the meeting of the people's poet, hardheaded Homeless (acted by M. Lebedev) and the literary consultant from the Writer's Union, the confirmed atheist Berlioz (acted by A. Sabinin) at the Patriarch's Ponds. The latter heatedly proves that there is no randomness in nature, that there are materialistic explanations for everything; but, in a minute, he himself becomes a victim of faith, slipping on spilt sunflower oil and falling under a trolley car.

Later we find ourselves in a Moscow psychiatric hospital where the unlucky poet, shaken by the mysterious death of Berlioz, is transported in just his underwear after a futile attempt to bathe in the Moscow River. Then we attend the scandal at the Writer's Club. Next we move to apartment 302B where a dangerous company of foreign touring artists headed by the magician Woland (acted by V. Smekhov) make their home. We see them mock "hard-working Soviet people" and the corrupt superintendent, humorously played by S. Farada.

When the other provincial Soviet office worker Poplavsky (acted by G. Roninson) arrives in Moscow for his nephew's funeral, the foreigners do something really outrageous: They seat a live white mouse on the bald head of this simple Soviet man.

A moment later they shock the audience as well; one of the magician's helpers, the cat Behemoth (acted by Yu. Smirnov), an ordinary man except with a feline tail, cleverly switches the live mouse with a plaster one, bites its head off and chews it with good appetite. Squealing is heard throughout the auditorium. This phantasmagoria is completed by another of Satan's helpers, the terrorist Azazello (acted by Z. Slavina) who, dressed in a black pants suit, expels shafts of flame from his mouth. The theater brings a hackneyed newspaper thesis to the point of absurdity.

And so goes this incredible production from one attraction to another—from elevated epic scenes, to vulgar, low scenes, to the most fantastic. Poetry is grounded in prose and myth in reality until the finale, Satan's farewell ball, when everything merges into one general metaphor: Life is the most absurd theater.

The artist's fate in the world, although kept in the background, nevertheless continually intersects with the Biblical hero's fate. Herein lies some miscalculation on the part of the director and error on the part of the performer, who, in this grotesque production, gave the Master tones that were too pastel-like. The artist and the Biblical hero simultaneously win and lose. Both are crushed and crucified by reality, and both found immortality in that they did not betray themselves or give up their internal commandments. The difference between them lies more in their scope and, of course, in the historical circumstances than in the quality of their actions.

The more attentively one observes Lyubimov's production the more obvious it becomes that he prefers to bring together distant eras through theatrical means rather than mere juxtaposition. This is exactly what *Pravda* faulted Lyubimov for when they said he was "lacking the semblance of a historical method," as if one were not talking about a work of art but a serious sociological investigation. In this lies Lyubimov's service; through theatrical means he managed to show the connection between epochs, repeating man's behavior in analogous historical circumstances. Numerous examples exist of theater, using the conditional language of art, representing its own time through other, remote epochs.

In his soul, the all-mighty procurator Pilate admits Yeshua's innocence but frightens himself with his human weakness. He suspiciously glances at the walls of his Jerusalem courtyard as if searching out spies. He articulates the clichéd text in a deliberately loud voice without having any faith in it: "There has not been and there will not be a power on earth greater than Caesar's!" The actor Shapovalov, playing without make-up (as did everyone in the production), with his kind, wide Russian face and characteristic smirk, first slyly and quickly glances at the walls that "listen," then furtively, mockingly at the auditorium. Everyone belongs to him, our contemporary Shapovalov, not to some Biblical Pilate.

It is also easy to recognize contemporary prototypes among Satan's underlings: the pushy Koroviev (acted by I. Dykhovichny), "Citizens! Why are you upsetting the tourist?"; Azazello (acted by Z. Slavina), "No documents—no man"; the thievish cat Behemoth (acted by Yu. Smirnov) meows, "My paws would sooner shrivel up than touch something that didn't belong to me." The black magician Woland himself is fully recognizable in the resounding line: "Every department must mind its own affairs." All of this "re-upholstering" of the text with the "new Soviet speech" culled from newspaper clichés creates, in sum (accompanied by the actors' mimicry and intonations), that social and psychological environment characterizing the Soviet image of life as a higher mysticism, a result of healthy reasoning.

The Biblical theme concerning Yeshua and Pilate is strikingly superimposed on contemporary life, creating one allusion after another. This stage focus helps us penetrate the timeless connection between man and his environment and understand the real factors that bring into motion the hidden mechanisms of life's circumstances. The past and the present become so interconnected in Lyubimov's production that one stops focusing on the transitions; only the pendulum, which lives by a special rhythm—leisurely stiffening in hard times or becoming feverishly crazed in periods of shock—will implacably count out the minutes and hours of man's centuries as they depart into oblivion.

The spectator, accustomed to ready-made ideas, will ask "What is this production about?" recalling the old theater joke in which an actor complains to the director that he cannot quite grasp the role's through line of action. The director answers: "Look, brother, what's this about action and through line. You have to know how to act!"

The last scene in the production seems to move the action along least, and also seems least necessary. However, in my opinion, it reveals the director's idea from an unexpected angle. Writes Lyubimov in the preface to his 1985 published adaptation of *Master and Margarita*: "I wanted to stage one of my favorite books. I heard a great deal about the sorrowful life of that brilliant master, M. A. Bulgakov, from my late friend N. R. Erdman. I wanted to give the entire cumulative experience of the theater, the best of its theatrical discoveries to that man with that sad fate."[11]

Lyubimov's admission indicates the main source of his inspiration in working on *Master and Margarita*—admiration for the lofty act of the artist with the "sad fate" who, in Soviet times, managed to resurrect the concept of *kalokagatii*: the ethic victory of beauty over the outrageous and false. Forgotten in our century, this category of Greek esthetics, which believes that an ethical deed gains an esthetic quality and, in and of itself, arouses a feeling of beauty, was expressed by Lyubimov in the Satan's farewell ball scene. Here Margarita, saving the world from dirt and lies, becomes the central figure as the embodiment of pure beauty. She accepts Woland's conditions to become the hostess of the ball, receiving guests in the nude (the custom of evil spirits), in exchange for the rescue of the Master's burned manuscript.

It is well known that in the Soviet theater nudity is viewed unfavorably as a product of decadent culture. The Taganka Theater allowed itself some doubt about this principle of socialist morality. For a long time the theater showed a Soviet woman naked, though granted only from the back. Was it not strange that nothing horrible happened? No one fainted, the government did not collapse. The idea was put metaphysically: Beauty runs the ball. She, not "class consciousness" or other wordly powers, emerges as victor in the duel between good and evil.

The actress Shatskaya, possessing an exceptional physique and a halo of short, golden curls, receives guests courageously, sitting with importance at the edge of the stage on a wooden executioner's block between two picturesquely plunged axes.

Her wonderful, marble body radiates in the projectors' bright rays. Next the last, main miracle occurs. After being blinded with feminine beauty, your eyes start to adjust, and you begin to perceive the spectacle from a purely esthetic point of view as a work of art, similar to looking at Venus's torso in the museum.

Some will interpret Margarita's nudity, in concert with their narrow-minded tastes, as a cheap attraction designed for the "spectator's poverty"—a view akin to that of the *Pravda* reviewer. But Lyubimov knows that other types of people are not yet extinct in Moscow, people for whom the beautiful is not foreign, for whom Margarita's sacrificial nudity is a lofty deed.

Even Satan, for whom nothing is sacred, falls under beauty's power. He exclaims in the quieted auditorium: "Manuscripts don't burn!" resurrecting the Master's novel from ashes.

"Manuscripts don't burn!"; beauty is imperishable; real art will find its way to the people no matter how it is strangled, burned, or trampled by those in power. This is what the Taganka production is about.

The performance ends. Yeshua and Woland appear from either side of the curtain. The pendulum with the increasing force of time moves between them. A chalice burns with eternal fire for the poor Master. Holding portraits of Bulgakov, the actors come out on stage, wearing sad looks that ask: "Will they understand me?"

Lyubimov, in exile, described his work on this production:

No one believed that I would be allowed to do it, not even the actors. As always, the administration announced that our people do not need this, and that they wouldn't give any money for the production.

I took pieces of old sets: the curtain from *Hamlet*, which could fling itself about the stage in any direction, like us sinners, the balcony from Y. Trifonov's *The Exchange*, the pendulum-clock, on which Woland and his entourage ride, the platform from poor, banned *Alive*, a splendid story by B. Mozhaev, who is, fortunately, alive. Solzhenitsyn, Erdman, Trifonov, and millions of readers regarded it highly. The blocks from the production on Mayakovsky, *Listen!* The gold frame from Molière's *Tartuffe*, in which Pilate formally sat. Unfortunately, we had to rent his favorite dog, Banga. And that's how we got by without Soviet money. I went to countless departments, to the Central Committee, to ministries, to the committee on cultural heritage, to the chairman, K. Simonov; the whole committee gave a favorable response, showing courage.

Having spent three years, on the thirteenth year of the theater, we were finally able to perform the production, in spite of the threats and discontent of the administration.[12]

Lyubimov and His Time: Before the Taganka

YURI PETROVICH LYUBIMOV'S BIOGRAPHY COMPRISES TWO halves: Prior to 1964 he was one of the successful, loyal Soviet actor-laureates, one of the domestics of the party, affectionately glorified, awarded and blessed; after 1964 he was an artist-rebel, the enfant terrible of Soviet art, who declared a war against apathy, lies, party bureaucracy and government leadership.

The outward circumstances of his life previous to his heading the experimental theater-studio at the Taganka do not tell how official Soviet art found someone who would overthrow it. "No one predicted the swift directorial take-off of Yuri Lyubimov," wrote the patriarch of Soviet theater criticism and shrewd connoisseur, P. A. Markov. "Among the Vakhtangov youths in the forties, he was one of the most promising actors—thanks to his temperament and charm he was *made good use of* [my emphasis], as they used to say in the old days, playing the young hero."[1] However, even Markov in his brilliant essay on Lyubimov does not go into detail about the circumstances of his life, his self-education, and his development as an individual and artist. Soviet criticism generally disregards these "trifles" though it occasionally likes to repeat the familiar expression of Saint Exupéry that "a man is a product of his childhood."

Yuri Lyubimov is the same age as the October Revolution. He, along with his country, went through all the stages of the "big path"—from the epoch of War Communism, through Stalin's five-year plans and purges, to the unmasking of the personality cult, to Andropov's policy of "developing" or "realistic" socialism. In a way, Lyubimov's path is the same as that of the first generation artistic intelligentsia, which, as the product of Soviet education, became disillusioned in its declining years with Soviet utopias. Its recovery of insight was long and agonizing. Not everyone found enough strength and decisiveness within themselves to be consistent to the end. But many of those who hid their dissent even from themselves could say, in the words of Boris Pasternak, that life was spent "in a struggle with one's self / with one's self."[2]

The second atypical—in the Soviet understanding—half of Lyubimov's creative journey begins in the spring of 1964. It forces a more intense look at those personal experiences and circumstances that one fine day awakened the rebel in him. If this second hypostasis of Lyubimov did not exist, perhaps his early successes would have long been forgotten, like his acting partners from stage and screen of the forties and fifties.

The Taganka illuminated Lyubimov with its never-fading light, leading him into world theater history. However, do we know much about that which preceded his rise? Information about it needs to be gathered like crumbs. Without taking the past into account, it is hard to understand what we call today "Lyubimov the phenomenon." Let's try to construct a chronology.

On his father's side Lyubimov belongs to an old peasant family. His grandfather and grandmother remembered serfdom and *corvée*.[3] After the 1861 decree his grandfather and his sons received an allotment of land in the village of Abramovo near Yaroslavl, and in a half century of management turned it into a strong, self-sufficient farm. Lyubimov's grandfather had a stern temper but was fair, and was respected as a hard-working farmer and family man. The family members were Christians.

Lyubimov's mother descended from gypsies. Her marriage caused a storm in her husband's patriarchal family, affecting his relationship with his grandfather. However, Lyubimov's father insisted and, settling down to married life, separated from his parents, moved to Yaroslavl, and took up a trading business. Lyubimov recalls his father having a strong, independent personality and a passionate love of books, which he collected, especially those on Russian history.[4] On the shelves at home stood yellowing volumes of Karamzin and Soloviev that Yuri inherited and preserved many years later. The volumes remained in Moscow when Lyubimov left the country.

On the eve of World War I the newlyweds had their first-born, giving him the Biblical name David. Soon after a daughter, Natalia, was born. By that time Lyubimov's mother finished her education and became a teacher. At first family life in Yaroslavl fell happily into place, with his strict grandfather and stubborn father reconciled.

September 30, 1917. The day, according to the Russian Orthodox calendar, of Saint Sofia and her daughters Faith, Hope, and Love, a second son, Yuri, is born.

At that time Yaroslavl still had the look of one of old Russia's most beautiful towns. It is located some 125 miles from Moscow on the banks of the upper Volga, surrounded by a gentle landscape—water-meadows and forests—very dear to the Russian heart.

The town's special pride was the local theater, established during Catherine II's reign, when the Yaroslavl merchant Fyodor Volkov started his "comedic" business. He created the first Russian acting troupe in the country, giving rise to the professional, native theater.

1918. Yaroslavl answered the October Revolution with a revolt heard throughout Russia. In July the townspeople, with the help of the military and even the local monks, rose up against the Bolsheviks, rescinded all of Lenin's decrees, and for a short period restored the old power structure that existed previously. The mutiny was, however, mercilessly crushed, and Soviet power once again triumphed in Yaroslavl, creating an especially savage order there.

1922. The Lyubimov family abandons Yaroslavl and moves to Moscow. The reason for the move is withheld from the children, though it soon becomes clear. The Lyubimovs settled into what was then the outskirts of the capital, a working-class neighborhood near Taganka where Yuri's father's sister lived. The country moves out of War Communism and enters into the New Economic Policy (NEP). Summers the children visit their grandfather in the village of Abramovo, help him with his work, look after the apple trees— their grandfather's pride—have long discussions with him, and delight in the clear and simple everyday life of the traditional Russian countryside as it lived out its last days. David became interested in painting and took Yuri with him when sketching. Yuri learned how to hold a brush.

1926–27. NEP ends with massive repressions against the "NEP-men," those who believed in the policy and lifted the country from collapse and hunger. Lyubimov's father was arrested first, then his mother and aunt. The three children, ranging in age from ten to fourteen, were left alone in a strange, huge city with almost no means of support. The "NEP-men" were thrown into jail so that their money, so necessary for the building of socialism, could be squeezed out of them. The people joked: "If you don't have money, why bother building?" A ransom is demanded of Yuri's parents as a condition for freedom. His mother buys her freedom, giving up her last savings to her imprisoners, and returns home. His father remains in jail a few years longer. The children bring him parcels.

Yuri, David, and Natalia go to school, carrying with them the label "disenfranchised ones," as those lacking civil rights were called.

1928. The dispossession of the *kulaks'* begins. Lyubimov's grandfather is expelled from his home in Abramovo, from the familiar old spot where he long lived and worked. Though eighty years old, he is still independent and works in the fields. Lyubimov, remembering his grandfather's story, tells what happened: A few strangers appeared at his home and demanded that he leave the village. As someone from the old regime he did not understand what they wanted from him, taking them for ordinary bandits and wanting to push them out the door. The old man was brutally beaten and physically thrown from the house without a chance to take anything with him.

Lyubimov's grandfather joined his son's family in Moscow. Yuri met him at the train station. They travelled on a horse-drawn tram. His grandfather gave him a ruble for meeting him. Yuri refused it, but his grandfather insisted. Yuri remembers his words: "Every labor earns its payment. If they begin to rob a person's labor, he will have nothing left." These words engraved themselves in the young boy's memory for a long time, though he would not make it known until many years later.

1931–32. The country is gripped with enthusiasm for five-year plans. David enters the Young Communist League and becomes an active participant in the new life. Yuri accompanies him to meetings and listens to the endless speeches, absorbing the essence of the League era. We do not know if he joined the League or not, but following his older brother's example he professes to communist ideals and wants to be just like all those around him—a real fighter for the bright future.

The relationship of the children to their father, released from prison, remains unchanged; they do not reproach their parents for their past. Family ties prove more lasting than the new morals. Their parents devote a great deal of attention to them, and true understanding reigns.

Yuri's father takes him to the theater for the first time to see Maeterlinck's *Blue Bird* at the Moscow Art Theatre and later Stanislavsky's famous *Woe From Wit*, in which the renowned Moskvin, Kachalov, and Luzhsky perform. The symbolism of *Blue Bird* and the realism of *Woe From Wit* are the first contacts Yuri Lyubimov has with the sacred fire of theatrical art, to which he is drawn from that day forward.

1933. Yuri quits his studies and enters an electromechanical training school located at Taganka Square, a few steps from the spot where, thirty years later, he will settle into his own theater.

In the evenings he visits classes at the choreographic studio, learning stage movement based on Isadora Duncan's method. He decides to become an actor.

1934. Lyubimov takes an examination at the theater school of the Second Moscow Art Theatre, which grew out of the First Studio of the Moscow Art Theatre under the direction of Stanislavsky's favorite students, Evgeny Vakhtangov and Mikhail Chekhov. The former had died long before; the latter had fled Soviet Russia and lived in the United States. The theater's leadership now consisted of Stanislavsky's capable later students, Bersenev, Diky, and Birman, among others. The Second Moscow Art Theatre distinguished itself from its forefather studio through its searching atmosphere, aspiring to develop Stanislavsky's teachings while counteracting the dogmatic training of his system.

Lyubimov surprises the selection committee at his entrance examination; instead of the usual fable, poem, or monologue, he chooses a speech, written by Yuri Olesha, from the recently concluded First Constituent Congress of Soviet Writers (August-September). The speech was ideologically "inconsistent," calling a series of censures upon itself, as was Boris Pasternak's presentation at the Congress. Instead of the devotional glorification of Stalin, the party, and the government, Olesha admitted to not understanding Soviet "newness," and being unable and unwilling to write about it because he does not feel it as an artist. He asks what moves the new generation of Soviet people before him. He also speaks of the eternal laws of creativity, irreplaceable by opportunism without threatening the extinction of inspiration within the writer's or poet's soul. To his future teachers the seventeen-year-old Lyubimov read the following:

An artist is often asked: How do you know this? Did you think this up yourself? Yes, the artist thinks everything up himself. Of course, nothing can be thought up that isn't in nature. The relationship between the artist and nature, however, is such that she reveals some of her secrets to him, she is more sociable with him than with others . . . .

The first young generation is growing in this State, the young Soviet man is growing. As an artist, I throw myself on him: who are you, what colors do you see, do you dream dreams, what do you dream about, how do you perceive yourself, how do you love, what feelings do you have, what do you reject, what do you admit, what kind of person are you, what prevails in you—feeling or reason, do you know how to cry, are you tender, did you understand what frightened me, what I didn't understand, what I feared, what kind of person are you—a young man from a socialist society?"[6]

Lyubimov is accepted into the studio. Many years later, at his sixtieth birthday celebration, Yuri Trifonov, who shares Lyubimov's views on art, will remember this episode as an early symptom of the future director's divergent views: "He liked this speech a lot. In it were pointed words, thoughts, dignity, pain and contemporaneity. Out of this, thirty years later, he would make theater."[7]

1936. Lyubimov becomes familiar with the elements of the actor's craft according to the Stanislavsky system and takes his first independent steps on stage, performing in episodic roles such as Jacques Duvale's *Compassion for Life.*

A campaign to fight formalism develops, directed primarily against Meyerhold, but also affecting other supporters of the sole method for Soviet theater, announced as the Moscow Art Theatre "method." On February 28 a resolution of the USSR and the Central Committee of the Communist Party of the Soviet Union is made public concerning the dissolution of the Second Moscow Art Theatre, finding it does not answer the demands of its time. The party assumes the role of supreme judge in matters of art.

K. S. Stanislavsky, ill, gives up leadership of the theater, locking himself up in his private residence and communicating with the outside world in his spacious study. He fought for the Second Moscow Art Theatre prior to the resolution. Expressing his dissatisfaction with its activities, reproaching his leading actors for breaking laws of nature and in striving for the externals that lead to success (he asked the actors who had come to visit him: "What do you believe in? What do you consider to be theater?"), Stanislavsky was, along with this, against the closing of the theater and agreed to write the government a petitioning letter. However, Radomyslensky[8] recalls him "consulting higher organs," finding out that the closing of the Second Moscow Art Theatre has already been decided; he does not send the letter. The authorities stop considering Stanislavsky's opinion and use his name as a screen in order to carry out the political line.

After the Second Moscow Art Theatre closes, part of the troupe goes to the Moscow Art Theatre, others to the Maly, and a group headed by Diky to the Massoviet Theater. Yuri Lyubimov makes his own choice, and to conclude his education enters the institute at the Vakhtangov Theater.

1937–38. The country is gripped in a wave of mass repressions—terror rules Moscow. Art competes with itself in subservience to the regime. The composer I. Dunaevsky produces the song "Oh, It's Great to Live in the Soviet Land."

The Vakhtangov Theater, headed by Ruben Simonov, betrays the tenets of its teacher in creating a series of frankly opportunistic productions specializing in Leninist themes. The production *Man with a Rifle* by N. Pogodin begins a "Leniniana" in Soviet art, the actor B. Shchukin, famous for his comic role as Tartaglia in Vakhtangov's *Princess Turandot*, sets a standard for Soviet theater in his idealized portrayal of Lenin.

Lyubimov, still a student, appears in this production in a small role. He, like many of the actors, is carried away with the craft and expressiveness of the talented Shchukin's Lenin. Lyubimov is staggered by the explanation Shchukin gives his scene partners about the secret to his success in this role: "I am indebted in this to my own Tartaglia."

Lyubimov attends a few rehearsals conducted by Meyerhold, who is preparing a production of *Boris Godunov*. The authorities will never let him complete it.

In January 1938 the Moscow theater world is shocked with the news that the Meyerhold Theater, deemed harmful and foreign to Soviet art, is to be dissolved. The resolution runs as follows:

The Committee on Matters of Art under the Sov-nar-kom of the USSR recognized that the Meyerhold Theater has completely lowered itself to positions foreign to Soviet art and has become foreign to the Soviet spectator. This was expressed in the following:

1. The Meyerhold Theater, during the course of its entire existence, could not free itself from completely bourgeois, formalistic positions foreign to Soviet art. The result of which, in subservience

to leftist trickery and formalistic affectations, even classic works of Russian dramaturgy were shown in this theater in a distorted, anti-artistic manner, with a perversion of their ideological essence (*The Inspector General, Woe From Wit, The Death of Tarelkin* and others.)

2. The Meyerhold Theater showed itself to be fully bankrupt when producing plays from the Soviet dramaturgy. Productions of these plays gave perverted and defamatory presentations of Soviet reality, permeated with double meanings and even with straightforward anti-Soviet malevolence. (*The Suicide, A Window to the Country, Comandarm 2* and others.)

3. The Meyerhold Theater not only did not prepare any productions for the twentieth anniversary of the October Revolution, but made a politically hostile attempt to stage a play by Gabrilovich *(One Life)*, an anti-Soviet perversion of N. Ostrovsky's famous work, *How Steel Is Tempered.* In addition to the preceding, this production abused the government's support of the theater, which is accustomed to living on the government's financial subsidies. In view of all this, the Committee on Matters of Art under the Sov-narkom of the USSR resolves to: (a) liquidate the Meyerhold Theater as foreign to Soviet art (b) utilize the theater's troupe at other theaters (c) give special attention to the question concerning the possibility of Vsevolod Meyerhold's future employment in the field of theater.[9]

Under orders of the party Moscow theaters hold meetings to support this resolution. Personal letters are demanded from Honored Artists of the USSR deploring the harmful activity of the brilliant director Meyerhold and thanking the party and Comrade Stalin for his wise direction of art. Lyubimov witnesses Boris Shchukin, his favorite actor and a big admirer of Meyerhold, sign a letter accusing him of sabotage. At the same time Lyubimov discovers that V. I. Nemirovich-Danchenko, the de facto head of the Moscow Art Theatre and Meyerhold's ideological opposite, threw out of his office those seeking his signature on a letter condemning Meyerhold. "I don't hit a man when he's down!" Nemirovich answered them.

On January 18, a gravely ill Stanislavsky, who had severed relations with Meyerhold many years before, calls the unemployed director and invites him to drop by and discuss matters. Stanislavsky—after a lengthy discussion about which little is known—offers Meyerhold, who has been daily awaiting arrest, directorial work in his Opera Studio.[10] "Who, today, would come to my productions?" Meyerhold wonders. "You underestimate the Moscow audience," Stanislavsky responds.

1939. The disgraceful Soviet-German friendship pact is formed. World War II begins. Poland is divided. Richard Wagner's *Valkyrie* is being prepared at the Bolshoy Theater, and its staging is offered to Sergei Eisenstein.

Lyubimov begins his final year as student at the Theater Institute and substitutes for the actor Abrikosov, who has taken ill. His role is Claudio in Shakespeare's *Much Ado About Nothing.* It is in this role that Lyubimov first subdues the audience with his particularly charming smile; laughing at his friend Benedict, who vows not to "look pale with love," Lyubimov-Claudio replies, glancing mischievously at the audience: "In time the savage bull doth bear the yoke."

After his successful debut, noted in the central press, Lyubimov is allowed to join the theater staff. Ample opportunities to play young socialist heroes open before him.

1940. During the winter war with the White Finns,[11] the People's Commissar of the NKVD,[12] Beriya, who replaces Yezhov, creates an NKVD Ensemble of Song and Dance to lift the fallen morale of the troops. It attracts the best artistic energy; composer D. D. Shostakovich and playwright N. Erdman collaborate with the ensemble.

Lyubimov dresses up in a military uniform. He is master of ceremonies and performs the interludes. Lyubimov the actor invariably calls forth "the spectator's sympathy with his youth and simple slyness."[13] Later Lyubimov will remember his service in the NKVD Ensemble by paraphrasing from the then popular operetta *Rose-Marie*:

A flower from the fragrant prairie-a
Lavrenty Palych Beri-ya. . . .

1941–46. Lyubimov spends the war years as master of ceremonies for the NKVD Ensemble. He performs at the front, near Moscow, in Leningrad, which was under siege. He is confronted with the heaviness of everyday life during the war even though he, like other leading actors, were not fighting in brigades at the front. Nevertheless, the war left a deep impression on his consciousness and stimulated a desire to tell the truth about it, as he later did on stage at the Taganka. In one later interview he said:

> I remember they put on a play about the war. . . . The brutality of the fascists had to be shown. The fascists were torturing a boy, and the boy was played by a short, fat woman. And every time that this woman would appear, I would die laughing. Such a war had passed and the director tried to move the audience to pity by using a fat woman, who was short in height. It seemed like lies and nonsense to me. And what was I doing there myself? What was I, a grown man, smearing my mug and ridiculously painting my lips for? It was unbearably shameful. It was, as I understand it now, the director fermenting within me. I started searching for a safety-valve. . . .[14]

1947. Lyubimov is demobilized from the army and returns to the Vakhtangov theater troupe. The theater building, blown up by the first wave of German bombers over Moscow in July 1941, was being rebuilt. Located in noisy old Arbat, the theater is well attended by Muscovites. The repertoire over the last few years included thirty-one Soviet plays, nine Russian classic, six Western, and twelve European plays. The theater devours all genres, but gives preference to playful, carnival-like spectacles, putting on Soviet plays primarily to "give an accounting."

The young actor gets the best roles in the repertoire. The head of the theater, People's Artist of the USSR, Ruben Simonov, hands his roles of Benedict in *Much Ado About Nothing* and Cyrano de Bergerac from Rostand's comedy to Lyubimov. That same year Lyubimov enthusiastically plays Oleg Koshevoy, a member of the Young Communist League underground organization, in A. Fadeev's *The Young Guard* (directed by V. Zakhava). He is nominated for the Stalin Prize for his performance.

He begins to appear in the movies with success, in the films of A. Stolper and N. Yarov; he is especially well received as Friday in a film based on *Robinson Crusoe*.

1949. Due to the government's growing anti-Semitism, a campaign develops against cosmopolitanism and subservience to the West. *Pravda*, newspaper of the Central Organ of the Central Committee of the All-Union Communist Party (Bolsheviks), publishes the tendentious article "On One Group of Unpatriotic Theater Critics," singling out leading critics with Jewish names:

> What conception can A. Gurvich have about the national character of the Russian Soviet man? The depraved opinions of the critics: Borshchagovsky, Gurvich, Yuzovsky, Varshavsky, Boyadzhiev, which are founded on unpatriotic positions, feed all sorts of perversions foreign to our people. It is necessary to decisively end this liberal permissiveness in regard to all of these esthetisizing nobodies once and for all . . . who have nothing in the soul, except for malevolence and an inflated opinion of themselves. It is necessary to cleanse the artistic atmosphere of its unpatriotic philistines.[15]

The Jewish Theater in Moscow is closed down soon after the People's Artist of the USSR, Solomon Mikhoels, is killed in Minsk. The actor Zuskin and other members of the Jewish anti-fascist committee are arrested. Lyubimov will later commemorate this campaign in *The House on the Embankment* at the Taganka in 1980.

1950. Lyubimov appears in the regrettably famous ornamental film *Kuban Cossacks*, directed by I. Pyriev. It glorified the prosperous life in Stalin's countryside after the war. The film is described in a Soviet advertisement:

> Having given out bread to the government ahead of schedule, the workers of Kuban gathered for their traditional collectivized market. Among them were two chairmen of opposing collective farms—Galina Peresvetova and Gordey Voron. Their coming marriage is the talk of the neighborhood. But there is no agreement among the neighbors. During the war years, Peresvetova managed to grow into a progressive and experienced leader. Recently, her collective farm won Voron's Red Banner away from him. Now, with complete support from her board of directors, Peresvetova announced a reduction in the prices of her collective's products. Voron, along with other chairmen, unsuccessfully tries to keep the current market prices. . . . Voron is bitterly upset over his inability to become equal to Galina, whom he loves as much as before. Soon, however, he learns from friends that Galina returns his love. Encouraged with the joyous news, Voron rushes after Peresvetova's two-wheeled cart on horseback. Finally understanding one another, the heroes continue their journey across the steppe, together—daydreaming about their future happiness.[16]

The film is awarded the Stalin Prize and the main award at the International Film Festival in Karlovy Vary.

Everything in the film is a lie: the dolled-up, cheerful members of the collective farm who sing songs while harvesting, the tables that break under the weight of the victuals, the continuing conflict between the two chairmen that supposedly made an independent decision to lower prices, the trivial love story, the Kuban sky that remained cloudless through the entire picture. Isaak Dunaevsky's music, first fervent, then lyrical, adorns the picture with a romantic veil: "Who you were, is how you are," sings the heroine, Galina Peresvetova, played by M. Ladynina. Millions of Soviet spectators accept these lies with joy and emotion: "Make life beautiful for us," the spectators seem to say as they come to the theater in droves.

Lyubimov plays the role of Andrey, the bright little Cossack and inseparable buddy of local strongman Fedya Grusha, acted by Boris Andreev, who has a powerful build and a face as round as the moon. They are a good comic pair that do not support the film's theme of strength and liberty. Lyubimov's doubts begin with a moment he will later recall more than once:

> They were filming the collective market: mountains of pretzels, some kind of dolls, thousands of balloons. An old peasant woman comes up to me and says, "Tell me, my dear, what life are they filming?" I tell her: "Ours, mamma, ours." And at that moment, my heart was so that I wished the earth would swallow me up. It was then that I made a promise to myself—never to take part in a similar swindle.[17]

1951. Lyubimov is awarded the Stalin Prize for the lead role in the adaptation of K. Fedin's novel *Kirill Izvekov* and for his Tyatin in M. Gorky's play *Egor Bulychev*, both productions directed by V. Zakhava. P. A. Markov reviews Lyubimov's role as the Red Commissar Izvekov as his most significant achievement:

> In terms of conviction, in terms of control, he carried the play's theme with dignity—the image became significant and filled from within, more in the Moscow Art Theatre than the Vakhtangov tradition. Lyubimov was cloaked in charm, the quality of which is so hard to explain.[18]

1953. In March Stalin dies; in September Khrushchev is selected General Secretary of the Central Committee of the Communist

Party. Rehabilitation begins for the victims of Stalin's repressions. Lyubimov joins the ranks of the Communist Party. Later he explains his decision:

> I was educated in the moral values of a great Russian culture. . . . When I was relatively young, my older communist friends, whom I believed in, talked me into joining the party. . . . They consider me to be an honest person and convinced me that right now the Party needs more honest people in it, and I believed them.[19]

1956–59. The year starts with an epoch-making event, the XX Congress of the Communist Party of the Soviet Union at which N. S. Khrushchev comes forward to expose the crimes of Stalin's regime. In June a document on the struggle with the consequences of the personality cult is accepted. In October a revolutionary uprising breaks out in Hungary. It is prepared by the "Petefi Circle" comprised of students and the liberal intelligentsia. Soviet tanks brutally crush the uprising.

In Moscow, a group of young actors (O. Yefremov, O. Tabakov, E. Yevstigneev, and others), graduates of the Moscow Art Theatre studios, get permission to open their own permanent theater-studio, the Sovremennik on Mayakovsky Square, formerly the Satiric Theater. The theater group proposes to begin work with a production of *Sailor's Silence*, based on A. Galich, but the censor bans it and they show V. Rozov's *Eternally Living* instead.

Lyubimov creates a slew of his best roles at the Vakhtangov Theater: Romeo, Juliet is played by Lyubimov's wife, the popular L. Tselikovskaya, (directed by I. Rapoport, 1956), Ivolgin in Dostoevsky's *The Idiot* (directed by A. Remizova 1958), Mozart in Pushkin's *Mozart and Salieri* (directed by E. Simonov, 1959), Victor in A. Arbuzov's *The Irkutsk Story* (directed by E. Simonov, 1959), and others. Also belonging to this period is his acquaintance, eventually becoming a friendship both creative and personal, with distinguished playwright Nikolay Robertovich Erdman (1902–1970), author of the prohibited satiric plays *The Suicide* and *The Mandate*. After his return from Siberian exile, the rehabilitated Erdman, who had worked with Meyerhold, takes an active part in Yuri Lyubimov's artistic fate.

Boris Pasternak is excluded from the Writer's Union in 1957–58 because of the overseas publication of his novel *Dr. Zhivago*. The best European theaters tour Moscow one after another: "The Berliner Ensemble" under the direction of B. Brecht, "NTR" headed by John Vilar, "D-34" headed by Yu. Burian, a troupe from the Comédie-Française . . . Brecht's epic theater causes a particular sensation. Many Moscow theater lovers see in it the development of Meyerhold's experiments of the 1920s. Lyubimov is with a Vakhtangov Theater troupe in Germany on an exchange of tours. Returning to the agitated theatrical world of Moscow, Lyubimov attends Kedrov's seminar on Stanislavsky's theory of "physical actions" at the All-Russian Theater Society and begins to teach at the Vakhtangov Theater's Shchukin Theatre Institute. He stages his first independent directorial work at the Vakhtangov—a production of A. Galich's *Does a Person Really Need A Lot?*

1961–62. Yuri Gagarin takes his space flight. The XXII Congress of the Communist Party of the Soviet Union decides to remove Stalin's body from the mausoleum. The chief editor of *Novy Mir* (*The New World*), A. Tvardovsky, by-passes the censor and with Khrushchev's personal approval publishes Solzhenitsyn's *One Day in the Life of Ivan Denisovich.*

Lyubimov plunges into his teaching at the Shchukin Theatre Institute. His class was chosen in 1959–60 without his input,[20] but among his students are such capable people as Z. Slavina, A. Demidova, T. Zhukova, B. Khmelnitsky, Yu. Smirnov, and others representing the core of the future Taganka Theater. His course of study includes not only elements of the actor's craft but a new creative approach to Stanislavsky's teachings as an open esthetic system, allowing for the combination of "psychological" and "conditional" theater.

> . . . the first ones to object to what I was doing were my own students. . . . They had a grudge against me because I wasn't teaching them the right way, according to the Stanislavsky system. That I was, well, destroying the system. Then they declared that Brecht was, in general, ill suited for the Russian school: he is too rational and foreign to deep emotional experiences.[21]

Lyubimov tries to vindicate his method of work, deciding to stage Brecht's *The Good Woman of Setzuan* as his class's graduation production. He uses the experiments of Stanislavsky, Vakhtangov, Brecht, and Meyerhold.

He appears in the satiric film *Caine XVIII*, based on Erdman's scenario. He discusses with Erdman the problems in educating the actor and forming a repertoire for a new "synthetic" type of theater.

1963. He is selected chairman of the Section on Young Actors of the All-Russian Theater Society. Lyubimov is named Honored Artist of the Russian Soviet Federal Socialist Republic.

After a difficult fight with the Institute heads, he gets permission to put up the graduation production in the third year and not the fourth, as is prescribed by the curriculum. Despite *Good Woman's* thundering success, the institute's director considers the production unworthy of the diploma. The central press, however, supports Lyubimov: K. Simonov's *Pravda* article states that it would be good to "preserve so alive an occurrence as *Good Woman.*" Due to pressure from the liberal community Lyubimov's course receives the diploma one year early and with it the right to independent work in the theater. A great deal is decided in this year.

1964. Called out for a discussion with the Moscow City Committee of the Communist Party of the Soviet Union, Lyubimov is asked to direct the Lenin Komsomol Theater, but, soon after, party officials change their minds, naming the director A. V. Efros to that position. They give Lyubimov the Theater of Drama and Comedy at Taganka, which is in an extremely sorry state; there is no troupe, repertoire, or audience, and the theater owes the government 70,000 rubles.

Lyubimov puts on his transfer to the Taganka the following conditions: complete reorganization of the troupe, the closing of old productions, a completely new repertoire under his supervision, and a staff of actors that he selects.[22] In his first few days of work at the Taganka, Lyubimov, along with the graduates of his course, accepts Vladimir Vysotsky from the Pushkin Theater in Moscow, introducing him into the productions of his own studio (the pilot in *Good Woman*, Kerensky in *Ten Days.*)

On April 23 the Theater of Drama and Comedy at Taganka opens its doors with Brecht's *The Good Woman of Setzuan*. The following season *Ten Days* secures the theater's success. The critic G. Boyadzhiev welcomes the new theater with the newspaper article "A Young Flock Picks Up Altitude," *Sovetskaya Kultura* (*Soviet Culture*), April 3, 1965. It is the first official recognition of the Taganka.

On October 13 the Presidium of the Central Committee of the

Communist Party of the Soviet Union, in accordance with M. Suslov's motion, retires Khrushchev and excludes him from the Central Committee, selecting L. I. Brezhnev as his replacement. The Khrushchev "thaw" ends, and with it the hope of the regime's tolerance of artistic freedom.

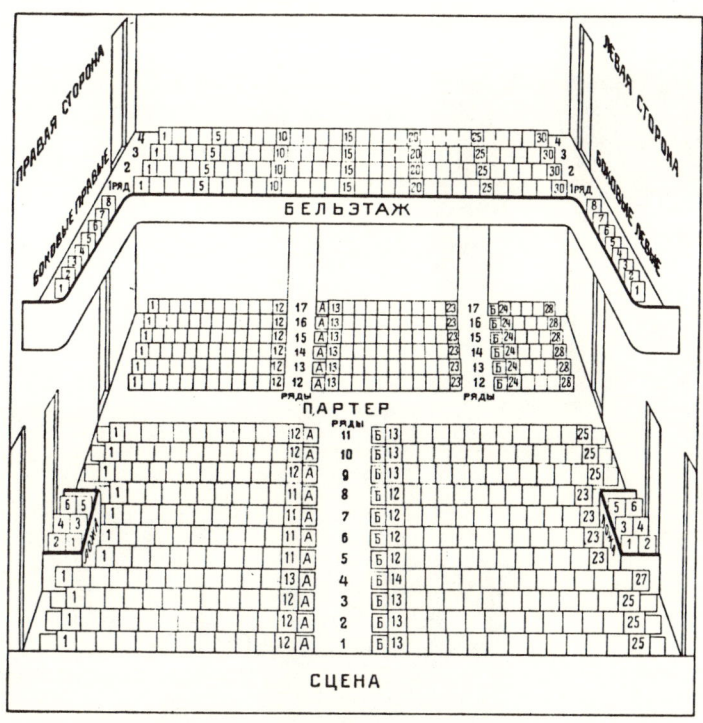

Exterior view of the Taganka Theater.

Diagram of the old Taganka Theater auditorium.

Above: Yuri Lyubimov (1960s).
Left and below: Scenes from
Good Woman of Setzuan (1963–64).

PHOTO COURTESY OF THE ALMA H. LAW ARCHIVE.

Scenes from *Ten Days That Shook the World* (1965).

Above: A scene from *The Dawns Are Quiet Here . . .* (1971).
Below: A scene from Bulgakov's *Master and Margarita* (1977).

Yuri Lyubimov (at head of table) and a group of his actors and friends (1970s).

Above: Vladimir Vysotsky as Raskolnikov in *Crime and Punishment* (Moscow, 1979). Below: Randle Mell as Raskolnikov and Kate Fuglei as Sonya in *Crime and Punishment* (Arena Stage, Washington, D.C., 1987).

PHOTO COURTESY OF THE ALMA H. LAW ARCHIVE.

Scenes from *The Three Sisters* (Moscow, 1981).

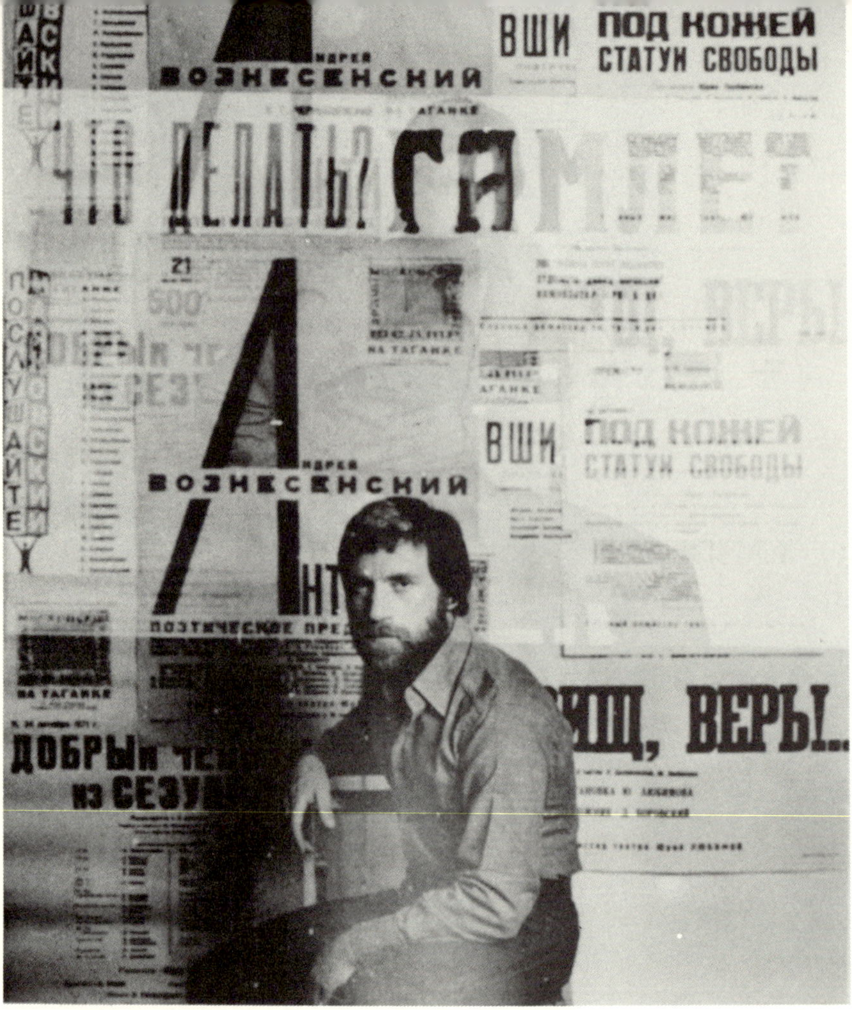

Above: Vladimir Vysotsky in front of Taganka Theater posters (1970s). Below left: Vysotsky with his wife, Marina Vladi (1972). Below right: Vysotsky (late 1960s).

Above: Vysotsky and Lyubimov in the director's study (late 1970s).
Below: Vysotsky's funeral (Moscow 1980).

Above: A scene from *Boris Godunov* (1982). Right: V. Zolotukhin as The Imposter (False Demetrius) in *Boris Godunov*. Below: Final scene from *Boris Godunov*.

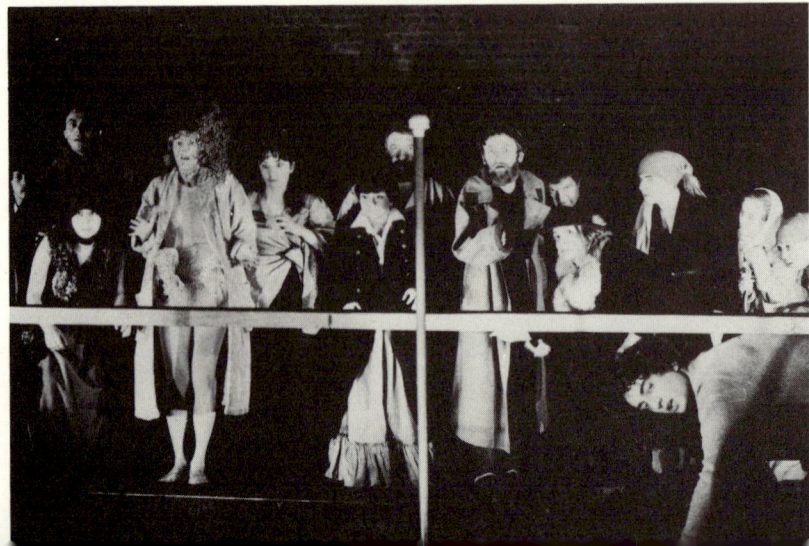

Yuri Lyubimov and his family (1985).

Lyubimov meets with his actors in Madrid (March 1988).

The Stage and the Audience

How *the* Taganka Began

NINETEEN SIXTY-THREE WAS THE LAST YEAR OF THE CELEBRATED "thaw"—liberal times by Soviet standards. Of course, they were only relatively liberal. After Stalin and Yezhov even the new Administration of Corrective-Labor Colonies seemed liberal compared to the previous Chief Administration of Labor Camps known as the Gulag.

Nevertheless, during this time Soviet art took a deep breath of fresh air. Evenings of poetry with Yevtushenko, Voznesensky, and Akhmadulina brought thousands of people together in clubs, stadiums, dormitories, leading research centers, and the academic institutes similar to the nuclear energy institute at Kurchatov's in Dubna.[1] New theater-studios were working successfully, the Sovremennik with the two Olegs, Yefremov and Tabakov, and the Moscow State University club with the two Marks, Rozov and Zakharov. The later works of Vasily Grossman and the early works of Aleksandr Solzhenitsyn were still being published. The writings of Yuri Trifonov and Vasily Aksenov acquired a new dimension. Every issue of the emboldened *Novy Mir* (*The New World*), edited by the rejuvenated Andrey Tvardovsky, was in great demand. The Manezh art exhibition made noise. It was there that the sculptor Ernst Neizvestny, former member of an amphibious landing force, committed an unheard-of act of daring. With soldierly straightforwardness he told Khrushchev that he did not know a thing about art, that he had better stick to corn and not enter an artist's workshop with commands.

The songs of Galich and Okudzhava, accompanied by a six-string guitar, broke through the barrier of censorship thanks to audio cassette recordings. By-passing editors and censors these songs circulated this immense country's towns and cities as contraband, thereby reaching the general populace from the intelligentsia's bohemian tables. It was difficult, from a scholarly viewpoint, to sort mass art from elite, or art for the people from art for the soul. Everything from the heart was for the people.

Somehow, on its own, without directives from the top or conspiracies from the bottom, a special stratum of society appeared spontaneous, unsanctioned, and unorganized, expressing public

51

opinion for the first time in Soviet history. In retrospect, V. Aksenov recalls:

> Aside from the artistic doers—old and young alike—a large vanguard of the politically conscious scientific and technical intelligentsia entered this stratum and, at that time, even within the party bureaucracy a considerable number of people appeared who could more easily be placed with a liberal stratum than with the moss-covered ideological rhinos. . . . The liberal opinion, the discussions in private homes or, let's say, at resorts or in the famous Moscow "kitchen salons" should not be overestimated, nor should they be underestimated. In many critical situations, the opinion of the patriotic, liberal stratum put more pressure on the authorities, than even the world press.[2]

The intelligentsia unexpectedly gained its own voice, sensing its right to its own opinion in a country of peasants and workers. The famous *kolkhoznitsa*[3] Zaglada, a master at growing beets, was incited by party instructions to reproach some Moscow theaters at an official conference, lecturing them as to how they should work. The usually quiet Moscow Art Theatre actor and director Mikhail Yanshin rose to respond. Round and goodnatured, he first seemed a bit clumsy next to the aggressive medal-covered *kolkhoznitsa*. No one had ever heard a loud or pointed word from Yanshin; even now, in the presence of party members, he answered her calmly, but not without humor:

> With all respects, I don't teach you how to grow lettuce. I like lettuce a lot, but it's very expensive. Couldn't you produce it more cheaply? But you're trying to teach me. . . . I'll figure out how to stage productions. And you figure out the lettuce.[4]

At a meeting of the Board of the Ministry of Culture, where the work of amateur folk theaters was discussed, an even more piquant scene played. The Minister of Culture, Ekaterina Furtseva, carelessly used amateur folk theater as a model for professional theater, asking Moscow actors to learn from it. From behind the long ministerial table covered with green cloth a tall graying man stood up— the famous and well-loved Moscow Art Theatre actor Boris Livanov. In a rumbling bass he asked the minister: "When you, Ekaterina Alekseevna, God forbid, feel sick, do you go to a professional doctor or to a witch doctor?" Furtseva, red and confused, adjourned the meeting.[5]

Such liberties, unthinkable in Stalinist times, caused a great deal of anxiety "at the top." The country's chief ideologue, Mikhail Suslov—nicknamed in the West "the Gray Cardinal"—suggested that Khrushchev arrange a conference with the intelligentsia. Since Stalinist times Suslov gained much experience in ideological reprisals against those of a different mind. In the post-war years, together with Zhdanov, he campaigned against writer Mikhail Zoshchenko and poet Anna Akhmatova. Suslov was also the motivating spirit of the fight against cosmopolitanism and an organizer of the anti-semitic campaign known as the "Doctors' Plot."

In the Khrushchev era this evil, colorless, half-crazed party bureaucrat, aged and with a cataract in one eye, nevertheless continued to hold the ideological machinery in his dry, toughened hands.

Characterizing him as the embodiment of creative sterility and party intrigue, A. Zinoviev wrote: "He . . . was a brilliant example that within Soviet society even a half-dead, half-witted creature was capable of playing a decisive role."

There were two meetings between party leaders and the artistic intelligentsia, in December 1962 and March 1963. They gathered triumphantly in the Kremlin, in the new Palace of Congresses. An orchestra played *The Blue Danube Waltz*. Everyone sat at tables with refreshments. Khrushchev delivered a forty-minute toast. Earnest conversation began. The main targets this time were Ilia Ehrenburg of the older generation and Yevtushenko, Voznesensky, and Aksenov of the younger. Criticizing Yevtushenko for his presentation at the first meeting, Khrushchev reminded him: "Times aren't what they were."[6]

"Yes, times aren't what they were," said the First Secretary of the Central Committee of the Communist Party of the Soviet Union, "but, they also aren't the time when the Petefi group existed. Moscow is not Budapest. There won't be a Petefi group. And there'll be no end to the struggle. Stifling even faithless thoughts is not right. Let the faithless thought ripen." With enviable openness, he outlined the party's new tactic: "There shouldn't be any police actions in art. Otherwise, the traffic light might break down and everyone will have a red light." Later on, he brilliantly formulated the concept that to the present day specifies the principles of the new Soviet cultural policy. "Even Chekhov's peasant," said

Khrushchev, "didn't unscrew every nut, in order not to cause a train wreck. *So we too will unscrew one and tighten another* [my emphasis]." He continued: "Do you think that there will be complete freedom under communism? Communism is an orderly, organized society. There'll be automation, cybernetics. But there will also be people invested with trust, who *will direct who does what*. Someone has to look after the little screws. Who?" And he answered himself: "A person invested with a high degree of trust."

At this conference Khrushchev first formulated a new, cynical base for the government's relation with artists—built on the principle of a secret public agreement. "You do things for us, we'll do things for you." Addressing Ehrenburg, Nikita declared that he is not made happy by the revolution, but suffers from it. "So," said Khrushchev, "as you treat us, we will treat you, Comrade Ehrenburg."

Mikhail Sholokhov, head of the opposing camp in Soviet literature, stood up and declared that if Ehrenburg shared "unrequited love" with Stalin, "we with the current make-up of the government have mutual love." This farcical scene concluded with an instantaneous response from Khrushchev, who welcomed this declaration of love by a living Russian legend. Turning to Sholokhov, Nikita humorlessly said: "We love you, and we hope that you will love us." This is how the new alliance between the party and its literary lackeys was cemented.

The only thing left was to restrain and scare off the young "*frondeurs*" who were holding to the middle of the road in art. Yevtushenko, Chukhray, Khutsiev, Tovstonogov, and Elizar Maltsev were taken to task by the head of the party and government. Khrushchev unflatteringly called Grigory Tovstonogov's Leningrad production of *Woe From Wit* "a, well, moldy idea":

> You're afraid to speak out yourselves, so Griboedov becomes a programmatic writer. And leave the Scottish Queen alone. Shakespeare was great, but everything has its time. Show us the pathos of labor, something new. . . .

The main blow at the 1963 conference was dealt to the vacillating Voznesensky. In his speech he ended up making a fool of himself. He had barely started with the words: "Like my favorite poet and

54

teacher, Mayakovsky, I am not a member of the Party." Khrushchev blew up and, banging his fist on the table, screamed:

No valor! You're challenging us! I can't calmly listen to those who pander to our enemies! He wants to create a Party of non-Party men and women! We are fighting a historic battle, Mr. Voznesensky!"

The young timid poet backed off immediately and said in justification: "I wasn't given a chance to finish the sentence, there's a comma here—but, like Mayakovsky, I am not separating myself from the Party." Khrushchev did not let him develop his thought and, seeing his weakness, threatened the following:

We will apply the strictest measures to people like you. We are precisely those who helped the Hungarians crush the rebellion. We have a lot of experience. We'll teach you all over again!

The most frightening thing in this scene, eyewitnesses record, was the applause. This egged Khrushchev on, so that he completely let himself go, screaming at those writers who did not applaud: "You young people over there, why aren't you applauding? You in the eyeglasses!"

Then, turning anger into kindness, the party chief said to Voznesensky:

There aren't any hopeless cases. . . . We will always have time to take measures. . . . Our youth is with the Party. . . . *And if not, then under the millstone!* Those like Voznesensky don't need to be talked into it. . . . Only modesty can help him. . . . He was born a prince. . . . I give you my hand, so that you become a soldier. [He lowers his hand.] I won't speak words, the work will show. . . .

That was how the party conducted conversations with artists at the end of the famous thaw. "Are you with us or against us?" the First Secretary screamed at artists in 1963. "There won't be any kind of a thaw—either summer or frost!"

However, this meeting, called to consolidate the power of Soviet literature, unexpectedly brought the opposite result. After the "Ides of March" the same artists for whom Khrushchev and Suslov had arranged "a bath" at the Kremlin gathered a little later at a small auditorium in the old Arbat section of Moscow, where Yuri Lyubimov and his pupils were presenting a modest graduation production.

Soviet theater had not seen such a select crowd in a long time. Ilia Ehrenburg, Yuri Zavadsky, Nikolay Erdman, who had known Stanislavsky and Meyerhold, and Konstantin Simonov came. Of course, the younger generation also showed up: Yevtushenko, Voznesensky, Trifonov, Akhmadulina, Okudzhava, Galich, Yefremov. The ballerina Plisetskaya and the composer Shchedrin came. The literary and theatrical stars of Moscow gathered.

The atmosphere in the hall was animated even before the production. The liberal circles of the Moscow artistic intelligentsia expected a lot from Lyubimov's production and they were not disappointed. In Yuri Lyubimov the qualities of both artist and fighter were successfully combined. He picked the best moment for his rise; Soviet society was showing signs of life after many years of fear-induced vegetation. Lyubimov had an uncontrollable hunger for creation. As Trifonov said, "at the age of forty-five [Lyubimov] stopped tolerating things." He was capable of heading a theatrical explosion.

In that unforgettable evening *The Good Woman of Setzuan* probably made as great an impression on the Muscovites of the 1960s as the famous Vakhtangov production of *Princess Turandot* did in the 1920s. It is amazing that, by a twist of fate, an Eastern parable very distant from daily Moscow was at the core of both productions, allowing wild theatrical fancy to run high. Lyubimov's young actors did not for a moment deny that they were performing theater, improvising a Chinese walk, and Chinese gestures and speech. Unbroken currents of life's stinging truths were sent from the stage into the auditorium. The actors addressed the spectators as co-participants in the production, delivered passionate monologues, performed genre scenes, and interrupted the action with songs accompanied by guitar. They laughed, despaired, cried, and laughed again with the spectators.

A new theater unlike any other was born in Moscow—innovative, daring, and passionate. It recalled the best traditions of the Russian stage; at the same time it was a keenly contemporary theater, without which present-day Moscow would be unimaginable.

Ten Days That Shook the World

PREMIÈRE: APRIL 2, 1965

THIS WAS THE TAGANKA COLLECTIVE'S SECOND PRODUCTION AS it continued its search for synthesis. It showed that the transition to a new stylistics of theatrical language at Lyubimov's studio was not an accident. "A Young Flock Picks Up Altitude," as the well-known critic G. Boyadzhiev titled his review of *Ten Days* the day after its première. In the journal *Teatr* (*Theater*) illustrious critic and theoretician Aleksandr Anikst wrote in support of the theater:

> Yu. Lyubimov brought a stream of theatricality down upon us. Everything that is possible on stage is demonstrated for us in the production, *Ten Days That Shook the World*. . . . We have genuine realism, episodes permeated with deep emotion and real drama here, as well as purely conditional theater. There's psychological drama, caricature, the grotesque, farce, low farce, slogans, pantomime, circus and shadow theater.
>
> The emotional scope of this production is enormous. I have the emotions of the audience in mind, not the emotions on stage. A feeling of genuine tragedy, sadness, melancholy, skeptical smiles, subtle irony, humorous moods, just laughter, or as some here derisively call it—"sheer laughter"—together all of this takes hold of us, while we watch the production. And somehow a feeling of immense satisfaction comes over us at play's end. The theater has fulfilled one of its most important missions—it aroused all of our feelings, and gave us a sense of relief. The production is really staggering.[7]

However, by no means did all Soviet critics welcome Lyubimov's drive for poignancy of form, for an organic unification of theater, music, pantomime, and eccentricity with vivid marketplace theater. The well-known dogmatic and orthodox critics Yu. Zubkov, N. Abalkin, and others representing the official point of view immediately sensed a threat to their antiquated views and primitive tastes in the new theatrical initiative. They were especially indignant that

Lyubimov displayed a portrait of Stanislavsky next to one of Meyerhold. Soviet ideology still stubbornly considered them antipodes and irreconcilable enemies. The offensive against the new theater began under the banner: "In Defense of Stanislavsky." The last word, however, belonged to the spectator: Will he support or reject the new theatrical program of Lyubimov's artel?

On the *Ten Days* poster the production was vaguely described as a "popular show in two parts with pantomime, circus, buffonade and shootings—based on themes from John Reed's book."

The spontaneous national uprising in 1917 unfolds on and off stage in a broken montage of short, colorful scenes that use all the means of expression available to theater. The actors recreate the atmosphere of the stormy and chaotic time that determined Russia's fate. Not just an illustration of events of a bygone era, it is a distillation of their most revealing facets, seen through the magnifying prism of the stage. In the chaos and variance of the impetuously changing scenes the familiar historical events, suddenly dropped from their bookish shell, are filled with living human flesh and the crude texture of everyday life, becoming startling and new.

Lyubimov constructed an unexpected shock for the pacified, disciplined Soviet audience, a spectacle occasionally bordering on theatrical hooliganism. Sudden, deafening gunshots force the spectators to shudder and sink in their seats, and the auditorium actually smells of gunpowder.

Vasily Aksenov recalled the first performance:

> I was sitting with Nayman, the poet, in the first row: I simply began to feel ill at ease. All of a sudden a grenade would blast in your ear, or sailors would run out with bayonets—right at our throats.
> "I think they're going to shoot us to death today, Tolya," I surmised.
> "Or stab us to death," surmised Nayman.[8]

This joke reflects the Taganka's characteristically particular poetics, inherent in its other productions as well. Lyubimov's theater strived to create a sense of involvement between the spectators and the action. Lyubimov's direction consciously brought the dozing spectator out of his subliminal state of passive contemplation, making him a participant in the performance.

In this sense *Ten Days* serves as a classic example of the consistency of a director's search. The whole production was built on this involvement effect, which began on the square in front of the theater's entrance and ended in a unique referendum at the auditorium exit where two urns, black and red, were placed. The spectators were asked to place their tickets in one of them, depending upon whether or not they liked the production. Perhaps this was the only direct, democratic, and free election in the Soviet country.

I saw *Ten Days* several times, at the première, when Lyubimov's theater was in its first spring in April 1965, and fifteen years later, in May 1980, as the theater approached its critical boundary.

I wanted to see *Ten Days* during a revolutionary holiday, not a regular workday. How does it sound in the non-revolutionary Moscow of today? On May 1, 1980, the production played in the afternoon—after the May Day parade on Red Square. It was unusually quiet in the festive city; no music, cheerful songs, or noise could be heard from Red Square. I was riding along Sadovoy Circle. There were no people on the street. I grew more and more amazed at the lifeless city with its spots of red calico slogans hanging about until I drove up to the familiar grayish-white pre-revolutionary building. It was only here, at the theater's entrance, that I saw a crowd of dressed-up Muscovites, taking up almost the whole pavement. They were basically young. It was not a regular evening crowd; moreover, it was not a première. There were no familiar theatrical faces, usually seen at the Taganka, but ordinary Muscovites of the 1980s who, on a revolutionary holiday, wanted to be carried from quiet, melancholy Moscow to a theatrical imagination of a distant and stormy era when all this started . . . .

There was still half an hour before the performance, so the crowd was not hurrying into the theater. Enjoying spring in the city and anticipating the coming show, people were talking animatedly and listening to the almost forgotten and now strange words of the hearty songs carried over the powerful amplifier above the theater entrance:

Our locomotive, fly ahead,
To the Kommun Station. . . .

The words and rhythms of the old revolutionary marches gained another, almost ironic sense:

Boldly, comrades, keep the pace
We'll strengthen our souls in battle. . . .

The young people, smiling, were especially animated at the song:

We'll boldly go to battle
To put the Soviets in power
And we'll all die as one
In the fight that's ours. . . .

"Why go into battle, if everyone—as if one—is going to die?" joked a man standing next to me.

No, clearly, no one among those who came to the Taganka that day wanted to die for "ours" or "someone else's." This new breed wanted to live and enjoy life. Puzzled by the whims of their fathers and grandfathers, they tried to understand and imagine their impulses.

A group of tipsy demonstrators returning from Red Square pointedly ignored the crowd, providing a strong dissonance to the mood at the theater, and underlining their own estrangement. These people with sweaty, pink faces, tired from lack of sleep, carried luxuriant bouquets of paper flowers and rolled up banners. Staggering and slurring curses, a political leader came from Red Square; he was a descendant of those to whom the production was dedicated. As if neither noticing nor showing any interest in the theater crowd, the demonstrators for a moment blended in as they passed, creating a varied, motley group. Presently the two streams separated. The theater-goers stayed put, while the demonstrators continued home or to the nearest bar. It looked as if all were staged by an invisible director.

Finally the doors to the theater open wide. The ticket collectors are armed members of the Red Guard, not civilians. Smiling, they spear the tickets on their bayonets, give out red bows for the spectators' buttonholes. The spectators smile confusedly; they are lively and laughing.

In the foyer more unexpected events await the spectator. A band of sailors in pea jackets playing an accordion sing ditties of those distant years. An actress in a striped sailor's vest dances frenetically in a circle, singing to herself: "Mother saw me off—a soldier I'd become / All my matchmakers came by—and then some. . . ."

Faded red panels with slogans hung near the ceiling stretched from one wall to the other; they read: "All power to the soviets," "The revolution welcomes workers, soldiers and peasants." Later

60

in the auditorium actor Mikhail Shtraukh will read them with Lenin's burr.

The performance had not started yet—or maybe it had. In the foyer a row of sailor-agitators with an accordion and a priest in cassock and red goatee appear on a roped off wooden platform blocked by a pyramid of rifles. The priest blows into a police whistle, calling attention to topical ditties.

> To the grief of all bourgeois
> We will set the world on fire,
> The burning world is in my blood—
> Oh please bless me, God!

Behind the priest a young woman in a red kerchief sings beautifully:

> My darling is a Menshevik
> And me—I'm a Bolshevik.

The low, clownish, ditty-like view of life has through the centuries made up the underside of the dull "high-style" government structure. At one time it seemed that in Soviet art, which is strictly regulated, this clownish view had been completely blunted, but— wait! It still lives and the slightest provocation, the slightest weakness will cause its folkloric spontaneity to break out and wake up the people's dozing free will.

> In nineteen hundred and eighteen
> There was a revolution—
> And my darling out of fear
> Bore a pig and not a son. . . .

The priest's police whistle cuts short this blasphemy.

With ditties and accordion accompaniment, played jauntily by the capable Valery Zolotukhin, the spectators—involuntary participants in a mass meeting provoked by the theater—break into the auditorium. There are clearly more spectators than seats; many take advantage of the Red Guard ticket collectors' recklessness and get in without tickets. All the aisles are occupied. A wall of people stand in the gallery. This overcrowded, rumbling, narrow auditorium creates a special atmosphere, precisely that needed for the production. The actors become infected by the spectators' gaiety. Like a whirlwind from the aisles the actors break out into the rows and shoot their rifles while the faint of heart scream. The performance begins.

A popular show by its own nature is an open, marketplace action where people are simultaneously their own artists and characters. Its view of history cannot be impartial like a ballad or a fairy tale where the stepmother is always evil and the orphan unlucky and kind; where the merchant is pot-bellied and the idiot smarter than the smartest. At the Taganka this popular and naive view was demonstrated thoroughly, clearly, simply, and playfully.

The whole production is conducted in two intersecting planes: the elevated and the grotesque; there is no middle ground. The artistic material of the performance-revue, the performance-attraction, is woven from a montage of short and colorful genre and buffonade scenes. I counted twenty-two in all, as in Pushkin's *Boris Godunov*. Here are a few of their titles as they appeared in the program: "Eternal Fire" (pantomime), "The Interrogation of John Reed" (buffonade), "A Hard Fate"—Russian ploughman (pantomime), "Crosses" (genre), "Assembly of the Nobility" (buffonade), "Jails" (genre), "The Fathers of the City" (buffonade), "The Fall of the Romanovs" (genre), "Bread Line" (pantomime), "The White Guard" (genre), "Chaos" (genre), "Shadows of the Past" (shadow theater), "Hands of the Fathers" (buffonade), "Counter-Revolutionary Lair" (genre), "Trenches" (genre), "The Last Meeting of the Provisional Government" (buffonade), "To the Capital for Truth" (genre).

Yuri Lyubimov carried out the complex montage by threading them onto one idea that ran through the production: the special atmosphere of the time and the spirit of the people who made the revolution. The director picked what seemed to be the most difficult method: showing elusive time through the palpable plasticity of space.

How can Russia's boundless expanse be conveyed on the cramped and narrow Taganka stage, without any wings or pockets? How can the primordial feeling ruling the hearts of people who, for centuries, have tolerated forced labor on free soil be presented?

On the stage open to all the winds, we see the naked steppe. Thanks to the lighting effects it fades into the endless distance that reddens first in a bloody sunset, then in an early dawn. In center stage appears a black relief of an anvil flanked by two blacksmiths. A woman's hands (A. Chernova) wriggling in the red light create tongues of fire in the furnace. With this theatrical illumination Lyubimov begins his endless spatial variations. The stage platform will widen before our eyes, moving the theater walls and involving us in its maelstrom.

Building the *mise en scènes* in different perspectives Lyubimov found unlimited possibilities for showing the Russian expanse. There is a Russian ploughman—barefoot, sinewy, in coarse trousers, with a muscular torso—walking behind a plough along the harvest field diagonally from right to left; there are some war invalids with outstretched arms moving toward us; in the depths of the stage there are the crosses of soldiers' graves drawn in shadow. Then, after a few minutes, in the center of the stage, a mother and her son, who is to be executed, perform a short farewell. Later, from the left portal, almost the corner of the auditorium and in the depth of the stage, along the diagonal (as if a mirror image of the ploughman *mise en scène*, a silent bread line of hungry women and children stretches out. These scenes continue to the end of the production. There are soldiers in semi-profile in a trench up to their chests; an officers' stopping place on the proscenium; a patrol of sailors in the front rows of the orchestra. Above the stage takes place the faceless scene "The Fathers of the City," where the hands of those running the country speak from behind black velvet—lustful, evil, dry, indifferent, nervous. There is "Shadows of the Past": Behind a transparent, matted curtain pass a gallery of social masks of the era, including anarchists, nuns, decadent young women, delegates from the Duma, a patrol of the Red Guard. . . .

These selected scenes, varied and instructive, gain a parable-like meaning on the stage, and individual, familiar, historical figures gain their own inner essence and imagery, and more—their own necessity. They all take their place in the flow of history: the soldier with the rifle, the pot-bellied bourgeois in the beaver coat, the Socialist Revolutionary party member with the little beard, the hysterical Kerensky, the ladies from the "Death Battalion," the soldier-cripples, the peasant-envoys, the sailor-fellows, and the sinewy ploughman behind the plough. . . .

Gradually, in the mixed character and driving tempo of this pic-

turesque spectacle, the historical life of a people thrown by someone's iron will into a boiling, revolutionary cauldron is drawn
through placards and the grotesque.

The methods of everyday, psychological theater are insufficient
for such a presentation. And Lyubimov, boldly violating the dogmatic precepts of socialist realism, takes much from the conditional
theater of Meyerhold, condemned by the party for "formalism."
Each actor plays several roles. By no means do they consider the
art of representation inferior to the art of experience. They are not
inclined to psychologically dig within themselves—the false understanding of the Stanislavsky system. Remaining slightly aloof
from their characters, looking at them from the side, generalizing,
reinterpreting, and finishing the composition enables them to create
an atmosphere of genuine theatricality—an unruliness of color, life,
and play.

In *Ten Days* at the Taganka actors free of clichés and dogma perform in the revolution. They do not stop feeling themselves to be
free creators at every moment, easily going from experiencing to
representation, from the grotesque to eccentricity. The director's
strong hand helps them, guiding their action toward the main goal,
to the uncovering of the main conception. With the director the
actors look at the revolution from today's distance, slightly aloof,
with romantic irony, as people to whom a few things are known
that were hidden from their contemporaries. Such a perspective
allows one to see not only the elevated in distant historical events
but also the base, not only the tragic, but the funny and awkward.
Just as the people who made the revolution were truly great, the
distance between the heroic and the base in the theater's portrayal
is great in equal measure.

The new type of spectacle offered by Lyubimov demanded not
only different laws of embodiment but a new perception from the
spectator, in contrast to the usual propositional drama. The Soviet
spectator was used to canonical plays on revolutionary themes like
the popular *Lyubov Yarovaya* and *The Kremlin Chimes*. Not all of them
accepted the conditional esthetic of *Ten Days* at the Taganka.

A respectable, graying citizen resembling a well-placed official
from the ministry sat in front of me in the first row of the orchestra.
During the play he expressed his displeasure to the portly woman
sitting next to him.

"What the hell! God knows what they heaped together. No connection. Some kind of excerpts from fragments. Remember *Lyubov Yarovaya* at the Maly Theatre—there was a show!"

"Well, the Maly's the Maly," answered the woman evasively.

The important citizen would not calm down. "And what do they have here? Look what a dustbowl they've got. They couldn't even vacuum properly, not even that."

The monumental production, beginning so loudly and colorfully and with such epic sweep ends on an unexpectedly quiet, cleverly confidential note. Three Russian peasants—V. Zolotukhin, Yu. Smirnov, and V. Semyonov—plunge us into a pointed characteristic of the psychological theater. The revolution has ended. Envoys from the countryside go "to the capital for truth." They tentatively enter the proscenium in bast shoes and tattered sheepskin coats and hesitate by the office door at the Smolny Institute where a navy-guard stands. They remove their hats as if in the presence of their master. The sailor asks them what they want. The clever peasant, Zolotukhin, first glancing over his shoulder at his countrymen, then with distrust at the auditorium, folds his hat in his hands and says: "Well, we're looking for . . . the a . . . Well, what's it called . . . well, what everybody's looking for, but can't . . . find . . . Good Lord, I've forgotten. . . ."

The sailor tries to help: "The truth?"

"Th-that's it, brother, that's just it. . . ."

Explosive laughter in the auditorium at this concluding dialogue constructs an invisible bridge from the past to the present, the purpose of the show.

We walk out of the theater onto the empty square of May Day Moscow still too weak to deal with all the impressions. The question that resounded in the finale—"What're we looking for?"—remained. It is not theater's business to give an answer. It is enough that theater awakens our feelings, fantasies, and thoughts. Understanding what art can do and what it cannot enriches us. We saw an unusual spectacle and believed that the theater, born in the marketplace, would sooner or later return to it.

Postscript: The resurrection of mass, revolutionary spectacles in today's national, marketplace theater is not at all convenient for the Soviet authorities. In America I interviewed a famous director of mass spectacles, former chief designer for the Moscow Circus and

Honored Artist of the Russian Soviet Federal Socialist Republic, Leonid Aleksandrovich Okun. He told me how he had repeatedly tried to revive this early tradition of the Soviet theater:

There was a Party person, active in art, by the name of Pokarzhev-sky. . . . I think he commands art even now. So anyway, for the next anniversary of the revolution, in the seventies, I proposed a scenario for a mass, theatrical presentation on the streets of Moscow, dedicated to the anniversary of the uprising on Red Presnya. At first, everyone liked it. They formed a committee, and went for recon-naissance. They examined the whole route of the upcoming presen-tation—from Gorky Street, through Mayakovsky Square, from there along Sadovoy Circle to the place of battle at Red Presnya. And then suddenly, a question arose in the administration: how do you block the streets so that people wouldn't be able to get to the place of battle from the side streets? "Cordons have to be put up," suggested Po-karzhevsky. I didn't understand at first: what cordons, what for? After all, we're organizing the mass theatrical presentation so that everyone who wants to can see how the uprising on Red Presnya occurred! But the administration had doubts, streams of people would go to a place of a mass action—who knows what might happen! It turned out that today's administration was afraid to revive the revolutionary spirit of the Muscovites. On the one hand they'd like to, but on the other . . . nevertheless a mob. And so, nothing came of this idea.[9]

The Fallen and the Living

PREMIÈRE: NOVEMBER 4, 1965

IN THE TAGANKA'S REPERTOIRE THREE MAIN LINES, AT TIMES intersecting, can be traced, though they cannot be mixed up with one another. Lyubimov said there is only one tree trunk to theater, but that the branches are varied. The first branch, the marketplace, is carnival-like theater of the street and square, puppet booths and *skomorokhs*[10]. These include productions like *The Good Woman of Setzuan, Ten Days That Shook the World, Mother, What Is to Be Done?*, and *Alive!* (B. Mozhaev's *The Life of Fyodor Kuzkin*), which was banned by the censors.

The second branch is the modernized classics, such as *Tartuffe, Hamlet, Crime and Punishment, The Three Sisters*, the banned *Boris Godunov*.

The third and final branch is poetic theater, or as Lyubimov said, "a chain of poetic presentations" that began with Voznesensky's *Anti-Worlds* and continued through *The Fallen and the Living*, Mayakovsky's *Listen!*, Yesenin's *Pugachev*, Pushkin's *Comrade, Believe*, and Lyubimov's penultimate production, *The Poet Vladimir Vysotsky* (sometimes called *In Memory of Vysotsky*), also banned by the authorities.

The form of poetic presentation naturally derived from that system of conditional, metaphoric theater Lyubimov developed on the Taganka stage as a continuation of the Meyerhold-Brecht line. Both were drawn toward the production-revue form. For Lyubimov, understanding of poetry as an epoch's lyrical revelation is organically connected to the moral-esthetic program of his theater. Because of this he did not strive to create an attractive surface action in his poetic productions, but primarily to recreate the era's atmosphere and impulses that also served to inspire the poet. In *Listen!* five Mayakovskys appeared on stage as a metaphor for the complex, contradictory personality of the artist who does not fit into the strict frame of one portrayal.

The actors performing in the poetic evenings at the Taganka did not try to concretely imitate someone through make-up, which was

67

generally not respected at the Taganka. Before all of the incandescence of socially civic feelings, poetry lived anxiously and nervously in the performances of the Taganka actors, as a personal, almost intimate, experience. It was as if the make-up was also taken off the poetry, appearing in its unusual, ungainly key, though always in an intelligent, lively, and individual expression.

The particular manner of reading poetry, which Lyubimov had worked out with great difficulty, consisted in rejecting the false declamation established long ago on the Soviet stage, when they sought to pre-digest the idea for the listener, disregarding the creator's form and personality. The artist's individuality played a huge role in selecting the means. The frenzied possession of Slavina, the epic calm of Kuznetsova, the street charm of Vysotsky, Khmelnitsky's intelligent manner of the professional reciter served as a faithful support for communicating the poetic intonations of Samoylov, Gudzenko, Kulchitsky, Kogan, and Mayorov. From this wealth of colors, timbres, rhythms, varied intonations, and anomalous and untheatrical inner experiences of the performers a multicolored picture emerged.

At rehearsals, Lyubimov demanded:

Read the poems about him, not about yourselves, so that everyone's heart would bleed for him! Don't rush the words . . .
Don't color the poems! Don't overplay! Speak simply, as simply as possible, like intelligent people . . .
Read from the situation . . .
Don't be declamatory . . . .

In *The Fallen and the Living*, one of the best poetic productions, there were no directorial innovations, minimal theatrical devices, and no scenery, only naked stage and the actor on it its complete master. Nothing distracted the spectator from the word. There was guitar music; pantomime in the intermezzos. Everything was completely simple and natural. The actors came out in their usual clothing and read the verses of poets who had fallen during the war, or who by chance luck had survived it but preserve its memory as a difficult but happy time.

The critic K. Rudnitsky wrote:

At the beginning of the production, the spectators are invited to stand for a moment of silence in memory of those who died. Uncertain, the spectators stand. Flames ignite at the edge of the stage. The war looks out into the auditorium.

And suddenly, V. Zolotukhin joyously, freely and with rapture reads Samoylov's poems:

The forties, the fateful,
The war and the front. . . .

This whole big musical suite is put together simply and without cleverness from separate episodes, even, if you like, from separate variety show numbers. . . . But, in the end, all of this is unimportant. Why are there tears in your eyes? Why does pain penetrate your soul? Why is there such a silence. . . .

There was silence in the auditorium. From the first minute a staggering, unusual *mise en scène* of the production created the impression of a spontaneous, evening party of young people. Young fellows gathered together somewhere by chance—in a dormitory or in a forest clearing—and arranged themselves every which way. Some sat, others stood, still others walked about as if they were wound up. All had books in hand, spoke, interrupted, engaged in polemics to one another. Their thin, boyish necks hiccupped or gulped from the enthusiasm and nervous, unsteady rhythm of their voices. Some of them like what Kolya Mayorov wrote:

Will we really forget how to love
And on holidays, throwing open the couches,
We'll start greeting guests and ceremonially drinking
The old, Caucasian mineral waters?

More to the hearts of others were the provocative lines of Pavel Kogan:

And once again it's quiet.
And once again there's peace.
Like indifference, like an oval.
I hated ovals since I was a child!
I drew squares since I was a child!

The one who likes Kogan argues, referring to his friends' reminiscences: "He desperately loved gay, honest, and brave people." What do ovals and squares have to do with it? Why precisely a square? Because, answers another actor in the words of Mikhail Kulchitsky:

The most frightening thing in the world—
is to be placid.

Gradually these boyish quarrels are tied into one knot: One can be different in poetic taste, temperament, or personal life, but the main thing is one's attitude toward life. Here everyone professes one faith and there is no dissent among them. They are all incorrigible optimists, heroes, romantics. They are all handsome. There are no whiners among them. The bright future is before them; they believe in victory as do all the people. Kulchitsky, a refined and intelligent poet, in a patriotic fog foretells the following:

Only the Soviet nation will be!
And there will be only people of the Soviet race!

In those years he was not the only one to think like that.
They all love Russia, no matter their race. Pavel Kogan, the son of Jewish parents, admits his love in the following heartfelt words:

I am a patriot. I am the Russian air,
I love the Russian soil.
Where else will you find such
Birch trees, as in my corner?
I would drop dead, just like a dog, from nostalgia
In any paradise of coconuts.

Will you find many such sincere confessions similar to that of this Jewish lad who believed in Russia to the end? The recovery of insight was more frightening for those who were rejected by their first love. Kogan, Kulchitsky, and Mayorov did not live long enough. To make up for it, we, who sat in the Taganka auditorium for that performance, lived to see it. The theater knows it. The actors read these poems composed in "the forties, the fateful" for us, the people of the 1960s, so that we may recover our insight, understand, and compare.

Is the history of a country the history of an illness? One can reason this way. The poetry of the 1940s was a poetry sensing future misfortune, not only from the expected storms of war but also from broken dreams. Their poems indicate that it is better to die young and whole rather than split in two, disillusioned in youthful ideals. Wrote Kogan:

We'll lay down, where we lay down,
And won't get up, where we lay down—

The poets that we love for their wholeness did not present themselves as such; they even laughed at themselves.
Mayorov warned:

The portraits will lie,
where our life's path is depicted—

And Pavel Kogan, with characteristic irony, wrote:

They'll make us up as wise ones,
We'll be strict and straight,
They'll paint and powder us.

The Taganka Theater remembered them, wiping the powder and paint of time from their faces, showing them the way they were in the 1940s. Selfless, unbusinesslike, interested, vulnerable, and wholeheartedly faithful to Russia, they humbly stepped to the side when the time came for others. Said Boris Slutsky about his friend Kulchitsky:

Some are true to Russia because of this,
Others are true to her because of that,
But he did not think how or why.
She was his daily work.
She was his lucky moment.
She was a native land to him—

He contrasts him with poets of another sort and time:

There are horses for war
and for parades.
In literature
there are also breeds.

The poetry of Kulchitsky, Kogan, and Mayorov was not for parades. Their horses carried riders through cross-fire from both sides. Kulchitsky directly declared:

It is essential to fall a youth.

Vsevolod Bagritsky, son of the famous poet Eduard Bagritsky, was perhaps the weakest poet of this constellation and probably the most enthusiastic. On the eve of war he wrote that he was prepared to:

Rejoice that I lived on this earth for less than
Twenty. . . .

He seemed to see the future, this boy who died in 1942 at the front near Leningrad. The history of a country is a history of an illness. That the theater does not color history gives the production its power and effectiveness. It cuts into history fearlessly, divides things without judgment, understands the delusions and wonderfully youthful impulses of these not yet grown, pure, enthusiastic poets—the children of their time. That is why the student parties *mise en scène*, the interrupted stories, the untheatrical but also anomalous manner of reading, and the prosaic interruptions of the poems with documents, letters, and friends' reminiscences were so pointed here.

"The distinguishing characteristic of this generation," recalls D. Samoylov, one of the few from this constellation to survive, "was its wholeness. Wholeness and the fullness of their attitude."

Yes, they were Soviet patriots. Yes, they believed that in the first few days of war Budenny would take Warsaw and Voroshilov Berlin by storm: "Only the Soviet nation will be! And there will be only people of the Soviet race!"

Wasn't this wholeness also a form of illness? The Soviet authorities artificially inculcated infantilism in their citizens; even poets were not insured against it. They carried the mark of their time and divided their common fate with the people. The theater reminds us of this in the final scene when, after a long pause, with a funeral ring, the following information is given blandly:

Pavel Kogan died in 1942 near Novorossiysk.
Nikolay Mayorov in 1942 near Smolensk.

Vsevolod Bagritsky in 1942 in the Leningrad area.
Mikhail Kulchitsky in 1943 near Stalingrad.

There is no sentimentality, no false significance. No actor strives to squeeze tears out of the spectators, as is often the case at similar "memorial" evenings. Nevertheless, the production is deeply moving; tears come against our will. Maybe this is precisely because Lyubimov does not allow posturing, banal words or pathos. His conception turns out exactly. The theater conducted the unconstrained, open, and intimate discussion about the 1940s' poetry from the 1960s' viewpoint, dispelling many hopes, impulses, and delusions. Before our eyes, the broken, temporal connection between the poetry of two generations is restored. Wrote D. Samoylov:

I myself must depend on them,
Although sometimes I'd rather not—

The connection between his own fate and the fate of those who completed the path is revealed by a poet of another generation— Vladimir Vysotsky. In the somnolent 1970s he wrote, like a will, two enigmatic lines:

We will not die by tortured life
We'd best just come to life through honest death.

The production of *The Fallen and the Living*, aside from everything mentioned, conveys other important lessons to its spectator—the ability to listen to and feel poetry, and the grand ability to be astonished. The poet's words are born spontaneously on stage at the moment the actor-poet articulates them, as if he does not know the next line, rhyme, and thought being created. We see the actor-poet at the moment of creation, inspiration, and composition. This is all but the most difficult to achieve in art.

Rush Hour

PREMIÈRE: DECEMBER 4, 1969

IN THE TAGANKA'S REPERTOIRE, IF YOU DO NOT COUNT Brecht's plays, you will almost never encounter contemporary foreign playwrights. The unsuccessful production of Peter Weiss's *The Investigation*, directed by P. Fomenko, showed that the Taganka actors have difficulty with themes that do not deal with Russia and particularly with the real character of Western people, their way of thinking, habits, and lifestyle. The strong criticism in Weiss's documentary "anti-play" did not suit the expressive acting style of the Taganka actors. Even with its noble goal (*The Investigation* is about a judicial proceeding on Nazism) the production looked like a pathetic declamation. The static manner of the actors who performed behind music stands, like an orchestral oratorio, proved to be a device alien to the Taganka's spontaneity. The production became dull and edifying. The Taganka has its own personality, its productions held together by a loose, literary foundation that invites bright, theatrical spectacles. This is the source of Lyubimov's passion.

There is one other reason why foreign drama experienced trouble on the Russian stage. Soviet theater had been artificially protected from the best works of European theatrical thinking for decades. Even during the most liberal period, F. Durenmatt and Arthur Miller were staged only with great difficulty. Soviet theater was not allowed to perform Rolf Hochhuth's *Namestnik (Deputy)*, Mrozek's satires, or the absurdist dramaturgy of Ionesco and Beckett. The Soviet spectator never got to see the anti-drama *Waiting for Godot*, which toured the world over. All this passed Soviet theater by and, of course, brought a noticeable loss to its esthetics and the development of the director's and actor's art.

At one time Soviet theater tried to compensate for this noticeable gap with productions of East European playwrights; Czechoslovakian, Polish, and Hungarian authors experimented under more favorable conditions with relative creative freedom, but soon this source also dried up. At the end of the 1950s and beginning of the

74

1960s many Soviet stages performed the plays of Czech dramatist Pavel Kohout *(Such Love, The Third Sister)* and the pointed, anti-fascistic play *Keepers of the Keys* by his countryman Milan Kundera. They were hailed by Soviet critics as the best playwrights of socialist Czechoslovakia, describing them as innovative artists one could learn from. Soon, however, the participation of these honest writers in the "Prague Spring" brought a taboo upon them and, despite their success with audiences, censors ordered that their names disappear from posters.

Lyubimov attempted to get closer to general European themes through East European drama. He chose *Rush Hour*, a comedy by Polish author Jerzy Stawiński. The action of the play develops as if on the border of two worlds—East and West. The ancestry, education and mentality of the characters belong undoubtedly to the "rotting" West, but because of their social position and habits they were fully prepared for life in the "socialist paradise." The duplicity of the characters in Stawiński's play induced the director to take a sharply theatrical approach, becoming the condition for the production's ironic subtext. Lyubimov directed the actors to live a double life on stage. With this goal in mind the actors speak not only their fixed lines but also their own commentary. The result proved bitingly funny.

"How are you? I asked in boredom, thinking only of myself," said one of the characters as he greeted a friend from childhood.

"What illness did you have as a child? asked the indifferent doctor, listening to the patient, right then and there ordering him: Shut up!" And so on.

Similar self-commentaries reveal a general symptom in man; living in a lying world, he is used to saying one thing, thinking another, and then doing something else entirely. Cunningly, the theater says it is understood that all of this is inherent in a society with survivors of capitalism, and that it does not have any relation to the moral code of those "building communism."

D. Borovsky built a set of a large establishment during the workday rush hour. The set included countless doors and long corridors, a crazed elevator rushing up and down, a carousel of people accompanied by a taut, ceaseless rumble behind the windows where lives the big hive-like city. People feel lost and lonely in all the confusion and congestion.

The crazed rhythms of the production assault the spectator in the first few minutes. The flow of white collars and mini-skirts appearing and disappearing in the countless doors creates an impression of wild, obsessive flashing and confusion. During the first ten or fifteen minutes the auditorium too is in a confused state: you are waiting for an event, but what kind—you do not know . . .

Unexpected things await us. Suddenly, one of the elevators runs not vertically but horizontally across the stage. It is so crammed with people that the door can't close. These government officials, who look alike in their white collars, seem as though they are about to be thrown from the elevator. There is whispering in the auditorium. It is only after the second or third run of this horizontal, ministerial elevator that we notice that life-size dolls, not people, are closely pressed up to one another; the dolls look very much like us spectators . . . Later, each of these mannequin-people appears in the proscenium and quite properly introduces himself and not without self-criticism; everyone knows that in our society self-criticism is a motivating force and the order of things as well.

Finally, out of this faceless crowd, the main character distinguishes himself—the successful manager Krzysztof Maksimowicz, played by Veniamin Smekhov, who leads the production in the author's person. He acquaints us with his inner circle, fast and business-like, as is fitting for a modern bureaucrat. His portly, civic-minded wife (acted by I. Kuznetsova) joins in the fight against alcoholism. Addressing the audience, Smekhov-Krzysztof comments on her pursuits: "Fighting alcoholism in our country simply makes no sense—" and, after a short pause, adds: "I'm speaking, of course, about Poland."

He introduces us to his girl Friday, as he jokingly calls his lover (A. Savchenko): "I only see her on Fridays," he tells us secretly.

We go with him to his office to meet the featureless boss (A. Sabinin), Krzysztof's deputies, the ever-gloomy Obukhovsky (A. Porovshchikov), and the young careerist, Radnevsky (D. Shcherbakov), whose face always wears an obsequious smirk. The old bookkeeper, Davidovich (G. Roninson) gets our special sympathy. He has been through many difficulties in his day but now faces the most insurmountable of all; with all his cleverness he cannot get a decent coffin for his deceased relative. "They make them all unpainted—to meet production," he complains to us. "The production of coffins in our country is still lagging behind buyers' inquiries—and, unfortunately, stoppages occur." Last but not least, we meet Krzysztof's long-legged secretary, Bozhena (T. Sidorenko). She is not a good typist, but she is wonderfully grounded in everything else required of her. Our hero explains his selection: "Show me your secretary and I'll tell you who you are." In sum, we plunge into the personal and business life of the successful manager, Krzysztof. In quick scenes we see his home life and his official surroundings and learn how he divides himself between his wife and his lover, his boss and his subordinates; we see him dodge, behave rudely and like a scoundrel, and indulge himself. However, he does not do any of this crudely, but in a thoroughly elegant manner—in European packaging, so to speak.

The theatrical feelings of the characters as performed by the Taganka are best categorized by the phrase "for show." The actors make no secret of this; on the contrary, they play it up at every opportunity. The actors are very expressive when crossing the stage, having rehearsed their movements in the spirit of a fashion show. They do not simply walk; they turn their side, front, and back to us, freeze for a minute, stare at the audience, and gracefully open the right or left flap of their unbuttoned clothing as if showing the label. The theater does not stop short at self-parody: Krzysztof shows the inseam of his cream colored raincoat showing the familiar red and black emblem of the Taganka Theater.

With European ease and delicacy, the actors conduct a sociable dialogue, quickly changing from one psychological state to another. They range from rhetoric to cynicism, understanding each other without completing sentences. When making a telephone call they do not imitate, as in everyday theater; they do not dial the number but instead bring an invisible receiver to their ear, talking in full view of one another at different ends of the stage.

Everything "acts" in the production—even the props. We see a banquet table with a snow white tablecloth in a restaurant where Krzysztof is indulging his foreign client at state expense. Next the banqueters throw, with an elegant gesture, a corner of the wide tablecloth on the bottles and a bucket of champagne; as if by magic the table is covered with a shroud, changed into something like a deathbed.

Was it because of these tricks that Lyubimov staged this Polish play that ran for many consecutive seasons? Something Lyubimov-like had to be in it.

One short scene in the first act switched the production from a carnival-like spectacle to one with a serious purpose. The prospering Krzysztof meets Andrzej—a childhood friend and friend from the anti-fascist underground. He spent many long years in jail, first in fascist ones, then in anti-fascist ones. Once free he could not understand much of what was going on in his country. Krzysztof, tormented by the memory of how his faint-heartedness caused him to abandon Andrzej in a time of trouble, manages to cope with his feelings. Our nomenclatured hero is uninterested in this excursion into the past. He lives only for today and has adapted well to it. For the audience, however, this passing scene is very meaningful. Krzysztof's career appears in a new light. The light comedy turns to satire directed toward those who hide their guilty consciences under a party ticket and underground revolutionary service records.

The director, however, does not particularly stress this social motif. He continues the production in a comedic manner. In the end Krzysztof's rebirth is worthy more of farce than serious drama. Later the theater tells how capricious fate unexpectedly surprised its indulgent friend. At the peak of fame and happiness Krzysztof suddenly experiences sharp pain; the doctor reveals an incurable illness. Facing death, our hero sinks and bids farewell to life. No one needs him now. He is a burden to everyone—his party, friends, his wife, and even more so, his favorite girl Friday. In the end Krzysztof is the same as everyone else. Now he is ready to do some good deed, to repent—but, that's not what happens. A comedy is a comedy. On the operating table it becomes clear that the doctor has made a mistake; our hero has only an ordinary hernia. Davidovich the bookkeeper no longer needs to get his former boss a magnificent coffin.

Krzysztof's reaction to the medical mistake is funniest of all: He jumps up from his hospital bed angry at the misdiagnosis. He has missed his trip abroad, he's no longer a boss, his career has ended! He believes it all an underhanded plot by his enemies. He will not leave it alone; the party will look into everything!

The Polish playwright's unpretentious comedy is played with comic brilliance by Lyubimov's actors. A not-so-harmless idea is hidden in the subtext. In the foyer after the performance, a spectator, laughing, summed up what we had just seen: "Of course, this doesn't have the slightest relation to us. Even though we and Poland live in the same prison camp, the barracks are completely different."

The Dawns Are Quiet Here

PREMIÈRE: JANUARY 6, 1971

AN AIR RAID SIREN DRIVES THE SPECTATORS INTO THE AUDI-
torium as if into a shelter. A stiff piece of canvas hangs over the
entrance. Bending your head you inevitably touch the crude war
artifact. You enter the theater bowing.

The wooden body of a wartime truck, almost life-size, with the
number IX 16–06 on the side, stands on the empty stage. This is
the only scenery provided by David Borovsky, the new set designer,
introduced into the Taganka by the remarkable director and follower
of Meyerhold Leonid Viktorovich Varpakhovsky.[11] A talented ped-
agogue selflessly devoted to the theater, Leonid Viktorovich uncovered Borovsky's talents while still in Kiev, where he returned
to the theater to continue the work of his teacher Meyerhold after
imprisonment in Stalin's concentration camp, Magadan. Leonid
Viktorovich found in the young Borovsky the ideal designer for
Lyubimov's innovative productions; without hesitation and in det-
riment to his own plans he blessed the union of these innovative
men. Borovsky's light touch became an integral part of the Taganka.
From that time on all of Lyubimov's best productions at the Taganka
and many abroad were designed by David Borovsky, with his in-
fallible and original spatial vision.

The military truck "IX 16-06" in *The Dawns Are Quiet Here* is an
arresting and concise metaphor for war. This image is staggering
in its stark simplicity, expressiveness, and combination of natural
and theatrical symbolism. For two hours without interruption we
watch the stage amazed at its transformation through the simplest,
most laconic means. The body of the truck and a little imagination
turn the stage into a clearing in the woods, a dugout, or a field
bathhouse.

The wooden boards vertically hung on the bars of the half-ton
truck become, in the final scene, mysterious trees of the darkened
forest and spin, as if alive, with the women in their death waltz.

The inventive Borovsky has an acute sense of style and finds a
particular form for every Lyubimov production: the living curtain

in *Hamlet*, the white door with drops of blood in *Crime and Punishment*, the glass aquarium-vestibule in *The House on the Embankment*. His concise scenography imparts the director's conception with what seems to be the only theatrical conclusion possible. Without Borovsky the Taganka probably would never have become the Taganka we know. Borovsky remained faithful to the theater even after parting in London with its founder and sadly returning to Moscow. Borovsky and Lyubimov are friends sharing the same views on art.

The Dawns Are Quiet Here is perhaps Lyubimov's most poetic and harmonious production. In it he unites previously diverse stylistic categories—the conditional and psychological theater. There are no directorial excesses in it and the actors are on equal footing with the director. It was not by accident that after this production critics noticeably quieted their discussion about the Taganka as exclusively the director's theater, with no place for outstanding actors.

Lyubimov's account of the terrible war was amazingly tender and intimate. We watch as the sweet young women in soldier's blouses perish, one after the other, in the difficult August of 1942. The director, avoiding sentimentality, showed the unnaturalness of the force leading these women to leave their own affairs and to accomplish heroic deeds. Continuing the theme of *The Fallen and the Living*, Lyubimov and his actors debunk the myth of war as a great act. Brecht, one of the Taganka's teachers, once said: "Unfortunate is the country that needs heroes." In essence, this idea is advanced in *Dawns*. The Taganka actors enter into a secret argument with the cheap optimism of the State, which supposedly declared in the name of its patriots: "When the country orders us to be heroes, then everyone becomes a hero."

The theater's voice sounds dissonant compared to the chatter of official poetry and the thunder of kettle drums on Red Square, both muffling the truth about World War II, the Great Patriotic War, with its often senseless and vain sacrifices. Bard Bulat Okudzhava, a great friend of the theater, later expressed himself quite definitively on this theme:

> It was not a Great war, it was a Terrible war. A disgusting war. It ravaged our souls, made us cruel. We had to become adults before our time. . . . It is by no means the best thing that could happen to a person. It's not something to be proud of nor a merit.[12]

The production tells the story of the young women in Sergeant-Major Vaskov's anti-aircraft battalions, who do not feel like heroes and do not use grand words. Even at the front they behave like young women of their age. They joke, sing, reminisce, read poetry, sunbathe, love or daydream about love, squeal with delight in a soldier's bathhouse, and cry in fear in a dark forest. They are horrified at death yet meet it fearlessly, maybe because they do not know what death is; many of them have not yet known a kiss. Probably, they do not fear death because they have not yet had the chance to experience life. This makes the war even more monstrous. The image of silent, faceless soldier-automatons moving mechanically through the woods is frightening; they take one step forward, one to the side, two back into the shade of the trees and further from the light. We understand Vaskov, the Siberian Sergeant-Major (Shapovalov) who, alone and despairing, runs in a frenzied outburst into the thicket of enemy machine guns that had cold-bloodedly shot up the young women of his battalion.

Life perishes before our eyes. We witness the deaths of sickly Galya Chetvertak (T. Zhukova), who has lost her boot in a boggy swamp; the thin young woman in glasses, Sonya Gurvich (N. Sayko), who would not part with her small volume of symbolist poet Aleksandr Blok; Liza Brichkina (M. Politseymako), who passed her youth in a God-forsaken place; Zhenya Komelkova (N. Shatskaya), whose beautiful figure brings envious delight to her friends; and their Commanding Officer, Rita Osyanina (I. Kuznetsova) who, despite her stoicism, cannot crush her mystic horror as she pulls the boots off the murdered Sonya in order to give them to another fighter.

Lyubimov's direction is spare, energetic, and even lapidary. The whole action seems subordinate to the soldiers' regulated rhythm of 120 steps per minute. The resilient tempo is set at the beginning, when an aligned formation of women soldiers carrying rifles passes through the central aisle of the auditorium from the back doors.

Usually very liberal with inventive directorial ideas, Lyubimov this time forces himself and his actors to subordinate to a strict, inner discipline. He puts an interesting acting problem before his actors; he wants to show, within a military framework, the form man's spirit takes in war. Infallibly and with obvious pleasure the actors live through the atmosphere of war, from the dullest moments of a soldier's everyday life to the elevated, tragic scenes that leave their special mark on an otherwise normal life. There is no room for sentiment here; even though the young women sometimes talk about love there is no rhetoric. Sergeant-Major Vaskov cannot even finish giving them political information before they drop from exhaustion, weary from heavy battle. There are no extensive reminiscences at the moments of their deaths. In spite of this, the production is deeply lyrical from the beginning to its last metaphor. Only the lyricism is special; it is concentrated and bleak, dressed, so to speak, in a soldier's blouse and crude boots. Because of this it is more penetrating, bringing out fury and not tears, clearing the consciousness, not clouding it with sentimentality and rhetoric.

Each of the five deaths concludes with a short theatrical barrier— a reminiscence, that final outburst of consciousness or sub-consciousness illuminating the whole life of each woman at the moment of death. This takes up only a few minutes on stage. They recall the house they grew up in, a favorite person, parting with their mother, or, like Sonya Gurvich, a very recent, fleeting conversation with Sergeant-Major Vaskov, whose stern exterior hides a good heart. He asks her before battle: "Your parents are of the Jewish nation?" "Naturally," answers Sonya. "If it was natural, I wouldn't have asked you," counters Vaskov.

Why did Sonya Gurvich recall precisely this episode from her life at the hour of her death? Why did the director force us to listen to this short dialogue twice? The second time a reflection of the dying Sonya's consciousness gives each word a particularly significant meaning. This is the power of theater. What order is there to the thoughts of old soldier Vaskov, who asks this strange question? Having only finished the fourth grade with difficulty, he manages to construct his punctilious question very precisely: not you, Sonya, but your parents—your nation I do not question— your nation is the same as ours, the Soviet nation, that is established. But Sonya's answer, listened to carefully, especially the second time, merits some thought: "Naturally," she says. What is so strange, Comrade Sergeant-Major, that the daughter of Jewish parents fights for her native land like everyone else?

Most significant, however, in this brief dialogue is Vaskov's reply: "If it was natural, I wouldn't have asked you!" It is delivered like the crack of a rifle bolt on the count of three: One—he throws out the empty cartridge of age-old prejudices; two—he puts a good cartridge into the receiver of consciousness; three—he drives it into the barrel of his memory.

The ending is infinitely lyrical; the dance after death is a truly brilliant directorial idea. These young women are gone but still with us, like the pine trees with whom they have blended in a slow tango. Whirling, they disappear, dissolving into the darkened forest, leaving their admirers bewildered.

Shaken, we leave the auditorium slowly, and mechanically drag ourselves to the coat room, but Lyubimov does not let us go so simply. Before we completely don our modern clothing and again enter the fray, he forces us to pass through a row of blazing shell-like cartridges on the staircase steps extending to the top of the foyer and out to the Moscow evening sky.

As a rule, Lyubimov strives to continue his productions outside the theater's auditorium in order to tie theater to life.

Wooden Horses

PREMIÈRE: APRIL 16, 1974

ONE COULD SAY THAT THE TAGANKA THEATER FAVORS EXCLU-sively Russian themes. As a director Lyubimov is a man of one passion—Russia and her culture. He expresses both love and pain for her. No matter what he recounts in staging Brecht, Molière, or Shakespeare, he nevertheless thinks first of Russia, presenting a Russian *Galileo*, a Russian *Tartuffe*, and a Russian *Hamlet*.

However strange it seems, this devotion to native problems makes the Taganka, to a high degree, a European phenomenon. National narrow-mindedness is alien to Lyubimov and his actors. They show Russian history through a prism of national self-criticism, empha-sizing, sometimes disproportionately, their bitter remorse concern-ing events on Russian soil that have undermined the people's well-being and spirituality.

The Taganka Theater, maturing through the years, consciously fulfilled a special mission in Soviet art. In an atmosphere of forced silence the theater touched upon forbidden themes and discussed universal human values and a sense of justice to which the people have remained faithful. On the theater's tenth anniversary it turned to the country's collective farms and staged one of its best produc-tions, *Wooden Horses*, based on the work of F. Abramov. Through it, the theater took revenge for the banned *Alive*, which painfully recounted the Russian peasantry's destiny on Soviet soil.

We have already spoken about the connection between beginnings and endings in Lyubimov's productions. In *Wooden Horses* this di-rectorial device not only links theater to life but also carries a sig-nificant emotional burden, forcing the spectator to feel personally involved from the very beginning.

To get from the foyer to the auditorium in this production one has to cross the stage over a small, specially constructed bridge. The spectators ascend the bridge and continue to the right wing of the stage, made to look like a country porch, clean and spacious, with long cotton curtains. Passing by, the spectator enters the brightly lit chamber of the peasant hut, with birch bark moneyboxes and other household items on the shelves and in the corners. A real Russian stove is center stage, on a spotlessly clean painted wooden floor.

Somewhat puzzled you walk along the floorboards and step onto a colored runner made of crude hemp leading stage front, where there is another little bridge with rickety handrails. You descend the bridge, enter the auditorium, and sigh in relief; finding your row and seat you finally become an ordinary spectator.

While on stage, in the unusual surroundings of a peasant hut, you wonder whether you have become a victim of a sophisticated theatrical mystification. For a second you feel turned into an object for observation. After all, those who crossed the stage before you laugh quietly, glancing curiously at you from their seats, watching your behavior in this unexpected situation. Will you react good naturedly and joke, or will you act indifferent? Yes, you city-dwelling socialite, you have been away from the soil for a long time. You forget how to walk on the floor of a peasant hut and to wipe your feet on the canvas folded especially for you by the front door; you forget to look at the holy corner, choosing to ignore and walk around it. You are unaccustomed to the old, country ways. You do not know and apparently do not want to know who feeds you, whose milk you drink in the morning!

Until you get used to the emphatically naturalistic setting you will not be able to appreciate the production's provocative beginning. Perhaps some consider it another of Lyubimov's eccentricities, a theatrical attempt at cleverness. Only at the very end, upon leaving the auditorium through the regular doors and returning to city life, do we, without fail, recall our passage through the chambers of the peasant hut. Then, perhaps, the production reveals its hidden concept.

Wooden Horses is not as typical of Lyubimov as his other productions. Usually action boils over on the Taganka stage, rolling like waves, rushing, outstripping thought, hurrying to change impressions and leaving certain things unsaid. The expressiveness of the action, as a rule, does not come through the author's text as much as through the theatrical spectacle, the expressive montage of separate scenic-attractions, as in *Good Person* and *Ten Days*. Lyubimov's dynamic theater is considered mechanistic in contrast to the traditional psychological performance of the Russian actor. But theater does not keep still. Gradually deepening and enriching its theatrical language, the Taganka begins to value the power of the actor's inner experience and substantively broadens its creative methods.

In *Wooden Horses* the theater unites diverse stylistic categories— those of everyday and conditional theaters—in its art. The poetry is enriched by everyday life and everyday life is enriched by the poetry; a new quality is created. The impoverished, shunned world of Russian peasantry, lacking a proprietor and now a part of the Soviet treasury, is presented on stage with a tragic quality in ordinary life not seen before.

The principal means by which the theater achieves this portrayal is through the lively dialect of the northwestern Russian villages that had managed to preserve their selfhood in the face of lifeless Soviet idioms.

The action flows quietly in *Wooden Horses* like a sleepy stream in central Russia where the characters come from. There is no action in the usual sense of the word, uncharacteristic of Lyubimov's theater. With refined strokes and no superfluous theatrical metaphors, the theater lightly sketches simple peasant days and ways. The soft, pale, enchanting Russian landscape is the backdrop for a large, arresting, sepia portrait of two ordinary Russian women, Milentievna and Pelageya, undistinguished but for their troubled fate. Two parts of the production carry their names.

Alla Demidova draws Milentievna with great concentration, gently, and with inner warmth; she does not seem to have even a kernel of a dramatic role. The old woman comes out of the woods with a basket full of mushrooms. She goes through them, rests for a moment because of her rheumatism, and goes out into the bad weather though they try to dissuade her from it. She goes out into the rain because she promised to see her granddaughter. We meet Milentievna and fall in love with her solely based on her daughter-in-law's stories. The talkative Evgeniya (Tatiana Zhukova) adores her grandma.

"D'ya think she'll wanna eat or drink now?" she asks, indicating the old woman who has wandered through the forest from dawn until late morning.

> Not for anything! She's an old fashioned person. Until she cleans the mushrooms, you'd best not even peep about food. . . . That's our

grandma, for you! We're still sitt'n, stuff'n our faces, and she's already done a day's work![13]

The hearty speech of the people, so rarely heard in theater, attains its own importance. It is neither the plot nor the absorbing subject that pumps the production's lifeblood; it is the word.

The daughter-in-law eagerly tells her fellow villagers, arranged on benches along both sides of the stage as if at a village gathering, about Milentievna. The peasants function like the chorus in ancient theater, commenting on the main action with song or short lines of little importance. Despite Milentievna's outward passivity and tendency toward silence, she is precisely the one holding the audience's attention. Through some kind of inexplicable inner luminescence she is the center of our attention, even though she sits on the sidelines seemingly unconcerned.

Milentievna is the genuine dramatic figure. Her radiant, deep, tranquil gaze confirms the old observation that an actor's eyes are not just mirrors of the soul but generators of feelings, thoughts, and imperceptible spiritual impulses. The deep, blue color of De-midova's eyes, focused most often on the auditorium, on the last rows of the orchestra or the gallery, reveals her rich, sincere, inner life and her involvement with something higher, something eternal. Her gaze, fixed over our heads, reflects the whole of her difficult and unfortunate life as recounted by the talkative Evgeniya. From Evgeniya's words we learn about Milentievna's youth when she stirred up the peasants to root out the forest, clean up the stubble, and plant rye in the sterile soil. The rye, replete with the sweat of the peasants, sprang as high as pine trees in the vacant land received from the new authorities, giving the peasants a taste of work and the beauty of their land. In the first years after the revolution, carved wooden horses appeared on the peasants' roofs, symbols of a free and easy life.

Milentievna, silent, listens to what they say about her. Recounted are the cheerful times of her youth and the black day that dashed the peasants' hopes—the day their own new government began to dispossess the kulaks, the new "owners," who had refused to sign up for collectivization. All is reflected in the watery eyes that address the spectator.

"They've gone crazy," comments Evgeniya, "well, we don't want collective farms here! That's when they were sent to where the sun don't shine."

Again, Milentievna keeps quiet. We see only an inexpressible pain in her eyes. Was it by any chance the fault of this activist that the peasants got caught under Stalin's thresher?

Milentievna is also silent when her daughter-in-law, as if not noticing the old woman, tells of her ungainly family fortune. She tells how she was shoved into marriage at the age of sixteen with someone she did not love ("Maybe she didn't even have breasts yet?"), and how on the first day of their marriage, in order to win respect in a strange house, got up at dawn to go for mushrooms; she came out of the woods with a full bag and—bam—a shot hits her in the face: it was the stern husband greeting his young wife; she probably did not please him the night before . . .

Milentievna-Demidova, going through the mushrooms, looks out into the auditorium, her head shaking slightly. Her twitch, as we learn from Evgeniya, is a lifelong reminder of that morning. Milentievna offers only a conciliatory smile: "Anything can happen between one's own family." She does not wish her unloved husband harm, though he irrevocably robbed her youth. Quietly, reasonably, she brings out a moral of her daughter-in-law's account:

Old people love to praise bygone times, but I don't. Now, people are literate, stand up for themselves, but we haven't known freedom since we were young.

The wise old woman has calming explanations for everything; maybe that is why her young eyes sparkle? Maybe her secret to life, spiritual calm, and reconciliation is this all-forgiveness and integrity?

She does not seem moved by Evgeniya's account of her large family being swept away. Two sons perished in the war; her favorite daughter, Sanya, an exquisite, gentle beauty, took her own life when a scoundrel, after getting her pregnant, abandoned her.

This transparent, elegiacal account ends as it begins—on a quiet note, like a river running into sand. A miracle happens! It is the sense of having experienced the unfinished drama; it remains with the spectator and grows even though the heroine does not shout, argue, or ask questions. With her head slightly twitching and the shadow of a condescending smile on her clear, unwrinkled brow

Milentievna-Demidova wraps a kerchief around herself, ties her belongings in a small bundle, casts a farewell glance at her peasant hut, and goes out into the bad weather to her granddaughter as promised, revealing a new feature of her enigmatic character—not only meekness and great patience, but also a firmness of spirit . . .

Pelageya, Zinaida Slavina's temperamental incarnation, is the extreme opposite of Milentievna both outwardly and in her view of life. Angular, noisy, abrupt, and even aggressive, she is the sole master of the stage just as she is in her house. Everything revolves around her and her often unexpected and illogical decisions. Having come home from work tired, she refuses to go to the nameday celebration of her husband's sister, Anisya (E. Kornilova). She does not just refuse, she refuses reproachfully:

> When did you get up today?— she attacked her sister-in-law. I got up, lit the stove, cut the grass, milked the cow, went to the river— and you were still sleeping on your stomach with your ass up . . . no smoke coming out of the chimney. There's still a glow on your cheeks.
> So I'm to blame?
> And I went to the bake shop, Pelageya-Slavina continues her reproach, lit another stove—one log was as long as a sazhen.[14] I carried up thirty buckets of water, baked 100 loaves of dark bread and another 70 white ones. And how I stood by the stove and roasted myself— well I won't even talk about that. . . .

They are just going to bed when a young boy comes running in with a note from Peter Ivanovich, the local boss, saying "we await our dear guests." Somehow Pelageya gets her second wind, rouses her sick husband out of bed, dresses him, and gets herself dolled up. Away they go. The necessary people would be there and, after a bottle, personal matters could be resolved with the Chairman of the Village Soviet. Registering her husband Pavel as an invalid could get him a pension even though he was good for nothing; some hay for the cow would come in handy, and Alka, the daughter, needs to get a certificate to go to town. Pelageya's husband is sick and generally dumb; she has to think of everything herself.

Strangely, however, the more Pelageya fusses about everyday, mercantile matters, arranging them according to current, crooked rules, the less personal happiness she has. Troubles pile up in her household; there isn't even time to enjoy the good weather, the dew-covered grass, and the mushrooms of the forest. Her face is harsh from nature, her dark, restless eyes grow sharper, darting ever more anxiously, her cheeks are puffed, and her nervous hands drop everything. Her active nature, once useful in quarrels with the local bosses and carrying the household burden, now, more often than not, manifests itself in short-tempered outbursts at people, life, and herself. A woman's quarrel with Anisya (E. Kornilova) turns into a brawl. (One doesn't have to go to the movies!)

We see Pelageya's soul become embittered; we see her lose respect for people. She once took pride in her profession as baker. Everyone in the village hoped for an extra loaf from her. Her hard life discourages her desire to work; even though she is still sorceress of the community stove, ever trying to bake the bread better and more aromatically, she does not feel herself and the work weighs on her.

Pelageya really breaks down for the first time when her Alka, the "bitch," runs away to town with a handsome lieutenant without saying goodbye to her parents. Pelageya, for all her bragging, cannot recover from this blow. When Pavel dies three days later Pelageya completely loses her ground and involuntarily begins to think about the meaning of her life, perhaps for the first and only time. On stage there is a village funeral, speeches: "Hard-worker . . . honest . . . an example for us all . . . on watch from the very first day of collective life . . . we won't forget him. . . ."

Something turns upside down in Pelageya's soul. She stood up to everything, but she breaks down upon these speeches. She enters the proscenium and asks our advice. Everything in the speeches is true. Quiet Pavel worked unfailingly on the collective farm, like a horse, like a machine. And the thresher at the collective farm made him an invalid. But who valued his work? His superiors? She, Pelageya? As if in confession she admits she did not value her husband's work at all! After a pause she asks herself and us as well: How can work on the collective farm be valued when no one pays for it? Then, for the only time in the production, Pelageya lets out a hoarse, soulful wail. It is not clear why. Is it because of the motionless, waxy face of the man with the crossed arms, with whom, from hand to mouth, she lived her life? Is it self-pity for the vain, laughable pretension of sitting at the same table with the bosses?

"This company should go to hell!" Slavina cries in a frenzy. In the strange word "company," which does not suit her peasant's speech, the character hides another more precise definition, but she is careful even in anger.

In contrast to the silent, passive Milentievna, who also had her share of sorrow, Pelageya cannot find anything in her soul to hold onto at this moment of despair. The heroine thuds against the floor in her cursed house like she did in her first, happy entrance when, still energetic and strong, she runs home from work with a heavy bucket of pig slop and, wheezing, glances at the pale, sweaty face of her husband: "Here you are, Lord, he hasn't rested enough!" She throws off her boots and falls to the ground so that the painted floorboards absorb the heat of her broken body, but this time she will not get up.

When you leave the auditorium the tragedy of Russian destiny has been strikingly revealed to you. You will certainly remember the production's calm, ethnographically accurate introduction and the almost forgotten cult of everyday village life. It is then that the passage through the stage-hut gains its own meaning as an image of that foundation, the sub-soil that, with its destruction, begins Soviet reality.

Crime and Punishment

BUDAPEST PREMIÈRE: JANUARY 1978
MOSCOW PREMIÈRE: FEBRUARY 12, 1979

Yuri Lyubimov staged *Crime and punishment* in Budapest a year before its opening night in Moscow. Although the theater planned to stage Dostoevsky for a long time with the director publicly announcing it a few times, the administration opposed it and so rehearsals at the Taganka were put off from one year to another. Lyubimov's decision to first test his mettle on a foreign stage surprised many. Only later did it become apparent that in his *Crime and Punishment* Lyubimov was preparing to confront the world as well as his native theater.

Hungary presented suitable ground for such farsighted plans. Located between Western and Eastern European cultures, Hungary and its theater offered favorable conditions for theatrical experiments with a Russian classic popular in Europe.

Other, subjective circumstances tied Lyubimov's fate to Hungary. A short time earlier he married a young Hungarian journalist, Katalin, fluent in Russian and a fervent admirer of the Soviet director's talent. The marriage was a happy one; it rejuvenated the sixty-year-old director. Katalin became a faithful companion. The newlyweds soon had a son, Petya. Yuri Petrovich, like most parents who have children late in life, became absorbed in his heir beyond the realm of reason. (During détente mixed marriages became fashionable in Moscow. Vladimir Vysotsky started it off at the Taganka by marrying the French actress Marina Vladi.)

While such substantive and happy turns were occurring in Lyubimov's personal life, the outer circumstances of his work were not as favorable. His relations with Soviet authorities worsened and became more complicated. Cultural bureaucrats closed in on the obstinate director. I have said, in May 1977 he was attacked in

Pravda for his production of Bulgakov's *Master and Margarita*. In the summer of the same year Lyubimov was publicly condemned for an interview with the organizers of the Venetian biannual because he appeared disloyal to Soviet cultural policies. Later he was attacked for his statement in *Humanité* addressing the difficult working conditions of Soviet actors. In November an open conflict broke out between Lyubimov and *Literaturnaya Gazeta (Literary Gazette)*, which accused Lyubimov of slandering the Soviet system.[15]

This unsettling atmosphere accompanied Lyubimov's work in the Hungarian theater Vigszinhaz, where the actors did not at first accept his methods in conducting rehearsals, disdaining work on the mock-up of the set and following the Table of Ranks far too much. Using specious excuses some leading performers refused to play their roles at the very height of rehearsals. Lyubimov, however, did not lower his demands on the actors and continued to work with complete dedication in the way he was used to at his own Taganka Theater, sparing neither time nor energy. He won. The success of the Budapest première of *Crime and Punishment* exceeded the expectations of even the most benevolent critics. They all acknowledged that Lyubimov had given the Hungarian theater a graphic lesson in contemporary, innovative direction.

I saw this production in Hungary in March 1978 when, as if in revenge for his Hungarian success, dark clouds again began to hang over Lyubimov. In a *Pravda* article Zhyuraytis, a conductor at the Bolshoy Theater, spoke out against continuing *Queen of Spades* rehearsals at the Grand Opera in Paris, where Lyubimov was next invited. Lyubimov was scandalously accused of mocking the Russian classics, and this time, despite protests from the French, he was forced to halt his work and return to Moscow without finishing.

What was the production in Budapest like?

The Vigszinhaz, where Lyubimov's *Crime and Punishment* debuted, was striking in the splendor of its interior, contrasted to the austerity of the Taganka. The huge oval auditorium with its orchestra pit, velvety armchairs, and glittering boxes was built at the end of the nineteenth century, in the style Hungarian haberdashers and bankers preferred, in a respectable district of Budapest on the Danube River. The atmosphere in this theater and its actors and spectators totally differ from those at the Taganka. The parlor room, conversational style of the Vigszinhaz, in translation the comedy theater, traditionally preferred drawing room drama or light comedy built upon elegant dialogue with easily developing piquant intrigue. The theater's home playwright, Ferents Molnar, was at the peak of his fame a remarkable comedy writer. He wrote *The Devil* and *Lilliom*, both making the rounds of world theaters including Moscow and New York at the beginning of the century.

First, Lyubimov ordered the heavy, velvet curtain taken away and the orchestra pit covered to shorten the distance between actors and spectators. Hungarian theaters usually have an additional curtain of corrugated steel, a so-called "fire curtain." Lyubimov used its texture in his production.

When the steel curtain rose it was extended on stage by a metal, vaulted gateway through which the spectators entered as if into the courtyard of an old Petersburg house. The narrow, steel tunnel oppressed one with its heaviness. It occupied the left half of the stage at a small angle and overlooked throughout. A stream of light from the setting sun or a street light penetrated this dark entrance from somewhere behind the stage. In the gateway the light dispersed, the borders of the stage concealed by a mysterious semi-darkness in which one could guess the contours of a human dwelling. The tunnel was the only slit tying the lives of the inhabitants of the Petersburg slum with the external world. There were no doors or walls on stage. The characters appear either from the entrance or the dark corners and in the same way suddenly disappear. Only Raskolnikov obstinately comes on stage from the auditorium or from the wings. He is above law and Lyubimov, it seems, allows him everything.

The main action takes place center stage, which is scantily decorated. The scene designer, D. Borovsky, united coarse objectivity with convention, resulting in a specific, almost symbolic expression in the naturalistic details. Like the director, the designer did not limit himself to one meaning, nor did he fear accusations of primitivism. Borovsky's scenography helps the actor concentrate on the drama's internal conflicts.

Lyubimov felt his way through the composition that later became the core of his stage design in mature Moscow, London, Vienna, Bologna, and Washington productions. Man, driven into a dark corner and alone with his thoughts and conscience, opposes the foul, hostile, oddly arranged world. In the Hungarian production the boundaries between man and the world are not yet so strongly outlined; they are only implied. It seems that Lyubimov gives the Hungarian Raskolnikov an opportunity to choose more humane means to fulfill his ambitions. The stress is not on the struggle between ideas but on revealing the psychology of the Raskolnikovs, whose awakened consciences seek, if not justification, then compassion.

It is possible that, in some way, the Hungarian Raskolnikov is closer to Dostoevsky's hero than his Moscow counterpart. Kern, a young, nervous, high-strung actor with sunken cheeks and burning eyes, does indeed suffer for humanity, and the better he realizes his helplessness in changing anything in this life the more relentlessly he torments himself. His hurt vanity nurtured itself on the pain created by the evil in the world. He went for the crime with romantic notions. One does not feel in him the demonism of the Moscow Raskolnikov, portrayed by Trofimov. He is much younger, less experienced, and more naive. At some points in the role small, neurotic, and ardent Kern resembles the student-rebel of the 1950s and 1960s, passionately searching for a new faith to replace lost and trampled ideals. Tearing down the verbal disguises of life's worldly lies, the Hungarian Raskolnikov himself becomes a victim of maniacal ideas.

At the very beginning of the performance, Raskolnikov climbs up on stage from the auditorium with notebook in hand and quotes his young contemporary: "The old woman is a wicked person, she's a louse who's harmful to those around her. And young Raskolnikov is a fine fellow for killing the old woman. It's too bad he got caught. He doesn't even repent his theory at hard labor in Siberian exile." The actor reads these school essays to the audience as if they were written by himself, as he seeks justification for his own thoughts. His calculations are simple: by killing the old pawnbroker he performs an act of double goodness—he saves the people from evil and turns evil into good for the "insulted and injured."

The Budapest production was imbued with romantic compassion for Raskolnikov, perhaps despite the director's will, primarily due to Kern's artistic personality promoted by the Hungarian sensibility toward moral issues. In the Moscow production Lyubimov firmly refuses to discuss the "awakened conscience" of the murderer.

The director shocks the spectator with the sight of bloody plastercast corpses that lay on the proscenium during the whole action. The crime is on hand and there is no justification for it, the director seems to say through this naturalistic, Guignol vignette.

In Budapest Lyubimov is more subtle. The *leitmotif* is a street musician who appears at the beginning and at the end of the play. The poor, lonely violinist, like an echo of a different life somewhere else, appears in the steel gateway of the Budapest house and plays a sad, familiar melody so out of keeping with the brutality occurring on stage. Having touched the Hungarian spectator's weak spot, Lyubimov returns him to the sentimental thought that real life is fuller than the most daring artistic invention, and that life's richness and complexity cannot fit into one frame.

The Hungarian production of *Crime and Punishment* and the Moscow performance which took place a year later were compared and analyzed by the prominent Moscow critic K. Rudnitsky.[16] Because it is one of the best critical analyses of the Moscow production, I have cited the article almost entirely.

> As soon as you enter the auditorium, opening not the front door of the theater, but a typical, peeling, white apartment door, you immediately see two twisted corpses at the very edge of the stage on the right. A murder has occurred. The faces of the women killed were hurriedly covered with handkerchiefs, here and there one can see drops of dried blood on their cheap dresses, their hands have already yellowed, their legs in crude stockings and old shoes jut out like sticks. The murder took place right here, in the corner, where the most varied and completely unattractive things are crammed: a dresser, neatly covered with an old lace napkin and a small icon with a warm icon lamp can be seen. Higher up, on the mezzanine, some old suitcases, warped by time, are placed. Yes, there was a miserly old woman pawnbroker, who lived wretchedly, in filth. . . . A little bit further is a square mirror in a wooden frame. There is a spot of dried blood on the mirror. Books, covered in blood, with pages torn out, lie about on the floor. The whole set-up takes only a fraction of the proscenium—only one small part. On the left—complete emptiness, a naked stage wide open to the back brick wall. In the corner where the corpses lay and the things are concentrated, in the emptiness of the huge, cold space is another door. That is David Borovsky's entire, meager, laconic set.
>
> The brick wall, closing in the boundaries of the stage, is white. Colors have no access to these boundaries; the play of colors is for-

bidden—the director almost never uses color. The whole composition is black and white, all of the costumes hold completely to the black-gray-white scale. The battle between black and white, darkness and light gives the action a somber degree of concentration; moreover, the lighting is cold, abrupt, and never tender.

In contrast, the theme of blood, from time to time, in loudly howling red spots—the bloody trail of the murderer—inserts itself into the very center of the black and white world.

Human figures cast huge shadows against the white brick back-drop—all the way to the ceiling. The performance of the shadows, evil and threatening, echoes the performance of the actors, increasing their movements and intensifying the expressiveness of their gestures. The meaning of everything that happens on this empty canvas for us is increased a thousandfold however, by that first impression that sticks with us: the picture of a double murder, which we discovered just as soon as we entered the auditorium, and about which Lyubimov himself keeps reminding us again and again, throwing light in the right corner where the corpses are.

A strange thing though: the fact that the corpses that we saw were plastercasts was, of course, not in doubt. We knew very well that there were life-size mannequins lying on the floor, not people, that the whole Grand Guignol scene—the prostrate bodies of the women in the wretched clothing, the drops of dried blood, the mess—was arranged in the naive naturalism of a wax museum. Unconcerned, we walked past the scene of the crime, talking about our own problems and checking our tickets. By no means were we horrified by what we saw, nor did we inwardly shudder. But all of the sober details indicated by the director registered in our subconscious.

It became clear that this was more than enough, that starting *with this moment* everything that happened after would without fail be marked by *this moment* and we wouldn't be able to forget what it all was about for the entire production.

A very strange situation: Raskolnikov despises mankind, but desires to do it a great favor. But, in its blindness, ignoble, ungrateful mankind naively assumes it can get by without Raskolnikov. It can somehow get by, if only he'd leave it alone. Only he won't leave it alone, he's not that kind of a man. Raskolnikov—A. Trofimov—is a man of ideas. Somewhere inside, at the core of his soul, ideas took root and met-astastically grew. At first they promised to lift him high up, but then they tricked him and threw him against the ground. But this tall, young man in the worn out, almost beggarly black coat, in the black shirt and ripped open collar, with the foul, soiled hat, didn't feel the blow, he wasn't in need of sympathy, he did not ask for compassion. Just the opposite, he is still trying to save mankind, not only this, but his ideas have been strengthened for he overstepped the bounds, committed a crime, killed, which means the murder is already accomplished, giving him the opportunity to do a hundred—what's a hundred?—a thousand good deeds.

But is he capable of good deeds? That is the very question that comes up almost as soon as we meet him. These shifts of focus were generally unusual for Lyubimov, who is sensitive to the slightest social nuances, attentive to society's gradations and distinctions, but in this case they were intentional. Lyubimov knew that too strong an emphasis on the social contrasts and contradictions could cause, if not a justification of Raskolnikov, then some kind of a leaning toward him, some desire to understand, if not his crime, then his motives. It was exactly on this point that Lyubimov was unyielding. He didn't want to accept the twin murders simply as "information for a discussion" of socialist problems, at all costs.

Raskolnikov, who felt cramped within the limits of local news, who yearned to be on the pages of history books, thinks of himself as a hero and he craves to interpret the evil he created as a blessing and as a lesson to all of petty, pitiful, incapable mankind. Here he seemed more an unfinished man than a superman. The theater did not promise him redemption of guilt, did not attach significance to the flashes of his wakening conscience, did not foresee repentance.

In the finale, when Raskolnikov-Trofimov lit the candles clenched in the hands of the women he had murdered, two actresses, who had switched themselves with the mannequins, opened their eyes wide as if bidding him farewell. Just then Svidrigaylov appears and blows out the candles. This signified that there would be no forgiveness. Then, Svidrigaylov would go to center stage and Vysotsky, no longer in Svidrigaylov's name, but now in his own name, in Lyubimov's and the theater's, loudly proclaimed: "Well done, Raskolnikov—it's good that you killed the old woman. It's too bad you got caught!"

And, after a pause, explained: "That's from an elementary school composition."

We leafed through these compositions—real, authentic, present-day—collected from Moscow schools before the performance. They were piled up on school desks that had been carried out in the foyer: more often than not the kids admired Raskolnikov. After all, they weren't told of social plagues of the cursed past and of the wakening conscience for nothing. . . . Now the critics who got used to chewing these themes that were crammed down their throats were lost in guessing what Lyubimov had in mind?

What he had in mind was that no general idea is justified in its goal by paying with individual human lives. That there is nothing general which could be a whole death higher than your own? That "one death" is not compensated for by ideology.

That's what this theater wants to say and does say convincingly.

The Three Sisters

PREMIÈRE: DECEMBER 1981

I SAW *THE THREE SISTERS* FOR THE FIRST TIME IN PRE-WAR Moscow, on virtually my first visit to the Moscow Art Theatre. Being a young man I probably did not understand it all, but I do remember the screaming cranes very well and the heartrending, wishful cry of the older Olga at play's end: "If one could only know, if one could only know!" All of us then pitied *The Three Sisters* who dreamed of getting away to Moscow.

Forty years later, in another theater, I am again watching *The Three Sisters* but in a strikingly different production than the one at the Moscow Art Theatre. Tomorrow I leave my native Moscow for a long time, probably forever, but *The Three Sisters* still live and dream there and Olga again speaks the same words: "If one could only know, if one could only know!"

For some reason, this time, they sound completely different. They do not have the comforting, wishful thinking of the wonderful Moscow Art Theatre actress Yelanskaya. They are hard; there exists an ironic, sarcastic sub-text. Today's Olga despises sentimentality; she is a businesslike woman who tells the God's honest truth over her shoulder, like a man. "Time will go by," she says coldly, not so much to her sisters but to us, the spectators of the 1980s, "and we'll be gone for good, we'll be forgotten, our faces, our voices, and how many of us there were will be forgotten. . . ."

The actress pauses, steps to the edge of the proscenium, and slightly mocking, skeptically tosses questions at us: ". . . our sufferings will turn to joy for those who will live after[?], peace and happiness will be upon us[?], and they will remember with kind words and bless those who lived now[?]."

These questions are rhetorical, of course. It is understood that the theater will not give any simple answers. It does, however, pose these confounded questions of Russian life and force us to think about them. In the auditorium of the 1980s Chekhov's words fall with sarcasm and not with false comfort in this bleak, un-Chekhovian production.

The Taganka Theater categorically rejects the traditional sentimentality and starry-eyed idealism of Chekhov's stage interpretations. The theater rises up against the tradition, showing Chekhov's humanism as a reverie in imitation of "Gorky," casting a "golden dream" over people, clouding reason with a search for the "sacred truth." For *The Three Sisters* of the Taganka, the image of Moscow is merely a metaphor for the impossibility of their hope for another, more free and active life, unlikely anytime soon in the real Russia. *The Three Sisters* at the Taganka is a masculine, cruelly unwomanly, I would even say soldierly production. It is significant that the color of military gray overcoats dominates, contrasting sharply with the sweet, almost sugary charm of the real, gold-domed Moscow. We will say more about this shortly.

Lyubimov staged *The Three Sisters* in the newly built, modern style theater, not in the old, cramped building. A proud, red cliff stands flat against the thick old walls, constrained by the heaviness and imagination of the modern construction. Immediately the maternal building seemed to shrink and become effaced, yielding its space to the red brick beauty. The new auditorium is semi-circular and laid with a special sort of brick. The auditorium is striking but cold. The special, homey, workshop atmosphere of the old Taganka disappeared and in the new structure a certain theatrical stiffness and banality took its place.

Yuri Lyubimov was in no great hurry to move into the new space. Understandably attached to his very own old walls, he laughed at the zeal with which Nikolay Lukyanovich Duppak, the manager and main enthusiast of the new building, proceeded with construction. On the other hand, it really was becoming impossible for the old theater to handle the influx of spectators. Foreigners and others travelling on business or to conferences in Moscow herded into it.

Nikolay Lukyanovich Duppak, an actor once himself, was extremely active and secured government grants. Doubtlessly he loves the theater in his own way. He spent whole days and nights in his second floor office, which had turned into a captain's cabin, carefully delving into every detail right up to the distribution of tickets. Duppak had unusual talent in getting along with the administration and smoothed out the many conflicts that inevitably arise in so complex an undertaking. I remember that on one of my visits, he was disappointed that one of the actors—I think it was Dzhabrailov—was refused a visa for a touring trip to Poland. Duppak phoned someone, argued, and got his way.

By fair means or foul, Duppak got the new building project through. He interested builders and contractors, not an easy task, and before long the new building was ready. Lyubimov made concessions, winning only the right to change the soft velvet chairs with the usual hard seats ("so they won't fall asleep"). He also secured an agreement to perform old productions on the old stage, and to have only premières on the new one. Both stages are connected by a common corridor, foyer, and wardrobe.

The Three Sisters went on in the new Taganka building. Its entrance is at the top few rows of the amphitheater, the floor of which is wedged into the bald, brick walls descending to the stage. At the bottom is the tall opening of the stage with a wide, sweeping proscenium, which profoundly juts into the auditorium to the spectator's right.

The lights go out slowly, complete darkness and a mysterious silence falls over the auditorium. Then, just as slowly, the lights come up on the stage; simultaneously, somewhere far off, beyond the theater, the sound of an old wartime march reaches the spectator. We do not see the orchestra for a long time yet, but it plays ever closer and more distinctly. The performance begins.

A regiment leaves the small provincial town and life becomes quiet again in the Russian interior. Three charming Russian women come out on stage and part with their youth; carried away by their dreams of Moscow they yearn for a sensible, active life.

Then, to the right of the unsuspecting spectator for whom the architectural possibilities of the new building are yet unknown, a wall smoothly opens from that side facing the street coming out on Sadovoy Circle—the main road through the historical center of Moscow. The mute panel, imperceptibly integrated into the stage, lowers itself before our eyes and at first all we see is a corner of the Moscow sky, not yet dark. Slowly, a musical regiment of soldiers, arranged on the theater's outside street balcony, passes by this background.

The military band plays the old Russian march louder and more passionately; the soldier figures step more precisely in their Czar Nicholas uniforms, reaching their full height. The trumpet players wear long gray overcoats. The panel descends to its lowest level and the spectators exclaim at the stunning beauty that is revealed.

The real, non-theatrical, but still fairy tale-like Moscow, one that we had never before noticed, is presented before us. The city is bathed in the golden rays of a setting sun, and the cupola of a white brick church on the furthest hill looks almost unreal. Moscow looks so attractive and tranquil from the theater's auditorium, and the military band's music sounds so harmonious, that one wants to sit through the production bewitched and not think about anything further.

But the theater does not create this illusion for our passive delight. Having found our weakness, having caught us on its hook, the theater in the next moment begins to destroy the sweet myth of Moscow that they themselves created. The tranquil beginning strikes the spectators' feelings so forcibly that we resist this destruction for a long time, waiting for another supernatural occurrence. They believe that the innovative director will present them with another miracle that will allow the heroines' fate to be altered, giving them a chance to fulfill their secret desire. The spectators believe that nothing is impossible in the theater. After all, according to Chekhov, the sisters only want happiness, pure and simple. They so movingly hide their yearning from others; they give themselves over to youth, gaiety, and silly jokes; they sincerely try to color their despondent everyday lives, to ease parting from their friends. Did they not really earn a better chance than that prepared for them by Chekhov the realist?

The all-powerful theater, having interested us in the starry-eyed idealism of reverie, does not divide our sympathy for Chekhov's heroines or try to please our pastoral tastes. In sharp contrast to the emotional introduction, the theater builds a cold, heartless, especially rationalistic action illustrating Chekhov's stark thesis. It is a drama presenting hard times and barrack-like discipline in Russia, and people's estrangement and senseless hostility to each other.

At the hospitable, Russian table, the intelligent Colonel Vershinin asked Masha: "This liqueur is very good. What is it made from?"

The morbid lieutenant Solyony cuts him off like a soldier: "From cockroaches." It is, perhaps, precisely Solyony who becomes the mainspring of the action. His aggressiveness, boorishness, and impudent demonstrations of strength express the main idea of Lyubimov's production.

"A man without faith is empty." Masha's words serve the director as an epigraph. Several times on stage water pours out of a washbasin until it runs out, leaving it empty, no longer serving the one for whom it was intended. Now he has nothing to wash himself with. Lyubimov is not afraid of illustrative metaphors.

The central spot on stage is a platform in the officer's club. The characters in turn come out onto it and present their roles, overplaying their most repulsive traits. The psychology and atmosphere of the barracks permeate the stage action and the actions of the departing officers, as well as the behavior of the three sisters, especially Olga. M. Politseymako presents Olga as a callous and power hungry boss, a kind of head matron, unceremonious toward others. If a person giving her a bouquet of flowers does not suit her, she scornfully throws the bouquet into the trash basket in his presence.

Today's Russian avant-garde theater reads Chekhov's mournful play strangely and questionably. It deliberately rejects the charming Chekhovian subtext and the complexity and nuances of the spiritual movements. The actors do not play characters but intentional outlines. They act pointedly, categorically, and directly, unlike Lyubimov's theater where something is always left unsaid, unstressed, or brought out in brackets. At the tensest moments the famous refrain of kind Doctor Chebutykin, "Tara-ra-bum-biya . . . I'm sitting on a post, I am," underlines the senselessness and anxiety of an empty life and the utter futility of Chekhov's heroines who are trying to direct their life onto another, more intelligent course.

Nevertheless, despite the contradictory stylistics—or maybe precisely because of its contrast with the idyllic introduction—*The Three Sisters* lets us feel the true price of groundless reverie on Russian soil. Throughout the production the theater says that life is good, that Moscow can be beautiful, and that there isn't anyone alive who would not want to live there, but how do you live without faith? Everything in Russia ends in tears because nothing can be done and nothing can be changed.

Just before the finale, after Irina's line, "There will come a time, when everyone will realize what all this suffering is for . . ." the theater reopens its Moscow view, now in twilight; the church cannot be seen. It suddenly dawns on you why the theater turned to this old, overproduced Chekhov play in present-day, completely un-Chekhovian Moscow. You look anew at the military band that plays so loudly, sluggishly thundering its brass and drums. Accompanied by this sound a commandant's platoon, laconic fellows in long gray overcoats, enters the stage and blocks our view of Moscow with huge deathly mirrored panels. In them the audience suddenly sees its own sullen, slightly distorted reflection. Then, maybe, we involuntarily compare that somber Moscow of today, in which we live, work, love, and grow, to that bewitching Moscow of the beginning of the production that is now sinking into oblivion. We reflect on the Moscow existing only in pictures or in our fired imaginations, the peaceful city without banners, slogans, or red calico, the Moscow washed in simple rain mixed in with sunshine, with the gold-domed little church on the far hill, quieted, submissive, expectant . . .

It seems to me that the ending of *The Three Sisters* presents the spectators with one more alarming premonition—the impending end of the Taganka itself. In *The Three Sisters* Lyubimov's theater seems to part with its plans, dreams, youth, and ideals. Not even two years will pass before spectators and actors witness the theater's inner drama. The Chekhov production is the last work the theater and its director shows publicly in Moscow. The next première, Pushkin's *Boris Godunov*, does not pass the censor and Lyubimov leaves; the Taganka is no longer what it was. Ironically, in *The Three Sisters* Lyubimov, perhaps unknowingly, parts not only with Moscow but with his audience and his theater.

Maybe because of a premonition of misfortune this production came out so uneven, dishevelled, and thorny. It is the tragedy of the starry-eyed, idealistically wishful nice people with noble impulses unsupported by deeds, lives and spirits corrupted by barrack-like surroundings. Maybe because of this premonition the production mixed such varied styles and rhythms—old military marches and radio music, reflection and illustration, nature and abstraction.

In spite of certain flaws, this strange production—in some ways eclectic and completely un-Chekhovian in tone—tells us many interesting and substantively important things about post-Chekhovian Russia. Chekhov lives in this production as our contemporary. We speak to each other as equals, in plain terms. Maybe we even tell him more about Russia's fate than he could have told us in his own time. It was for a reason that Chekhov ended his play with the sigh: "If one could only know, if one could only know!"[17]

Vladimir Vysotsky: Actor and Poet

The Last Role

AT FOUR O'CLOCK IN THE MORNING OF JULY 25, 1980, AT THE height of the Olympic games in Moscow, Vladimir Vysotsky, a leading actor at the Taganka, died of a heart attack in his Moscow apartment.

The stresses of the city's noise and confusion consumed him. He always valued silence and seclusion. Behind his crude exterior and hoarse voice hid a tender, responsive, vulnerable heart. He took every injustice against him, his theater, and his country very hard, especially in his final years.

"What hurt you the last time?" his colleagues once asked him.

"Everything," was his short reply.

"In your opinion, what are the most offensive qualities in people?"

"Stupidity, mediocrity, vileness . . ."

"What do you want most out of life?"

"To be allowed everywhere, not to be forgotten . . ."

It was not easy to live with such demands. It was even harder to breathe. His chest became constrained and suddenly an evil, troublesome lump rose to his throat from his stomach.

"July 13th. We're playing *Hamlet* for the 217th time," recalls actress Alla Demidova:

> We're very tired. We've just finished the end of the season . . . and a tour to Poland. We played *Hamlet* there too. Volodya didn't feel well, he kept running off the stage to take his medicine. An "emergency services" doctor was kept in the wings. During the performance, Volodya often forgot his lines. In the scene with Gertrude, after Hamlet says, "You must confess," he quietly asked me: "How does it go—I forgot." I prompt him, he continues. He acts well. In this scene, a heavy curtain got caught on the coffin on which I was sitting; the coffin started to take off. . . . Volodya and I successfully covered this "addition". . . . Volodya was in a soft, kind state, which lately was very rare.[1]

On July 27 the last performance of *Hamlet* for the current season was announced. That same day, in the newspaper *Vechernaya Moskva (Evening Moscow)*, one line in small type appeared: "The performance of *Hamlet* has been cancelled." There was no explanation.

As soon as news of Vysotsky's death circled the city through some miracle—there were no newspaper announcements citing the day or hour of the funeral—people flowed out of the stadiums and away from their television sets onto the square, usually empty on Saturdays, to the nondescript theater building.

Driven by love and pain people in an endless stream, with their own inner debt to pay, came to part with the actor-poet whose songs were recorded and distributed in cassettes by his fans. These songs expressed their thoughts and feelings and became a part of the country's spiritual life in the 1960s and 1970s. In essence, Vysotsky's farewell, deprived of official pomp and publicity, turned into a spontaneous act of civil disobedience. All of this was, to some degree, reminiscent of a grand crowd scene staged by an invisible director. It seemed as if unseen, Vysotsky, on the day of his own funeral, played his newest and perhaps most important role.

We will not die by tortured life
We'd best just come to life through honest death.

These words of Vysotsky, accompanied by his photograph on thick paper, were displayed behind the glass of the theater's cashier's window, so that they could be seen from the street the morning after his death.

The mystery of these words was unsettling because of what they left unsaid. What does "die by tortured life" mean? How can one "through honest death" come to life? Finally, why did Yuri Lyubimov's theater, which never did anything by chance, choose these lines from Vysotsky's entire poetic heritage as an epitaph to his life and work?

In the evenings prior to the funeral people gathered in front of the theater's entrance. Silence hung over the square. There was only the sound of cars carefully passing. On the sidewalk, by the wall under Vysotsky's portrait, were his guitar and some posters from the productions he had performed in: *Ten Days, Pugachev, Galileo, Crime and Punishment*. A field of carnations, roses, forget-me-nots, and daisies, wet from rain, seemed to grow out of the asphalt. But most incredible for the usually cautious and silent Moscow were the hundreds of poems, some handwritten, some typed, posted on the walls, drainpipes, and windows of houses. Even Vysotsky's legendary guitar had two copies of his obituary attached to its finger board.

People crowded each other to read the poems and copy them, sometimes looking over their shoulders to see if they were being photographed. But the militia, strangely, was nowhere in sight, and the guys with the red "Voluntary People's Patrol" bands kept their distance. Someone under his breath read the following aloud so that those standing in the back could hear:

A heart was broken like the string of a guitar,
But you're alive, not gone, my dear Volodya . . .

Say farewell-forgive, Volodimer—the world, though—
You didn't finish singing your song.
For the burden you leave, you most know, firmly know
That in Russia there just are no shoulders so strong.

How many times has there been such an end
He's honor's slave, the poet's died!
As if it wasn't known at all—
In Russia, talent does not long reside . . .

Those participating in this unofficial memorial service, publicly creating uncensored literature, were, of course, aware that they were doing something illegal. The ticklish feeling of risking involvement in an "incident" united them and even, in their eyes, ennobled Vysotsky's bold poetry and life exploits, bringing them closer to him. But what about the authorities? They did not expect this unprecedented, spontaneous outburst. However, this was the city of the Olympics, overflowing with foreigners, and they were forced to act with care.

I saw Vysotsky on stage for the last time, in Dostoevsky's *Crime and Punishment*, two weeks before his death. After a long break brought on by an attack of his purely Russian illness, he "gave" us Svidrigaylov. This work, prepared with Lyubimov, was his last.

Vysotsky played Svidrigaylov with a sorrowful wrinkle by his mouth that was completely anomalous to his striking temperament. He appeared onstage in a snow white shirt with a wide, open collar and a long unbuttoned silk robe the color of a wilted, gray hollyhock. Everything did not tie together for the actor in the role of the in-

111

veterate scoundrel, tainted by grave sins. In contrast to the neur-
asthenic Raskolnikov, Vysotsky's Svidrigaylov conducted himself
comme il faut, observing social decorum and being a gentleman, even
when he said vulgar things or acted vilely. Only the vague smirk
at the corners of his mouth—the smirk of a cynic and a snob—
betrayed him to be a person who had long ago transgressed forbidden boundaries.

Vysotsky amazingly combined the appearance of a Siberian convict with breadth, delicacy, and depth of character. He looked like
a dockworker with his gray sweater and sailor's striped vest, and
his stocky, sinewy, and somewhat crude facial features. Once he
was barred from his own concert at a worker's club, where his fans
had to be held back: no one could believe an artist could look so
unassuming. Our Vysotsky really was a great dockworker; he lifted
onto his shoulders a burden beyond his strength and refused to
throw it off until his work was finished. Meanwhile, few knew that
he was born into an intelligent Moscow family, with a Russian
mother and a Russian-Jewish father, or that he grew up in a quiet
yard hungering for life and experience, but that he adored solitude
more than anything else. He stayed that way—open on the outside
and closed on the inside. Even in his roles he never fully blended
with the characters, thereby violating Stanislavsky's commandment.
On stage and on tour Vysotsky's priority was to express his personal
relationship—as an actor and a person—to the image; that is how
it was with Hamlet, Galileo, and Svidrigaylov. He was always true
to himself and his lyrical, temperamental song.

When he sang it seemed as if an organ sounded in his chest. Once
while playing Svidrigaylov he took a guitar in hand and, right before
our eyes, his character transformed. The actor sang something sorrowful and, reflected in Svidrigaylov's eyes, something long forgotten and hidden, something fated never to come true. He finished
the song and, still holding the guitar, spoke about his desire to go
to America. This represented a dream to settle accounts with the
past, start a new life, and once again become pure before God,
before others, and before himself. It seemed that he understood the
impracticability of this dream even though he passionately tried to
convince Dunya to share a fate of voluntary exile. At this moment
Vysotsky's Svidrigaylov seemed weak and sincere to us, completely
unlike the superhuman portrayed by Dostoevsky. Clearly, Vysotsky
enjoyed his character's measure of weakness and suffering, and with

genuine poetry and temperament played this small scene so that it seemed he would at any moment step out of character to debate with the author about making Svidrigaylov a romantic rebel.

Vysotsky received raging applause from the auditorium. He was tired, slightly condescending, not yet fully released from his role; his gaze wandered somewhere far away.

On Monday July 28, 1980, the day of Vysotsky's funeral, Taganka Square woke up earlier than usual. By eight o'clock Radishchev Street already overflowed with people wishing to pass Vysotsky's coffin. They stretched in a seemingly endless line of three or four miles and people still came. It became apparent a very small percent would be able to reach the coffin. People started to push on the steep street. There were heartrending screams. Some climbed fences and windows. At noon an announcement that ended access to Vysotsky's coffin was answered with a roar. Someone on a rooftop with binoculars told the crowd how the coffin was being carried out. An older woman screamed: "Stop them! Let us say goodbye, you nonbelievers!" A group of desperate young people called out: "Go to the cemetery!" Very few, probably only 100 or 200 of the many thousands who came, parted with Vysotsky in the way they wanted.

"After Vysotsky's funeral, I began to respect the people of Moscow," admitted Lyubimov in exile.

Vysotsky's funeral was a spontaneous, national referendum on freedom from censorship in Russian art. This was the last, maybe the most important role, that Vladimir Vysotsky played after death.[2]

The Banned Vysotsky

DRESS REHEARSAL: JULY 27, 1981

THIS PRODUCTION—UNLAWFULLY BORN, MARKED BY COURAGE and inspiration—is one of the remarkable events in the history of free Russian art.[3] It arose and, after a few public performances, faded away under the following unusual circumstances.

Immediately after Vysotsky's death his theater friends, headed by Lyubimov, planned a performance in his memory. In the course of a year the whole troupe, without asking permission, prepared a program above and beyond the planned repertory, giving it much time and energy. When the production was ready the Minister of Culture, P. Demichev, banned it. Vysotsky's popularity scared the ideological upper echelons. With great difficulty Lyubimov managed to get Andropov, then the head of the KGB, to permit the production twice yearly, on Vysotsky's birthday, January 25, and on the anniversary of his death, July 25. After two or three performances, however, even this "kindness" was removed.

On July 27, 1981, I went at the theater's invitation to the first preview of *The Poet Vladimir Vysotsky*. At twelve o'clock a crowd was already seething at the entrance to the theater. They were restrained by a police detail and the Voluntary People's Patrol. Not only were there no free seats in the auditorium, there was no standing room. The audience, however, kept growing. People broke through the controls and swept away the ticket collectors, delaying the production.

Yuri Lyubimov, aroused and irritated, stood up from his director's stand in the seventh row of the orchestra to address the auditorium. He spoke deliberately, slowly, and officially:

> We've arranged a preview for friends of the theater and sent out tickets to them. You've taken their seats and created a mob scene. Until all of those who do not have invitational tickets clear the auditorium, we won't start the production. It's an outrage! It's disgraceful! We aren't giving a performance; it's just a dress rehearsal. I ask everyone without invitations to leave the auditorium.

114

The auditorium quieted but no one, of course, even considered leaving. They knew Lyubimov spoke for order's sake and that everything would work itself out. That's why the Taganka is the Taganka, after all, for order to be born of disorder.

The darkened stage with only an empty row of chairs looks like a continuation of the auditorium. A white covering like a shroud has been thrown over them. The actors remove the covering from the right and it shoots upward like a sail, like the living curtain first used in *Hamlet*. Vysotsky was the only Hamlet at the Taganka.

A familiar voice is heard in the suppressed silence:

Someone wanted some fruit, what was ripe, what was not,
They shook at the tree—it fell, it fell.
Here's a song for you about him, who wasn't yet ripe, who didn't
    sing,
Who had a voice, but did not know it, did not know it.

It's funny, isn't it, it's funny, funny,
That he had joked—but hadn't finished,
He hadn't finished tasting wine,
And didn't even finishing sipping . . .

He wanted to know everything from to to fro,
But he didn't make it up to fro—
Nor to a guess, nor to a day, to a day,
He didn't dig into the depths, the depths,
And she, who was alone, alone,
He didn't finish loving, he didn't finish loving.

It's funny, isn't it, it's funny, funny,
That he had hurried—hadn't finished hurrying,
And everything he hadn't finished solving
Remained unsolved.[4]

Vysotsky's voice fades into the distance. The stage is lit and we begin to make out the actors' faces as they stand silently: Gubenko with a guitar, Demidova with a little umbrella from *The Cherry Orchard*, Zolotukhin, Khmelnitsky, Smekhov, Filatov, Antipov, Dzhabrailov, Zhukova—every co-worker and friend of Vysotsky in the Taganka's best years.

Nikolay Gubenko without leaving the row reads a poem by Vysotsky, one of few he had not set to music, that is his *ars poetica*, his poetic and civil credo: "I stay awake. . . ." Vysotsky's spirit in his friends' voices hovers over the auditorium. Who said that he is not here? The theater refutes this. Vysotsky's voice is arranged with the choir on stage, creating the illusion of his presence.

Vysotsky spiritedly starts a song: "Where are your seventeen years?" His friends' choir answers: "On Bolshoy Karetny Street."

"Where do your misfortunes start?" continues Vysotsky. The choir answers: "On Bolshoy Karetny Street."

Later they switch roles and the choir inquires: "Where are *your* seventeen years?" with the accent on "your". Vysotsky from somewhere above says: "On Bolshoy Karetny Street."

"And where's your black revolver?" Vysotsky answers laughingly: "On Bolshoy Karetny Street."

The actors' choir does not fall behind: "And where aren't you today?"

We wait for an answer but there is none.

Within the theater walls, which are filled with him, a grave silence sets in. This unexpected gap—a needed pause in the performance's tense introduction—gave the actors and spectators a breather, allowing thoughts to focus on the irreplaceable loss.

The concert-performance illustrated Vysotsky's life with his own words and songs, lovingly chosen and commented on by his friends in art. The performance consisted of five parts united by Vysotsky's main role, Hamlet. Fragments from *Hamlet* were separated from other scenes by the long drawn-out sound of an English horn, serving also as a connection between the times, a historical background tying the past to the present. These fragments together with a new text composed by the theater underscore the main theme of Lyubimov's composition: Vysotsky's life and work now belong to history as much as to the present.

The first part of the production tells of Vysotsky's place in the spiritual life of the Soviet people of the 1960s and 1970s. It culminates with a song Bulat Okudzhava wrote on Vysotsky's death and performed by Okudzhava himself:

For Volodya Vysotsky I decided to think up a song:
Here's another who'll never return from the tour.
They say that he sinned, that he put out his candle too soon . . .
As he knew, so he lived, nature knows not the sinless for sure.

116

VLADIMIR VYSOTSKY: ACTOR AND POET

Not for long do we part—not at all—for an instant and then
We ourselves set out on his trail, in his footsteps so deep.
Let his hoarse baritone circle Moscow, my friend,
While together with him we will laugh and then weep.

For Volodya Vysotsky I wanted to think up a song,
But my hand—it would tremble, the tune and the words wouldn't
      sound . . .
The white Moscow stork, flew up to the white Moscow sky,
The black Moscow stork, came down to the black Moscow ground.

The second part of the production is dedicated to early Vysotsky
and his well-known cycle of "street" or "outlaw" songs. The motif
fastening this cycle together is the famous: "A Guitar Is What I
Have."

A guitar is what I have, so you walls, make way,
Not see freedom for a century 'cause of evil fate.
Cut right through my throat, cut right through my veins,
But just don't tear these silver strings . . .

Volodya performed four of its short, choppy verses alternately
with genre scenes played by Zolotukhin, Gubenko, Antipov, and
Bortnik. A picture rises before the spectator showing the everyday
life of post-war Soviet youth who cast off the revolutionary romance
of their fathers.

In the middle of this noisy, reckless merriment Vysotsky's cry
is again heard from somewhere above:

They've crawled into my soul, ripping it in pieces,
Oh, just so they don't tear my silver strings.

The action irrepressibly begins to pick up rhythm. The friendly
get-together is at its height. Nikolay Gubenko runs from his place
and bangs out a frenzied tap-dance to the words of "Do You Remember Those Little Evening Parties. . . ." Again there is an unexpected change in rhythm and mood. Valery Zolotukhin, in a
ringing voice, reads:

So where do I get this sullen brow,
What's the reason for these white forelocks,

117

My papa gave me the constitution of an ox,
And he didn't just put forelocks in my little head.

In this poem the author wonders where he got his "vulgar manners." It seems he was happily born with "a silver spoon in his mouth," that his mother "girded him with a red sash," and that everything fell into place cleanly and well. He should sing and sing "of the meadow and beyond" but no—"God didn't give him a voice . . . clean as silver." The poet matured and grayed but could not get rid of his "sullen brow." He is not drawn toward singing "about the beautiful and pleasant for all" but

Just once about what's important, just once but even that . . .
And I hoarsely yelled, people didn't breathe,
And no one winced, really no one did.

At this moment, as if from the depths of history, there is the prolonged sound of a shepherd's horn, used to separate the contemporary scenes from the literary reminiscences in *Hamlet*. The actors, altering their voices and postures but without changing costume, perform a satiric dialogue on the theme of *Hamlet* written especially for the production.

The king and his courtiers discuss the harmfulness of "singing hooliganism" for the maturing young generation; it is understood that the scene takes place in Elizabethan England and that the conversation is only about the Danish prince:

King: So it means that you cannot get to the bottom of it, why he allows himself this whim, what he's worked up about, that he's not afraid of the consequences in wasting his peace and quiet in spiritual turbulence?
Polonius: He admitted that he's not quite himself, but for some reason he doesn't want to say . . . The conversation just barely touches on health, and he slips away with the cleverness of a lunatic.
King: Of course, a grown person doesn't need these songs. This singing hooliganism is, in general, offensive. This is, if you like, one method of spiritually breaking down the youth.
Polonius: Unfortunately, they're in fashion now.
King: Yes, these aren't just inoffensive songs. This is, if you like, spiritual poison.[5]

118

The third part of the production begins with the whistling of bombs and mines. The theme is war and Vysotsky's songs of war. They do not paint war with the ring of victory speeches and bold marches; they are hoarse songs, stories of the soldier's difficult work, of friendship at the front, and the death of friends. Vysotsky was reproached for this by the official critics who argued that he didn't experience the war at all, though he paints everything with such somber tones as if he did personally experience it.

It really is incredible that the post-war generation of Soviet artists and actors was able at times to convey the truth of those bleak times more pointedly and disturbingly than those who fought. There were those who portrayed the war pompously and falsely, as did Sergey Bondarchuk. However, Shukshin, Andrey Tarkovsky, Larisa Shepitko, Boris Plotnikov (in the film *Ascent*), V. Ivashev (Alesha from *Ballad of a Soldier*), and Aleksey Batalov never fought because they were only children, and they created the most authentic portrayals of Russian soldiers. What is the secret?

The white covering outstretched on stage turns into a snowy Russian field with drops of blood on the snow. Shots ring out from the only scenery on stage—the seats of the chairs. David Borovsky, with wizardly inventiveness, turns a hanging block of spectator's chairs first into an inaccessible elevation that needs to be taken by storm, then into a white plain, and then into a neutral zone between the "forbidden" and the "allowed," where "unusually beautiful" flowers grow. The actors Shapovalov, Smekhov, Bortnik, Zolotukhin, Demidova, and Gubenko rise from this row of hard chairs to read and sing Vysotsky's poems each in his or her own way.

This part is concluded by the reading of a form handed out among the Taganka actors in 1970. Vysotsky answered the questions like this:

Q: What question would you like answered?
A: How much is left? Years, months, weeks, days, hours.
Q: Your favorite painting?
A: Kuindzhi, *Moonlight.*
Q: Your favorite work of music?
A: Chopin, *Etude Number Twelve.*
Q: Your favorite flower?
A: A branch of blossoming cherries.
Q: Favorite expression?

119

A: We'll figure it out.
Q: Your favorite actor and film?
A: Charlie Chaplin, *City Lights*.
Q: Your distinguishing traits?
A: Others'll figure it out.
Q: What would you want more than anything?
A: To be remembered, to be allowed everywhere.

The choir concludes Vysotsky's last line inhaling: "Scared," and exhaling: "to death!"

In this concert-performance, the serious and the lofty organically intertwine with the happy and carnival-like without which Vysotsky is unthinkable. The fourth part of the production is devoted to Vysotsky's fantastic and allegorical songs. Grabbing some inflatable dolls—caricatures of Lyubimov and Vysotsky—the actors begin a round dance at the creek.

"There's Russian spirit there, it smells of Rus," Fyodor Antipov exclaims with pathos to the laughter in the auditorium. He is a great master of parody in this theme. He stands embracing "Uncle Vasya"—a Taganka stagehand in whom Lyubimov uncovered a comedic gift back in *The House on the Embankment*. There, "Uncle Vasya"—as a mimetic actor—portrays a silent, submissive "worker-boozer" who is ready to split a bottle at any moment. In a wrinkled cap and with a crushed cigarette in his lips, "Uncle Vasya" (unfortunately I don't remember his real name) brings a colorful feature of artlessness to the production.

At the height of the carnival the tall bearded Khmelnitsky, with an artsy scarf tossed over his shoulder, turns into the roving actor from *Hamlet*. Coming out onto the proscenium he speaks a maxim that would give the scene "At the Creek" an unexpectedly serious meaning.

> For some, theater is art, for others it is a realization of necessity. We can play anything for you that you want: heroes and scoundrels, hired killers, political schemers, debauched wives, chaste virgins . . . All this, of course, for a good *price*. All this, *of course*, under the banner of *socialist realism*, for which [a meaningful pause] . . . *special* demands exist.

It is possible that the actor did not say the word "socialist" at other previews (in my tape recordings the word is already gone), but it was clearly implied. Such "innocent" compromises were often made at the Taganka and the spectator easily forgave them, understanding that without compromises one could not survive.

The dual role of art in society—its ability to serve both truth and lies—is one of its amazing qualities. The Taganka actors and spectators successfully used art this way and laughed not only at those who determined the proportions of truth or lies but at themselves, forced also to play the game. They understand each other without completing sentences.

The fifth and perhaps most important part of the production begins. The themes are today's workday, everyday life, and the problems and worries of society in "socialist realism." It opens with the song "Dialogue at the Television." After a hard day Vanya the worker and his worker-wife, Zina, spend a "cultural" leisure at home. She in hair curlers and he with a glass in hand watch the circus on television and compare the clowns, parrots, and acrobats with situations from their own lives. This little genre scene is accompanied by uninterrupted laughter.

Oy, Vanya, I'll die from these acrobats,
Look how that bastard spins!
Our boss, that Comrade Satikov
Recently jumped like that at the club.
And you when you come home, Ivan,
Eat—and hit the couch right away.
Or scream, when you're not drunk.
What's with you, Ivan?

The actor F. Antipov sings in answer:

You, Zina, invite vulgarity.
You, Zina, aim to offend everyone.
All day I jump through the hoops,
I come home and you're sitting there.
Well, I am, of course, Zina,
Drawn to the store right away.
All my friends are there, and Zina,
You know that I don't drink alone.

A slew of other dialogues equally as colorful follow this one. The genre scenes paint a picture of Soviet life. F. Antipov and R. Dzhabrailov hilariously play a popular story about two alcoholics: "What Our Family and School Teach Us?" Once again a sharply dissonant, alarming, and serious voice unexpectedly breaks in: "We don't know," the familiar voice says into the microphone, "what goes on and what we should do down the road. We only know what they tell us, and that's not much. And all of this, as far as I know is a lie to boot."

Applause breaks out at these words.

The humorous story of the worker Kolya who goes through a briefing at the District Committee of the party before his pleasure tour of the Bulgarian-Polish city of Budapest concludes the cycle of Soviet workdays. Vysotsky's resounding voice finishes with a song about a crowded Moscow tram:

Citizens, why push.
Darlings, why grumble,
We're all passengers in this society,
We all live and pay our fares,
Because of life, we're all travelling by tram.

Like the choir in ancient theater, the choir on stage repeats:

We're all passengers in this society.

There is one more reminiscence from *Hamlet:* a conversation between the gravediggers.

"Well, what's happening at the court? Do you know the details?" asks F. Antipov hoarsely.

"Strong measures have been introduced inhibiting the citizens," complains R. Dzhabrailov.

Perhaps one of the strongest moments in this three-hour production filled with action and music is Valery Zolotukhin's story about his presence while Vysotsky composed his favorite song, "White-Hot Bath."[6] This happened in the remote, Siberian countryside, where fate had taken them to shoot the movie *The Taiga's Boss.* They lived in an old, deserted peasant hut without shutters or curtains. Outside, in the nettles and tall weeds, villagers—children and old men included—stood for hours wanting to see Vysotsky in person and to see how he worked.

A naked electric bulb of about 1,000 watts illuminates the empty, black stage. It hangs over the actor's head and gives off a blinding white light. Zolotukhin's high, thin voice carefully intertwines with the hoarse baritone of the main singer. Let us take note of the songwriter's emphases. The song's refrain is an appeal to the "landlady." (The words the singer stresses are italicized):

> Draw me a bath, a hot one, little landlady,
> I'll make myself white-hot, burning hot
> Right at the edge, on the sweating shelf
> I'll wipe out all doubts in myself.

In this refrain, Vysotsky develops a subject by no means inoffensive:

> I'll languish to indecency
> A cold ladle—and everything's behind me.
> And a tattoo from the *times of the personality cult*
> Becomes blue on my left breast.
>
> Draw, draw, *dr-r-raw* me a white-hot bath,
> So that I'll *get used to the white light of day*.
> I'll burn up, and the hot steam'll
> Loosen my *tongue*.

Vysotsky's voice achieves a tragic force in the next two verses:

> How much *faith* and forest have been *toppled*,
> How much *sorrow and travel was involved*.
> On the left breast a profile of . . . *Stalin*.[7]
> On the right—Marina in full face.
>
> I remember, how early in the morning,
> I managed to yell to my brother: *"He-elp!"*
> And two *handsome* secret policemen . . .
> Took me *out of Siberia and into Siberia*.

"Why 'out of Siberia and into Siberia'?" asked the man sitting next to me of his companion. "He probably lived in Siberia," she guessed. "We *all* live in Siberia," whispered someone from behind.

In the dual performance of Vysotsky-Zolotukhin, "White-Hot Bath" gains an unexpectedly dramatic subtext. When, in the long drawn-out refrain, Vysotsky demands: "Draw, draw, dr-r-raw me a white-hot bath," Zolotukhin breaks in with the desperate cry: "Don't do it, don't do it." Then the singers switch roles. It's as if two contradictory feelings struggle in one man: the desire to express the soul's accumulations and the fear of blurting out something forbidden. The Soviet people are well acquainted with this psychological state.

The production, it seems, has culminated, but the theater's main point is still to be made. Vysotsky's voice brings out the final words of "Bath" and, without any transition, as if it were one song, one theme, one thought, Boris Pasternak's translation of Hamlet's monologue begins. Vysotsky reads it swiftly without pauses:

> To be or not to be that is the question whether 'tis nobler in the mind
> to suffer the slings and arrows of outrageous fortune or to take arms
> against a sea of troubles and by opposing end them to die to sleep. . . .

Arranging these layers of different times and styles, Lyubimov turns to the "broken montage" method he often used in other works. Probably, to adherents of classical purity in form, this combination of seemingly unconnected phenomenons—the lyrical hero of our time and the Danish prince, Vysotsky and Shakespeare, the fates of Russia and Elizabethan England—appears blasphemous. From history's point of view, however, it makes sense.

Lyubimov continued to develop this parallel in the production and beyond. Vysotsky's song about the mythic bird Gamayun—an image from Russian folklore—intertwines short inserts from *Hamlet*. Vysotsky, having played Hamlet with a guitar on the Taganka stage, again takes a problem worthy of Hamlet: tying together the broken "chain of time." He sings:

> It's as if seven cherished strings
> Rang each in its turn.
> It's the bird, Gamayun
> Bringing hope.

> In the blue sky, pierced with steeples,
> A copper bell, a copper bell
> Grew happy or grew cross . . .
> Cupolas in Russia are covered in pure gold,
> So that the Lord would notice them more often.

Again without caesura or any rhythmic stop he turns to the story of the Taganka *Hamlet*, as if it is directly related to the Russian cupolas:

> So it means we did it like this: a gigantic curtain cuts through the stage like this: on this side, the King, Queen, and the whole retinue works, Rosencrantz and Guildenstern are there and Hamlet is here. . . .

A low guitar chord separates the past and the present, and a two-sided Vysotsky—Hamlet and Gamayun, Doubt and Hope—arises in our consciousness.

"So a thought turns all of us into cowards," Vysotsky's voice ardently whispers in the guarded auditorium. Who speaks now? Hamlet? Gamayun? "And our decisiveness withers like a flower in the sterility of an intellectual dead end. Thoughts that at first promised success die with a sweep of the hand. From long delays. . . . But be quiet, be quiet. . . ."

An English shepherd's horn weaves a strange, simple melody into a Russian song about Gamayun, reminding us for the last time of Hamlet's theme in the work of the all-Russian singer.

The production's finale is a resounding parable about hunting for a wolf, breaking a ban, and stepping beyond barriers:

> I came out of obedience—
> From behind the barriers, the thirst for life is stronger.
> Only behind me I joyously heard
> People's astonished cries.
>
> I'm bursting out of strength and out of my tendons,
> But today isn't like yesterday,
> They've cornered me, cornered me—
> But the huntsman isn't left with anything.

The actors stand in a semi-circle on stage, leaving a place in the center for Vysotsky. The lighting brightens. "We know you're here," someone says. Demidova asks him to come out. Smekhov asks him to speak. Then, from somewhere above, getting closer and louder like thunder peals, the heavy voice sings for the last time:

> There's somehow not enough air for me, I drink the wind,

I swallow fog,
I sense with fatal rapture—I am done for, done for. . . .

The voice collapses, then rises again, with an effort of the singer's will. (Vysotsky was asked on the form mentioned earlier what he would consider the greatest personal tragedy; he answered: "Losing my voice.")

A little slower, horses, a little slower,
I beg you to gallop, not fly.
But somehow I got persnickety horses,
And I didn't have time . . . to finish living, I won't have time to
    finish singing. . . .

The curtain of light disperses. The auditorium lights go on. There is silence within the old walls of the Taganka in which Vysotsky worked sixteen years, his entire creative life. The theater ended with him. Tired, the actors slowly seat themselves on the floor by the back wall, thinking, as are we, their unhappy thoughts. The silence lasts a very long time.

The Phenomenon of Vysotsky

VYSOTSKY CAME TO THE TAGANKA THEATER IN 1964 WITHOUT having completed Lyubimov's studio, but he felt himself to be in his element. Though he was an unknown in his very first production, *The Good Woman of Setzuan*, he smoothly joined the acting ensemble and attracted the intent attention of the audience. He then played Kerensky in *Ten Days* using devices of the grotesque; he found himself as a singer in *The Fallen and the Living*; and in the 1966 *Life of Galileo* he created a profound, psychological portrait of the great truth seeker. A year later in *Pugachev* he expressed in Yesenin's peasants a force both tragic and clownish, a force perhaps not yet known to the Russian stage. He contributed as though he co-authored the production. The spectator watched the peasants' revolt through his eyes, the eyes of a Russian *skomorokh* or clown for whom everything is allowed. From that time on no production at the Taganka, perceptibly or imperceptibly, was without Vysotsky's creative spirit hovering free.

Lyubimov's theater gave Vysotsky a great deal, but before his time was half over he repaid the Taganka's artistic artel with interest. His name was the password of the trend in Russian art that valued above all talent, courage, free scope, willpower, and spiritual strength.

He took his work very seriously. Wrote the critic N. Krymova: "In the theater—out of every, tiny role he elicited something that was disproportionate to its size, something that usually isn't carried away with you, but left behind like a costume in the wardrobe."[8]

Vysotsky's greatest accomplishment was his dark, aggressive, and easily wounded Hamlet who played guitar, sang contemporary songs, and laughed almost helplessly at the jokes of the Guildensterns and Rosencrantzes. To some he seemed stylized, crude, and shocking, not only Shakespeareans, but those of contemporary theatrical tastes as well—but they soon accepted him. Soon they could not imagine a Hamlet other than this frenzied philosopher who sits on the floor under a gigantic pendulum-clock.

The time is out of joint:—O cursed spite,
That ever I was born to set it right!

127

In this role he came out on stage as he was in his daily life, but with the mark of heavy thoughts on his brow. He played—everyone felt and understood it—his own fate and that of his era and his contemporaries, confronting the inevitable decision for himself and for others: "Whether 'tis nobler in the mind to suffer the slings and arrows of outrageous fortune or to take arms against a sea of troubles and by opposing end them?"

No one in the auditorium waited for or demanded an answer to this question. They were satisfied that it was asked, but Vysotsky would not stop mid-journey. In Hamlet he reveals himself completely; he feels it inevitable to answer. He knows the answer.

Before *Hamlet* he wrote the song "I don't like . . ."

> I don't like chilling cynicism . . . I don't like things that're done half way . . . I don't like confidence that's satisfied . . . I don't like, shootings in the back . . . I don't like violence, impotence . . . I'll never, never learn to like it.[9]

In his first years as Hamlet he proudly carried the poetics of negation; he was a nihilistic Hamlet. Many noticed his interchange with the famous Shakespearean sonnet that, as Shakespearean scholars note, reflects "Hamletism" as a phenomenon born of protest.

> Tir'd with all these, for restful death I cry,—
> As, to behold desert a beggar born,
> And needy nothing trimm'd in jollity,
> And purest faith unhappily forsworn,
> And gilded honor shamefully misplaced . . .

With the years Hamlet changed and grew wiser, concentrating more on a way out of the impasse. His maturing Hamlet began to see that this was worth "screaming his throat out," and that fighting should be "for something" and not just "against something." A few years after his première Vysotsky wrote his programmatic poem "My Hamlet," expressing his civil credo. Vysotsky did not set this intimate composition to music and never read it on stage. Part is quoted below.

128

My brain just as a spider—seeks knowledge out of greed,
I comprehend it all: inactive things and things that moved
But what's the point of thoughts and science, what's the need,
When everywhere they simply are disproved.

Through the silenced rumble, I heard my forebear's call,
I took the call, and from the rear these doubts would creep,
A load of gravest thoughts on top of me I caused to fall
But wings of flesh would drag me down into the grave to sleep.

I'm Hamlet, violence I despise,
I could care less about the Danish crown,
I screamed my throat out for the throne before their eyes,
And killed my rivals to the throne.

The poem ends with:

We all just give a tricky, double-dealing answer
And cannot find the necessary question.

A principled opponent of false answers Vysotsky shows life as
it is, with its questions and uncertainties at every step. His poetic
work gathered meaning in the very search for these necessary questions. Life in its most varied forms and characteristics entered into
his poetry as questions for which he did not yet have answers, but
the very act of posing them before an audience made him dominant
over these thoughts. "Vysotsky was essential. One could either think
of him or not think of him, but the thought that he existed brought
out some kind of constant, hopeful joy," wrote an ordinary reader
in a personal letter. This same thought was articulated in almost
the same words at one of the plenums of the Union of Soviet Cinematographers in December 1980, when the famous film director
Eldar Ryazanov announced to all: "The death of Vladimir Vysotsky
and Vasily Shukshin showed with enough clarity who today sways
the people's minds in our country."[10]
Vysotsky was not only a great poet and actor but also the living
soul and conscience of his time. He was a tuning fork for Soviet
artists of different esthetic movements and moral positions. They
checked their own voices and actions against his. Many were even
more famous than he. Through his songs and charm, if not in his

own personal conduct in art and life, he filled an exceptional place in Soviet art. He united poets, actors, and writers in the belief that if everyone worked together it would be possible to clear the air, which, in the art world, had gotten heavier in Brezhnev's last years.

When the Aksenov almanac, *Metropole*, was destroyed, Vysotsky appeared before its creators with his guitar to lift their fallen spirits. For the Taganka's tenth anniversary Volodya composed the song "Theatro-prison-like étude" in which he offers a toast "to collaboration, connection, cohesion / With my age-old friends, with the folks from the Taganka." He sang:

Our well-constructed ranks are growing thin,
Writers that we all respect.
It's said, from this, however, one matures.
Righteous work will be your motivation.

Taganka, be renowned! Laugh! Cry! And yell!
Live on, through suffering and also through delight
Let our bricks fall together and as they fall
Will form the cornerstone of our new building site.

It was only after he was gone that many understood how much Vysotsky meant for Russian culture in the Soviet period, what had been lost with him, what national love existed for him, and how much he achieved, almost single-handedly breaking through totalitarian control over art. After all, is it possible? Is there some hope that an artist can break through to the people to express himself openly under Soviet conditions? It is possible, answered Vysotsky by example, but at what cost! You have to pay for everything, either with your life or your art.

Life responded strongly to Vysotsky. The numbers wanting to see their singer were so huge that the authorities were not unduly alarmed. The officially sanctioned poets, R. Rozhdestvensky, S. Kunyaev, and others, tried to belittle his importance, arguing that Vysotsky was not exceptional amongst Soviet poets, and that he was just as patriotic as those who were "recruited by one idea." S. Kunyaev, in the journal *Nash Sovremennik (Our Contemporary)*, complained that popular taste had deteriorated, explaining the idolatry of Vysotsky. He argued that the poet had fallen victim to his own popularity, a short-lived fad. What a storm followed! The editorial staff received thousands of letters from every corner of the country cursing the author. Stanislav Kunyaev describes the readers' reactions:

> Nine out of ten cursed the author of the article with such passion that if words could turn into physical force, he would have long ago turned into ashes. At night the phone would shriek: "You're still alive," "Just you wait . . .," "You're jealous! Your own poems don't cut it," and so on.

Kunyaev attempted to prove his righteousness by bringing out some opinions:

> "It could be, that in one hundred years, Vysotsky will stand next to, or maybe, even higher than Shakespeare and Pushkin . . . National favorites, our heroes or idols should not be touched." (Milena Milkovskaya, Stavropol) "You, Salieri, are nobody." (R. Orlova, Magadan) "Aside from Vysotsky I don't believe any of today's poets." (V. Maksimova, city of Aldan). And so on.

What explains this passionate defense by millions who openly expressed their solidarity with him, his songs, his behavior, and his courage?

Kunyaev listed the social position of those who wrote letters in support of Vysotsky: "a student, a worker, an engineer, a schoolboy, a trade worker, a Ph.D. candidate. There were more women than men. . . ." He quotes one unsigned letter: "Millions of hands will stretch out and grope for you in the dark until they find you. . . ." The offended Kunyaev concludes his discussion: "The point isn't in taste—no one argues about that—but in something much larger: as it is said in Tolstoy's short story 'The Death of Ivan Ilyich' the question isn't in the kidney, but in life and . . . death."[11]

The decorated Soviet poet was absolutely right in trying to prove that Vysotsky, who had become extremely popular, was not free from the people in whom he inspired civilian courage through his poetry. A poet does not want to be free of people; he wants to always remain true to his ideas and worthy of his songs.

Vysotsky is known and well liked in the West, where he gave repeated concerts. He has close friends in Paris, including a widow,

Marina Vladi, who keeps a unique, partially unpublished archive of the actor-poet. Vysotsky has thousands of American fans, and not only former Soviet citizens. They grow in number every year. Vysotsky provides them with a full understanding of unofficial Soviet culture. I know several Americans who are anthologizing his songs, performances, and photographs. Here, in the United States, his first song collection was published on twenty cassettes and thousands of records. Two volumes of his works in Russian were first published in New York, publications significantly more complete than the single, thin little book of selected songs, vigorously sifted through the censor's sieve, that appeared in the USSR a year after his death. The Soviet collection was put together by the famous poet Robert Rozhdestvensky—Vysotsky's antagonist in art and life—who did everything possible to turn Vysotsky's "voice, torn from despair" into a "pleasant falsetto" *(Monument)*, something Vysotsky had predicted. The first American collection of Vysotsky's *Songs and Poems* includes more than 600 titles, compared to the Soviet edition's 140, and contains Vysotsky's prose along with remembrances of him. A third supplementary volume is now being prepared.

In the West at least three different full-length documentaries were filmed and shown on television to millions in America, West Germany, France, Denmark, and Sweden.

Scholarly presentations on Vysotsky are made at Western Slavic studies conferences; dissertations and lectures are presented in American and European universities. I do not know of similar cases in the artist's homeland—probably there just aren't any. This does not mean, however, that Vysotsky is forgotten among the people.

Vysotsky's songs can be heard coming out of windows in Soviet homes in the capital city, in large and small towns, in the country, and in workers' communities. Pilgrimages to his grave at the Vagankino Cemetery in Moscow continue without abating. In winter bouquets of uncommonly beautiful flowers are placed there, sometimes cut out of schoolchildren's notebooks or colored paper.

The more time that passes since Vysotsky's death, the more precious he becomes for all of us and the more irreplaceable and priceless his contribution to the present and future of Russian culture. For a long time to come, while the love for song lives, people of

Russian culture in and out of their homeland will gratefully remember Volodya Vysotsky.

Yuri Trifonov wrote in Vysotsky's obituary:

> He sang about much that was sorrowful about the times and about himself, and, at the same time, he rewarded us . . . with genuine poetry, passion and courage, so essential for life. He was a poet of legendary temperament, and he left—not having spent it all, not having drained himself, not having betrayed his gift.[12]

The End of the Taganka

Pushkin's Boris Godunov Banned

DRESS REHEARSAL: DECEMBER 1982

Something changed in the Taganka's mood after Vysotsky's death. Even the old, smooth running productions showed strain, like an instrument with a broken string. A cold wind blew in the brick walls of the new building. The actors' voices were lost in the last rows. They were worn out from unnerving worry. Anxiety and impatience were communicated from the stage to the auditorium. Everyone, actors and spectators, waited for something, no one knew what.

The year 1982 was coming to an end. In the Kremlin an old, weak, and undistinguished leader, notable only for his hairy eyebrows, thick speech, and infamous invasion of Czechoslovakia and Afghanistan, died slowly during the October Revolution's sixty-fifth anniversary.

The country's new boss announced himself. Climbing atop Red Square mausoleum, the head of Soviet Russia's secret police delivered a speech about the deceased leader. He spoke in roughly the same spirit that the Moscow boyar Masalsky asked the people to shout a toast to the new czar. The words were different because they derived from the lexicon of the twentieth century and not the seventeenth, but the essence was the same.

Coincidentally, at the same time on another Moscow hilltop in the Taganka section, a world-famous theater made final preparations on Pushkin's tragedy. Before the new leader settled into the Kremlin mansion, the Taganka comedians performed a "comedy about an imposter," as the author originally called his play.

A governmental committee saw the rehearsal and horrified—especially at the play's final scene—ran like mad out of the theater and categorically forbade the production to be shown publicly. News that the new Kremlin powers had initiated their cultural policy by banning Pushkin circulated instantly throughout snowy

137

Moscow, reaching newspapers abroad and causing scandal and gossip—not just of a literary nature.

What had happened? Why had a great Russian classic, studied in Soviet schools and universities, suddenly become offensive to the authorities? What sedition did they see in Lyubimov's production?

Those who aspired to reject the routine penetrated the depths of Pushkin's ideas and followed him in reforming old theatrical forms, now and for a long time after found their artistic spears breaking and their heads rolling because of *Boris Godunov*. The play's trying fate began during Pushkin's lifetime, though he never saw his favorite work on stage. *Boris Godunov* was staged for the first time in 1870, thirty-three years after the poet's death, at the Marinsky theater in St. Petersburg without any particular success. Later other theaters also suffered setbacks in staging *Boris Godunov*, including the Moscow Art Theatre, where it was staged by Nemirovich-Danchenko in 1907.

Meyerhold seriously attempted to solve the riddle of Pushkin's drama in the Soviet era. In 1937, with the appearance of Meyerhold's grandiose conception of national political drama, S. Prokofiev wrote music for it and V. Shestakov designed scenery. However, the Soviet press cruelly attacked the Meyerhold Theater and it soon closed; Meyerhold was dismissed from active work, then arrested and liquidated. Luckily, detailed accounts of his rehearsals and his contemporaries, recollections concerning his last love were preserved. At a meeting of his troupe on September 30, 1937, when, for all practical purposes, rehearsals were stopped, Meyerhold said: "Theater has such an expressive language that *between* [my emphasis] the words and gestures, it can concisely show the situation in such a light that for the modern spectator it will be expressed differently."[1]

Those who worked with Meyerhold recall the director demanding his actors to always keep in mind a phrase Pushkin wrote in a letter to P. Vyazemsky: ". . . there was no way I could hide all of my ears under the dunce cap. They stick out!"[2]

Pushkin's words seem to serve as an epigraph for Lyubimov's *Boris Godunov*. From beginning to end his direction was built on the theatrical laws of the *skomorokh*. The director openly created a free wheeling carnival-like spectacle, even bringing out two *skomorokhs* with forelocks wearing dunce caps who winked devilishly at the audience in what seemed the most tragic and inopportune moment of the final scene.

The Russian *skomorokh* is a special figure, the people's conscience in a joking mask. The *skomorokh* could be killed, bought, and made to dance or compose lying songs; if he resisted he could be trampled. One could do anything to the *skomorokh* but destroy his spirit. The dunce cap hence became an artistic image representing the indestructible irony of the people.

Pushkin pulled the dunce cap on himself in the relatively liberal times of Czar Alexander I, understanding its indispensable role in Russian art. In one scene (*Deviche Pole*, "Virgin's Field," thrown out by the czar's censors in the play's first publication), Pushkin depicts two simple men watching the selection of a new czar from the back of the crowd, farther from the police constables where it was safer to freely judge:

One (quietly): What're they crying about over there?
The Other: How should we know? The boyars know, we're no match for them.
One: Everyone's crying.
Brother, let's cry too.
The Other: I'm trying, brother,
but I can't.
The First: Me too. Is there any onion?
We'll rub our eyes.
The Second: No, I'll use my saliva.
Why fuss?
The First: Yeah, who'll know . . . figure it out. . . .[3]

As far back as 1973 Lyubimov worked on the Pushkin production *Comrade, Believe*, using this scene in his adaptation. He took aim at *Boris* for a long time, seeing in it a rare opportunity to sum up his esthetic and moral searches. The libertinism with which Pushkin depicted the common people was key to the tragedy's coarse elements. The idea matured and was put aside, but did not leave him in peace. The director seemed to chase it away like a hallucination or a premonition of the end, but it kept returning and ever more emphatically demanding its incarnation.

He seemed to decide on the production at the most inopportune moment, when the very existence of the theater was in question after the scandal over the Vysotsky production. He could not bear to wait any longer, however; the theater was losing faith in itself and the actors were growing old as was its director. Any way you look at it, Lyubimov was turning sixty-five and Pushkin demanded youthful energy.

In the winter of 1982 rehearsals began with the training of the choir. The composer, Dmitry Pokrovsky, was invited to the theater; he is a famous compiler of Russian musical folklore who spent a few months teaching the actors a special style of performing Russian songs. The choir became the critical element of the production. It remained on stage for the entire action, living its own life, relating indirectly to the czarist scenes. The choir seemed a florid national background against which intrigues were woven and the political power struggle in the Time of Troubles (1605–13) played. The choir dressed in costumes from different epochs, from national Russian sarafans to the long bohemian skirts, leather jackets, and blue jeans worn by people in the crowd scenes. This mixed choir, intentionally anachronistic, created an amazingly unified and dynamic representation of the people who carried Russian song through the different eras. The doleful and lyrical songs, the traditional Slavonic folk dances in the round, the weeping and laments performed by this unusual, free spirited, and mischievous choir carried the whole production as if on the waves of a national sea. From scene to scene they tied together the montage of freely constructed *mise en scènes*.

We still do not know everything about this banned production, but through various sources, above all the eyewitness accounts of those who attended two closed previews, we draw an outline of an unusually bright and large scale theatrical action. It surpassed in boldness everything known about previous interpretations of *Godunov* in the Russian or Soviet theater. The following is excerpted from a letter by one Moscow theater lover:

> I cannot remember any production making a similar impression on me. Everything seems to go according to Pushkin, who sounds incredibly real, especially in the folk scenes. In general, the individual parts aren't as strong as the crowd scenes, which are basically conducted in song (some kind of old Russian songs, exceptionally well studied with a very impressionable text). There aren't many of "Lyu-

bimov's devices"—for instance in the fountain scene an old, rusty bucket utilized more than once in other scenes plays a role; out of two streams the "fountain" sprinkles. (Marina—Alla Demidova, False Demetrius—the actor Zolotukhin.) But this is comic, unimportant, even though it cancels out some of the pathos. . . .

I don't think the fate of the production will be a lucky one. But God help it. It would be a shame for such a work to disappear. . . .[4]

Lyubimov's 1982 *Boris Godunov* lacks a central figure. The people, confused and without faith in their leaders, become the main character and unburden their hearts only in song. Lyubimov did not present a single production without a key metaphor (the floating curtain in *Hamlet*, the military truck in *The Dawns Are Quiet Here*, the swinging pendulum in *Master and Margarita*) and found the theatrical movement in the "conceptual" costumes for Pushkin's characters. Even though he employs this in other productions, Lyubimov used this in *Boris Godunov* for the first time as a consistent device. This entailed a whole system of metaphor for the costumes. False Demetrius dresses as a sailor-anarchist of the 1920s, in an unbuttoned pea jacket with a knitted vest showing underneath. The boyar Baratinsky wears an overcoat. The patriarch of Russia wears a hospital robe and walks on crutches. The deserter, Andrey Kurbsky, naturally wears foreign blue jeans. The hermit, Pimen, as one onlooker noted, resembles a modern day "zek" or political prisoner in his prison robe.[5]

This historical masquerade reaches its peak in the appearance of the main intriguer and experienced courtier, Vasily Shuyskoy. With a forceful walk the actor Ivan Bortnik enters the Taganka stage in a leather jacket and a military cap with a band around it. A somber shadow of a gallows is cast upon the backdrop at his appearance. Maybe the leather jacket of the Cheka does not say much to the Westerner, but it brings out familiar associations for the Russian spectator.

Perhaps most unexpected of all is Boris, the Czar played by the talented Nikolay Gubenko, a deep and reserved actor. Godunov's image withstands substantive changes and steps out of the interpretation of a killer-czar suffering a tortured conscience.

In Godunov Gubenko creates complex and contradictory characteristics. Wearing the Tatar quilted robe he establishes order in

Russia with Asiatic self-confidence. The country is gripped in a fear that results in his falling victim to palace intrigues—the fruit sown of lawlessness.

In Lyubimov's production Godunov suffers, especially at the end when, after the death of his character, Gubenko the actor presents himself differently before the spectator, in the name of the theater and the author. I will elaborate on this later.

The production was performed on an open platform almost without scenery. Lyubimov came up with a wooden platform reminiscent of old Russian platforms used for executions, open on three sides with the fourth supported by a blank white brick wall with encased windows. Only one narrow hole was left at the bottom. Through it the actors threw themselves out onto the stage wearing gray caftans, fur coats, or sheepskin coats, and huddled at the furthest edge of the platform. For most of the action it was very difficult to see them from the auditorium; they seemed to be kneeling. The higher part of the platform was accessible only to the czar and his attendants, but they too stepped to the back rows and mixed in with the commoners.

Lyubimov arranged the performance space in such a way that an actor entering up on the platform was level with the spectator and could easily address him. Intimate close-up scenes alternated with general scenes when the choir entered the action.

In the center of the platform, at the outer edge, the director, poking fun, placed a nondescript wooden post with two arrows: the left one pointed to Europe and the right one to Asia. With this device Lyubimov explained the production's special, unrestrained style that broke many traditional acting rules. On the Asia/Europe border the actors parody their roles; they act tough and aggressive, sharpening their characters to the point of the grotesque, consciously challenging the spectator to a passionate argument.

In one scene Lyubimov, as he told me himself, went for an openly shocking bit. He forced an actor to go down into the auditorium and chase a dumfounded "European" spectator from his folding chair in a nearby row because the chair was needed for the "quasi-Asiatic" on stage. Let him know that we do not stand on ceremony with Europeans!

Similar shocks occurred in other Taganka productions; you will recall that in *The House on the Embankment* the main "unmasker" of the cosmopolitans, that raving paralytic, was wheeled down a narrow passage in his wheelchair, crudely brushing against the spectators. In Lyubimov's opinion, it is sometimes healthy for the spectator to, even mildly, feel the physical discomforts of life that make the characters suffer.

The action winds down. Boris the czar has died, his offspring have been poisoned, and a new czar, Dmitry Ivanovich, is declared, but the people, as in Pushkin's famous quote, have already lost faith and are keeping silent. It is here, just before the curtain falls, that Lyubimov places his final, most important stroke. The whole play seems staged just for this. (This often happens in art. I know a prosperous Soviet director who admitted to me that he staged *King Lear* today for the sake of only one line: "There is no one in the world to blame!") From a side entrance Nikolay Gubenko appears, dressed now in his normal Moscow clothing, indistinguishable from the spectators. Unhurriedly he walks on stage and, almost without reproach or any great hope of getting an answer, he addresses the audience:

"Why do you keep silent? Scream: long live . . ."

The spectators keep silent.

Confused, the choir on stage also keeps silent. In the next instant they succumb to the drama's rhythm and break the silence by singing a toast, acting as the connection between stage and auditorium.

The last line of the play serves as a counterpoint for Lyubimov, tying together different eras into a unified whole.

Russian literature, as I've noted, is a literature of questions: "What is to be done? Who is to blame?" Our contemporary Lyubimov found one more confounded question of Russian life in Pushkin.

In the finale, after Boris's children are killed, the choir slowly moves toward the auditorium, freezing in horror at the very edge of the platform. Their mask-like faces with their glassy eyes, dilated pupils, and half opened mouths frozen in a mute scream stare at the spectator point blank. Only two *skomorokhs* who have not lost heart make a low, comic bow and with an energetic curiosity peer from time to time at the audience.

Lyubimov ended his last production at the Taganka with this dual finale, found in reading Pushkin.

What "seditious" idea did the theater bring out in its production of *Boris Godunov?* Why did the authorities label it anathema even before it became public? The answer is essentially simple. The production showed that Muscovites were not of one mind concerning the authorities and never were, and that they were not apt to be soon. There will always be those who naively yell "Hurray!" and others who, out of fear, prefer to remain silent, but jokesters will also be found who, in pretense, wet their eyes with saliva.

You say Pushkin is more complex? It is possible, but for various reasons the Russian theater has been unable to accommodate all of his complexity in 150 years of trying.

Lyubimov's Revolt

THE TWENTY-YEAR HISTORY OF THE TAGANKA THEATER records not only a selfless labor of devotion but an exhausting battle as well. A handful of like-minded actors fought Soviet conditions for survival and the right to create according to their personal convictions.

Lyubimov and his actors did not have any special requirements, except to be allowed to tell the truth as much as possible and to work in peace. They wanted to conduct a serious search in art, to tell people the truth, to show things that many did not notice or want to notice. The Taganka Theater did not ask its spectators to revolt or dissent; it did not advance any political demands. It addressed the audience's moral and esthetic feelings as is appropriate for the theater. It showed that the art world is richer than the precepts of socialist realism, moreover, that life does not fit into its plan.

The tragic paradox, however, lies in the fact that in a country where art is considered, as Lenin put it, "a part of the Party's general proletarian affairs," any artist's attempt to be independent of politics or experiment loosely with form inevitably leads to a clash with the predominant ideology. By the very conditions of its existence, art in the USSR is assigned an exaggerated role over and above its esthetic one. This role is simultaneously its strength and its weakness. People do not have other legal platforms from which to express their true thoughts, feelings, and moods, hence art's special mission for the people and the sheer panic and fear of the authorities.

In 1974 the authorities broke up with bulldozers an unofficial artists' exhibition organized by O. Rabin and A. Glezer on a vacant lot in Moscow. The president of the AFL-CIO, George Meany, exclaimed in amazement to the United States Senate: "God, what kind of society is it that must use bulldozers against paintings!"[6] An artist asserting his modest right to free creation according to normal, human standards needs superhuman nerves under Soviet conditions. This is understood only with great difficulty in the West. Alternatively, Easterners do not understand why Westerners cannot perceive it.

The Soviet artist's societal position makes him vulnerable to reprisals from the one-party government, often negating all his creative efforts. More often than not this forces talented people to capitulate and serve the regime or, less frequently, to master roundabout searches or alternative paths to government roadblocks. Wrote Andrey Dmitrievich Sakharov, one of the Taganka's admirers: "Every display of nonconformity under our circumstances demands exceptional courage, a readiness for deprivation and sacrifices, and precisely because of this, is very important."[7]

The Taganka's work was one such bright display of the spirit's courage, that is, nonconformity in art. The theater's immense popularity enraged the dogmatic and orthodox Soviets because it proved the defeat of party ideology and cultural policy. The Taganka's success showed that despite ideological treatment in the spirit of "class consciousness," the Soviet regime did not succeed in destroying, in a significant mass of people, a feeling for beauty, truth, fairness, or kindness.

The Taganka Theater's nonconformity was determined by its own esthetics and in the very fact of its existence on Soviet soil. Rumors often crept through Moscow that the Taganka would be closed down—after *Hamlet*, after *Tartuffe*, after the censored *Fyodor Kuzkin*, after *Master and Margarita*, and after the merciless *The House on the Embankment*. Lyubimov's friends asked him what he would do if the theater closed. He jokingly answered: "I'll become a cab driver."

He continued fighting for his theater and not only in Quixotic ways. Uncompromising with regard to principles or the general direction of his art, he gave in to the authorities on small things. He looked for support among the liberal intelligentsia in both academic and artistic circles, among cosmonauts, and unexpectedly, at the very top of government by writing to Brezhnev and Andropov. He knew that even at the top there wasn't complete agreement about what art should be in the atomic and space age. Vysotsky broke through the obstacle of censorship by reaching, not only students and workers, but the military, the KGB clubs, the frontier guards, and even the governmental summer homes of the ruling elite, thereby strengthening hope for change in the artist's situation.

Lyubimov was supported not only by green youth but by some old Bolsheviks who had spent time in Stalin's jails and concentration camps. At times they were particularly eager. They had nothing to lose, they were fussed over, they were fed in government cafeterias and from time to time invited for a meeting at the Central Committee "for advice." The people jokingly named them "the people's avengers." After John Reed's *Ten Days* in which Lyubimov resurrected the atmosphere of their youth, enthusiasm, and the chaos of October, they created their own club, Friends of the Theater, rallying around the energetic Lev Matveevich Portnov. After eighteen years in the Gulag he preserved his love of art even into his eighties; he was indeed tireless. He organized group viewings of new Taganka productions for old Bolsheviks, scholars, and the Moscow intelligentsia. He supplied the influential people with tickets and complimentary passes and formulated public opinion. Lenin's old guard wrote letters to the higher levels of government, right on up to Brezhnev and the Secretary of the Central Committee, demanding that the Taganka be saved and given the right to work the way it wanted to. A true friend of the theater showing great support for Lyubimov was the nobel laureate P. L. Kapitsa. In a well-known example, he let Lyubimov use his personal telephone to call someone inaccessible to mere mortals—the head of the KGB, Yuri Andropov. This conversation, Lyubimov later recalled, was significant. Andropov, having heard Lyubimov's request that the Vysotsky production be allowed to run, asked: "Why are you addressing this question to State Security and not to the Minister of Culture?" Lyubimov, not losing his head, replied: "Because I consider this a State Security matter." "Maybe you're right," Andropov said.[8]

The theater patrons should not be overestimated. They were all useful, but only up to a point. The ideological mechanism used to crush different views on art in those years was insidious and refined, but cautious at the same time. The cultural bureaucrats did not hurry events along, knowing their day would come. Opinions promulgated regarding the unsuitability of the Taganka for Soviet theater. Yuri Zubkov, editor of the journal *Teatralnaya Zhisn (Theatrical Life)*, was famous for his safeguarded position, stagnancy, and dogmatism. In 1971 he was already provoking accusations that the Taganka directly engaged in political sabotage. He wrote about their production of *Tartuffe* in the spirit of a police report: "Molière and his troupe were forced to stand on their knees before the king. But, as the production seems to say, to search for sincerity in the relations between an artist and the authorities is to search in vain."[9] The same pen denounced Brecht's *Galileo:* "the director suggests that the spectator's attention turn to the outer associations with our reality, sort of tempting Galileo with a toy model 'Volga.' " Many similar attacks appeared in the Soviet press and in oral presentations at various social forums.

For the time being, however, Brezhnev's principle of following the status quo included art and kept the Taganka's adversaries from open attacks. Everyone felt the gap between words and deeds that characterized the country's atmosphere in the last years of Brezhnev's leadership. Their sense of humor intact, Muscovites joked about their mistrust of the authorities. In one joke a crowd of people waits at a crosswalk for the light to change. The light turns green and everyone crosses except for one old woman holding a bag. Someone tenderheartedly asks: "Why aren't you crossing? The light is green!" The old woman answers, "You know dear, I don't trust them, in general."

Lyubimov had faith but did not sit with his hands folded; he looked for new patrons. Going over the Minister of Culture he turned to Brezhnev, who said "on the record": "Artists should be trusted. Let him work in peace." Using this indulgence, Lyubimov entered into open confrontations with cultural bureaucrats, acting through his own means. In *Tartuffe*, gold-framed portraits of the king and Cardinal Richelieu, the actual ruler who dominated the arts among other things, hung in the proscenium. It was not hard to recognize in the image of Molière's cardinal, wearing a wig and with a cataract in one eye, the "gray cardinal" of Soviet times— the omnipotent Suslov. The Taganka awaited a scandal, but everything turned out all right. The head ideologue had enough sense not to recognize himself in Lyubimov's Richelieu. Later, in 1979, a "limited contingent" of Soviet troops, responding to "a request by the Afghan government" invaded that country; Lyubimov showed Moscow Brecht's *Turandot, or the Congress of Whitewashers*. In it the theater performs a farce about the collective leadership of an imaginary government where self-righteous people find legal justification for all the mistakes and pompous triviality of their leaders, compete in glorifying each other, and award one another every possible medal and title. The audience swallowed it! ("This must be about the Chinese—everyone on stage is slanty-eyed and takes small steps—it's not Russian!")

Of course things could not go on like this for long. On March 11, 1978 *Pravda* opened fire on Lyubimov, who was then in Paris rehearsing Tchaikovsky's *The Queen of Spades* at the Grand Opera. The production had not yet been shown on stage, but *Pravda* already opposed it, publishing a letter by the conductor of the Bolshoy Theater, A. Zhyuraytis, under the misleading headline: "In Defense of *The Queen of Spades*."[10] It began ominously, as in the worst Stalinist times: "A monstrous action is being prepared! Its victim is a masterpiece by a genius of Russian music, P. I. Tchaikovsky." Using this provoker who had not seen the production or the rehearsals as a mouthpiece, an organ of the Central Committee of the Communist Party of the Soviet Union made the following accusations:

> Really, is it permissible for Soviet citizens to organize a Medieval auto-da-fé on Tchaikovsky who is adored by the Soviet people . . . appearing in the role of an inquisitor? Really, is it decent to betray things that are sacred to us, to the petty interests of cheap, foreign commercials?

A. Zhyuraytis, laureate of the USSR, called the director an imposter, demagogue, destroyer of Russian culture, and "a parasite on a perfect, living organism. . . ." The author, demonstrating his supposed objectivity, intentionally left out the director's name and the place where this "horrible crime" was being prepared. *Pravda* corrected this "forgetfulness" by supplying a letter with the expressive footnote: "Lyubimov the director is preparing a production of Tchaikovsky's opera *The Queen of Spades* 'modernized' by the composer A. Shnitke in Paris."[11]

"Didn't the responsible organizations show tolerance for such a mockery of a Russian classic?" the party newspaper demagogically inquired, clearly suggesting that the Taganka's director be restrained, at home and abroad.

The breaking scandal called Lyubimov back to Moscow, forcing him to interrupt work on the Paris production. Russian culture and prestige were of little concern to the Soviet bureaucrats. Lyubimov's successes on the world stage—in La Scala in 1975 with L. Nono's contemporary opera *Under the Warm Sun of Love*, the successful tours to Yugoslavia and France, the productions in Hungary and other countries—annoyed them. They continued their petty attacks despite French protests and the Italian Central Committee's declaration, in the person of Giorgio Napolitano, head of the Cultural Department, of the enormous significance of Yu. Lyubimov's work for "fruitful cooperation on a European scale."[12] Those who signed the Helsinki accords with one hand and with the other closed all paths to its fulfillment did not want this most of all. The Soviet bureaucrats once again showed themselves to be, as V. Aksenov expressed it, "unique creators of their own endless disgraces."

Lyubimov also drew his own conclusions from these lessons. He realized that his duel with the Soviet system was entering its final stage, that hoping for the best was unrealistic, that his obstructions were coming from all sides, and that it was time to make his choice. His student Vladimir Vysotsky and author of the song "Hunting for Wolves" set an example.

In 1980 Lyubimov undertook Trifonov's *The House on the Embankment*, a chronicle unmasking the Soviet image of life. By doing this Lyubimov accepted the challenge thrown down by the Soviet bureaucracy. The new hero of the Taganka production was Vadim Glebov—"balding, with breasts like a woman" and "sunken shoulders." He embodied a type of Soviet conformist, cynic, and time-server. Painful moments from recent Soviet social history were represented in the production: the 1937 arrests and the campaign against "cosmopolitanism" in 1949. These subjects were taboo in Soviet art. Lyubimov disregarded this, conceding to the censor only in omitting the name Yezhov—Stalin's executioner. In Lyubimov's production there is a scene where the Pioneers of the 1930s compose a poem in Yezhov's honor. The bureaucrats from the Ministry of Culture protested. In order to save the production Lyubimov agreed to remove Yezhov's name. The Pioneers recite the poem to just before the rhyming word "Yezhov"; they then pause significantly, clap their palms over their mouths, and look at the audience amused. It is doubly malicious. It is not wise to joke with Lyubimov. The Taganka Theater broke completely free from the higher ideological levels of command and became simply intolerable to them. It was time to finish the theater off.

After *House* premièred in the spring of 1980 the Taganka's conflicts with the authorities became more pointed. The theater collective headed by the director disobeyed the administration and entered into an open confrontation. It was indeed an unprecedented situation for Soviet art. In July a heavy blow was dealt the theater—Vladimir Vysotsky, pride of the Taganka, died. Despite this great loss, Vysotsky's friends felt a surge of strength and decided to follow in his footsteps. The spontaneous memorials for the poet were no joking matter for the ruling powers. The USSR Minister of Culture, P. Demichev—the same one who tried to curry favor with Khrushchev by suggesting the removal of Stalin's body from the mausoleum—now atoned for his sins and displayed a particular, ideological vigilance. An old enemy of the Taganka and of Lyubimov, he personally impeded the theater's work, thinking it the principal breeding ground of opposing views in Soviet art. The ignorant and cowardly party grandee did not scorn intrigue and slyly waited for a convenient moment to inflict the final blow. The change in leadership after Brezhnev's death and the naming of Chernenko as the country's chief ideologue presented that moment. The theater gave him additional grounds with its "disgraceful" *Boris Godunov* in December 1982. Demichev personally ordered the production banned. This was the last straw. Lyubimov lost all patience. The director wrote a letter to Andropov declaring his retirement if the ban remained.

While awaiting an answer Lyubimov continued his work, rehearsing Bulgakov's *Black Snow: A Theatrical Novel* and planning his future repertoire. In February 1983, in a discussion with American interpreter Dr. Nicholas Rzhevsky, he shares his conception for a production of *The Possessed*. Nothing foreshadowed the tragic outcome of the escalating conflict. After all, few situations in the Taganka's twenty-year history were as pointed. Lyubimov still hoped that Andropov, who was favorably disposed toward the director since he talked his offspring out of an acting career, would help change the current attitude.

Events, however, developed completely differently. Andropov's rival, Chernenko, assumed responsibility for ideology. The public quickly christened him with the nickname "coachman." (The Russian word "kucher" corresponds to Chernenko's initials and the first syllable of his last name: *K. U. Cher*nenko.) Indeed, a semi-literate, morose, laconic, puffed-up, and unsmiling Siberian coachman, very attentive to his business but completely ignorant in it, took the reins of government and self-importantly controlled the culture of Pushkin, Dostoevsky, Chekhov, Tolstoy.

The new leader revealed his plans for Soviet culture at an ideological plenary session of the Central Committee in June 1983. He formulated his policy with primitive straightforwardness: "There are truths," he loudly declared, *"that are not subject to examination, there are problems that have been decided unequivocally once and for all."*[13]

This translated from Soviet into Russian means: "Don't let them get through! Crush them!" In a hoarse voice, gasping for breath, the new chief said:

> We encounter examples when an author loses himself in complex problems or tries to flaunt his "unorthodox" interpretations; the result, however, is a distortion of our reality. . . . What was just said is fully applicable to the repertoire formed by the theater and the cinema.[14]

Since the main penalty of the last theater season, the ban on *Boris Godunov*, had Chernenko's approval and was possibly even ordered by him, Lyubimov knew where the new leader was headed.

The Soviet "coachman" gave these instructions to the cultural workers, urging them to help pull the collective load: "It is necessary to more actively press the great magnetic strength of communist ideals into the service of our educational goals."[15]

One can well ask, how much is enough? After sixty years there is still no change. Again, the whole trouble, it turns out, is not with the carriage or the coachman, but with the horses! A more desperate, humiliating, or hopeless situation would be hard to imagine.

The atmosphere in the theater heated up. The actors became exceedingly anxious. Lyubimov came down with a nervous eczema, a vexing and unpleasant disease. His heart began to trouble him from time to time. The theater did not give in, however, trusting in its director. The nineteenth and perhaps most difficult season was coming to an end. Two productions in which the theater showed the results of its esthetic and moral searches—*Vladimir Vysotsky* and *Boris Godunov*—were banned. This was too much. Just before summer vacation the theater unanimously decided to not accept the ban; working under these conditions was not only impossible but made no sense.

At this critical moment Lyubimov was offered the direction of *Crime and Punishment* in London. Negotiations, underway for more than five years, had seemed never ending, especially after the open conflict with the authorities. This time, however, he was being rushed to go and was even allowed to take his family. Something was hidden in this.

From Sheremetievo Airport Lyubimov sent another letter to Andropov (the first one remained unanswered, as would the second): "The conditions that have arisen at present mean that neither I nor the theater can work, if our productions continue to be banned. . . ."

With a light bag in his hand, and a heavy weight on his heart, Lyubimov boarded the Aeroflot plane and shot up into the Moscow sky, heading West. What he thought of as he flew over Soviet soil only he knows. I doubt he thought about parting with his native land forever.

Six weeks of intense rehearsals with the British actors flew by. On September 5 at the Lyric Theater in Hammersmith near London, Dostoevsky's *Crime and Punishment* successfully premièred. That same day a long interview between Lyubimov and *Times* correspondent Brian Appleyard was published. Called "The Crosses Yuri Lyubimov Bears" the article contained, in essence, nothing new, nothing that the well-known director would not say to his Moscow opponents; however, it abruptly altered his fate.

I am sixty-five years old and I simply don't have the time to wait until these government officials finally arrive at an understanding of a culture that will be worthy of my native land. . . . These works are shut down. I cannot accept this.[16]

In a few days he repeated this on the BBC for Soviet listeners and for his actors.

Pavel Filatov from the Soviet Embassy in London met Lyubimov at the Lyric Theatre auditorium and threatened: "The crime is completed, now punishment will follow." The indignant British showed the dull-witted diplomat the door. Lyubimov turned to the British authorities for protection.

I will never ask for political asylum. . . . I do not wish to become a defector. I love my country, I love Russian culture. However, I cannot work under the conditions dictated by the Soviet government.[17]

In another interview in January 1984 he elaborated:

I will wait until they guarantee me the conditions in which I can work. I'm waiting for them to remove Demichev, the Minister of Culture, and he's waiting for me to drop dead. We'll see who waits the longest.[18]

On March 6, 1984, a general meeting of the Taganka Theater troupe was called. A rank and file government official from the Board of Culture of the Moscow City Executive Committee, Vladimir Shadrin, read a short directive that said Lyubimov, who was then in Italy, was dismissed from his position as permanent director of the theater "for not fulfilling his official obligations without providing valid cause."

This bureaucratic formulation settled accounts with twenty years of inspired work by the founder of the Taganka Theater—the theater of the Russian avant-garde. His portrait in the foyer was taken down and his name crossed off all the posters of current productions he had staged. Leading actors of the troupe—Gubenko, Zolotukhin and Smekhov—demanded that the disgraceful directive be changed and objected to another director. A few people left the theater in protest, including Lyubimov's faithful comrade-in-arms, designer D. Borovsky.

The black deed was done, however. The Taganka and Lyubimov were separated. The government officials celebrated another martial victory over Russian culture and over the artist-rebel who had dared stand up for the right to create freely. In a few months, in the summer of 1984, Yuri Lyubimov was stripped of his citizenship.

What about the actors? They are the same, though in some ways different; after all, for them art is not always happiness. Often it is an urgent necessity, their daily bread. They laugh and cry as before, when necessary for the play, but of how they feel in their souls only they know. As before, they come out on stage every night to entertain the people of Moscow and maybe secretly think that which they once openly confessed in the Vysotsky production:

We can play anything for you that you want: heroes and scoundrels, hired killers, political schemers, debauched wives, chaste virgins . . . All this, it's understood, for a good price. All this, of course, under the banner of *realism*, for which *special* demands exist.

The theater continues.

At the Bottom

PREMIÈRE: DECEMBER 1984

IRONICALLY, THE FIRST WORK THE TAGANKA PRODUCED IN Lyubimov's absence had an almost symbolic title. Gorky's *At the Bottom* (also known as *The Lower Depths*) was staged by Anatoly Efros, who assumed the position of permanent director after three other candidates—M. Zakharov, N. Gubenko, and V. Dunaev—refused. This decision probably did not come easily for Efros, but his advisers and his situation pushed him into a fateful action. Efros explained his action in an open letter to the journal *Kontinent (Continent)*, No. 46:

> The theater has a hundred actors. All of them, with a very small exception, wanted to continue working and to preserve what was best about the theater and maybe to do something new; after all, their life isn't over, they're forty, forty-five years old. . . . They didn't want to go to different theaters so that the Taganka would cease to exist. A few of Lyubimov's students accepted me with caution, maybe even with hostility, because to them it seemed as if I came to wreck everything. They treated me with respect as a director, knew my previous work—I even staged things at the Taganka sometime ago—but they thought that I wanted to wipe out all that was old and to do my own thing without taking their individuality into account. Besides that, they were loyal to Lyubimov, their teacher. When they saw that I came without ill will, they quickly changed toward me. . . . Four people out of one hundred left. In short, many thought there would be no theater. . . . But now, I am convinced that people are happy that there is a theater and that they can go to it.[19]

This conciliatory statement made after two years somewhat differs with the program he presented in the *Literaturnaya Gazeta*[20] *(Literary Gazette)* right after his appointment. Coming into a troupe founded on workshop principles of creation, the new director called for reorganization:

> In some sense a strange time has come to pass for theatrical art. V. Rozov once said that in theatrical art there was a "time of unification,"

but now, and maybe not for long but for now, is a time of "separation."
And it is not at all necessary to hold on to the habitual organizational
frames of yesterday. Maybe a new and unexpected unification needs
to be found. Sometimes a collaboration that was put together long
ago turns into its own antithesis.[21]

Efros offered the following practical measures:

> . . . gather performers from different places. . . . Take Demidova
> from the Taganka, Yakovleva from the Bronnoy, Neelova from the
> Sovremennik, and Drobysheva from the Moscow Soviet Theatre and
> stage, let's say, a play by Williams with four women.

The authorities, forced to exile one talented artist, wanted to use
another to quietly turn the Taganka into a mediocre Soviet theater
like hundreds of others. For example the Sovremennik became mediocre when a group of leading actors were lured to the Moscow
Art Theatre with tempting salaries.

Reorganization inside the dead structure of Soviet art is characteristic of the 1980s not only for Efros, but for other artists
searching for compromise. Interestingly, the day after Lyubimov's
dismissal poet Andrey Voznesensky, one of the Taganka writers,
published an extensive article in the *Literaturnaya Gazeta (Literary
Gazette)* entitled "Managers of the Spiritual Works." There was not
one word in it about the conflict that took place between the artist
and the authorities, but, indirectly, he put forth a dubious theory
of how both sides could reconcile their differences. In Voznesensky's
opinion, a generous art patron could step forward as middleman;
this Maecenas was, supposedly, always crucial in art. Comparing
past patrons such as Savva Morozov, Diaghelev, and Tretiakov with
present "leaders of culture," Voznesensky called for mutual understanding and forgiveness. He exclaimed:

> How obligated our art world is to the Maecenases! The artist is fragile.
> He needs support, and not only material support in his relations with
> the world. He needs to be loaned spiritual energy, no less than mon-
> ey. . . .[22]

Claiming that art patrons, in all times and in all nations, create
their art through others, Voznesensky placed the patrons above even
the artists themselves. He wrote:

If these people didn't receive help, no masterpieces would appear. These martyrs, these cultural movers and shakers, these builders of the superstructure, these public men of culture—I would call them "managers of the spiritual works."

According to Voznesensky, art is created not by Raphael but by Medici, not by Surikov or Vasnetsov but by the respected P. M. Tretiakov. "Managers of the spiritual works," according to Voznesensky, are not Shostakovich, Meyerhold, Bulgakov, Lyubimov, Tarkovsky, or others; the real "builders of the superstructure" are those who run culture and "loan money and spiritual energy" to fragile artists, rewarding or punishing them according to their whim. (Zhdanov? Suslov? Demichev?)

Not to leave any doubt as to who he means, Voznesensky tells a touching story of Stalinist times. In the 1930s, while discussing a plan to reconstruct Moscow, someone's "decisive hand in a railroad soldier's shirt knocked down a model of St. Basil's Church," but another hand "in a Defense Department shirt stubbornly returned it to its place. This was," enthuses the author, "a deed worthy of Tretiakov."[23]

According to Voznesensky, there is no single approach to culture at the upper echelons of Soviet government. There are movers and shakers. The conclusion suggests itself. The Soviet artist, in order to exist and to create, must find his own Maecenas in the upper echelons of Soviet society. They exist, but the whole problem is in making the right choice.

In essence, the words and deeds of Voznesensky and Efros during the Taganka drama reflected the complete confusion among a segment of Soviet artists faced with an unprecedented situation. After leaders and artist-rebels left for the West—Solzhenitsyn, Neizvestny, Rostropovich, Aksenov, Nekrasov, Lyubimov, Tarkovsky, and many others—and after the deaths of Shukshin, Vysotsky, Trifonov, and Abramov—Soviet art slid back to its state ten years before when it served only a utilitarian purpose. The fate of Soviet culture was in the hands of minor artists, people who were weak, pacifist, compromising, and inconsistent, more interested in a career than in their work, incapable of withstanding pressure from the bureaucratic government. Those who left had no moral right to blame them, but they also could not close their eyes to the country's spiritual atmosphere for which they partly were responsible. Everything had to start from the beginning.

157

Efros's Taganka production of *At the Bottom* reflected the deep moral and esthetic conflicts of the theater, now entering the concluding phase of its development. The new production, without Lyubimov, was instantly announced as a great victory by all the Soviet critics from *Vechernaya Moskva* (*Evening Moscow*) to *Pravda*. Very likely no previous Taganka production had such press. The critics extolled Efros's new production as if to compensate for many years of silence about Lyubimov's work. This alone was suspicious. After many years of experience theatergoers in the USSR know that when all the newspapers praise anything as if they were on one team, the thing's garbage. The reverse—silence, or better yet, abuse of an out-of-the-ordinary production—is a true indicator of success.

Nothing can be done. The party approach to art is in operation. They vilified Meyerhold shamelessly for his *Inspector General* and even for his courageous attempt to breathe life into N. Ostrovsky's lifeless *How Steel Hardens;* they maligned the talented director Akimov for his innovative productions of Russian classics; they persecuted Eisenstein for *Ivan the Terrible;* they ripped apart Lyubimov's *Master and Margarita.* The young Efros, still full of strength and creative passion, was disgracefully thrown out of the Lenkomsomol Theatre in the 1960s for his creative productions of Chekhov.

Deprived of the pleasure of seeing this production, we can only judge it from the reviews and descriptions. A theater historian often has to reconstruct that which he has not seen himself. Let us try to recreate the new Taganka production from what the Soviet press gives us.

In 1903 Gorky wanted to call attention to people at the bottom by creating a naturalistic picture of everyday life at society's lowest levels. Stanislavsky's classic production at the Moscow Art Theatre scrupulously investigated the bottom, studying it for real at the Khitrov market where criminals lived. Today, theater offers a look at them eighty years later, after life has lifted them up. In Efros's production the people at the bottom settle into a communal apartment on the top floors of a red brick house, not, as in Gorky, in a flophouse basement.

Here are a few eloquent Soviet reviews delighting in the production about tramps, thieves, cheats, and killers in whom Gorky tried to find glimpses of humanity. G. Mikhailova wrote in *Vechernaya Moskva:*

No, these are not doomed or helpless people, even though it seems that they are completely lost, but those who, even under such horrifying conditions save within themselves a little island of light, faith in the idea that "man lives for a better life." This faith, this dream, this light is underlined by the director and the actors in their characters.[24]

She gave her article the pretty title: "A Little Island of Hope." Neither the reviewer nor the newspaper were troubled that this hope for a better future is the story of society's castaways. Their only concern was to praise Efros's production for "historical optimism," no matter what.

An even more inflated note was taken by *Isvestia* in its verbose review. A candidate for a degree in art criticism, I. Myagkova concluded her analysis with the following passage:

And the song that all of the people of the Bottom sing together in the finale becomes their "heavenly song"—a song of will and unity. Closely pushed up to one another, back to back, in the bright light of Truth, they all sit at Anna's death bed, like passengers on an ark, in an ocean of misfortune. Their salvation is in each other, within themselves, in the human community. . . .

Everything was heaped together in this critical opus. The only thing unexplained is what the truth was that with a "bright light" illuminated their souls and consciousness—a religious truth or a Marxist-Leninist truth. The reviewer learnedly informs us:

Between the sky and the lower earth, mankind is situated. The Taganka Theater production makes an attempt to somehow arrange the play's characters on all levels of the Mountain, to observe their path in hellish spheres in order to raise them to the Mountain in the finale and unite them in heavenly song.

Is the "mountain" reference to Sinai or to the "gaping heights" of communism? The confused thoughts of the reviewer seem to reflect the confusion of the production. Gorky's play, written at the very beginning of the century according to the rules of typical, naturalistic drama, clearly cannot withstand the burden of importance Soviet reviewers attached to it.

In the end all the ideological and artistic boundaries are washed away in an eclectic broth of the actors' interpretations and the director's tricks. Judging from the reviews, every actor performed independently. No consideration was given to who was good at what. Anna, played by T. Zhukova, "forced me to remember the Russian icon." Kvashnya (M. Politseymako) was "a genre painting of the old Flemish." Vasilisa (Z. Slavina) was "a portrait from Goya's brushes." Satin (I. Bortnik) reminded one of "some of Shukshin's characters." The whole spectacle, as asserted by the reviewer, rolls along like "a bright triumphant Strauss waltz."

Maksim Gorky, founder of socialist realism—tramps and drunkards in a flophouse—and . . . icons, "the Flemish," Goya, Shukshin, and even the carefree Strauss! Isn't it insulting to the actors of a once avant-garde Moscow theater that they are forced to act? Isn't it grotesque?

In Gorky's play the devout elder Luka tells Pepel the tramp: "What you believe in, that's what is. . . ." Vaska Pepel (played by Lyubimov's actor Zolotukhin with the curled forelock of a professional thief) plays the clown upon hearing this. His whole person seems to ask: "And if you don't believe in anything? What then?" Writes the reviewer: "His sly habit is to seem different from what he is, which forces him to act without interruption." One asks: "What do you do if you really don't believe in anything?"

The liberal Marianna Stroeva sounds a more serious note in the January 31, 1984 *Literaturnaya Gazeta (Literary Gazette)*. She saw the production's conception in the portrayal of the people:

> . . . having lowered themselves to the very bottom of life, having lost all sense of being on this sinful earth and vainly struggling in their search for a way out. If the sacred world is unable to find the path to truth—then regards to the madman who will blow a golden dream over mankind!
>
> The red brick of the new building takes up the whole stage. Straight ahead is a conventional wall, three floors with windows and weathered shutters (designed by Yuri Vasiliev). On the left—bunks, as bare as a skeleton. On the right—a cold arch. And that's it. Empty space, as if it were a brick sack where there are no signs of life, not even a hint of a comfortable everyday life. . . .[25]

M. Stroeva underlines the two-faced nature of the production. It starts out with circus clowning, "where, through a funny practical joke the truth is covered up, in an attempt to trick life with laughter, to color the rags with bright patches of jokes," but then in the second half of the production it's as if the actors rip off the joking cover, and show life as it is: "They look truth in the eye. . . . In the beginning it's as if no one lives, but only pretends to live, afraid to look life in the eye. However, the gaiety becomes colored with evil very soon."

This critic sees life in a brick well—life in prison—where people search vainly for truth, as the production's main idea. The locksmith Kleshch (V. Semenov) stretches out on Anna's deathbed and asks the audience: "Where is truth? There's no work . . . there's no shelter! To breathe one's last that's what's needed . . . there's the truth!"

The author of the *Literaturnaya Gazeta* article concludes:

A cruel accounting is going on here; one is led to results that aren't a laughing matter.

Satin does the bravest thing of all. His fateful hour comes. Ivan Bortnik portrays him with the frenzied, tragic sweep of Vysotsky's last roles. "Man—there is the truth. . . . Lies are the religion of slaves and masters. . . . Truth is the god of free man!" The actor throws out this compiled tirade from his soul as a sudden realization: "What do people live for? For a better life! . . . That's why any man should be respected . . . Especially children should be respected . . . the little ones! (On the radio, Luka's distant voice would answer him— "respect children!") No longer is there a killer, a convict, or a cheat in front of us, but a fanatic of the truth. Without any romanticized pathos, without any rhetoric, this Satin now boldly screams as a free man who has rejected all of the world's lies and opened up the "sacred truth"—before his last boundary.

And later he will go and sit next to everyone on the deathbed. There is no exit from this torture chamber.

The new permanent director of the Taganka Theater staged his first production as a candid fusion of this theater's devices with some of his own. The director came here not to destroy, but to carefully preserve the best of the theater's traditions. Efros begins the production with devices familiar to the actors of this theater and ends in a manner that demands a more extensive inner psychological expanse. It may be that not all of the stitches in this fusion fit at this time, not all the spiritual depths have been exhausted.

But the gravest symphonic harmony of the production reveals Gorky's humanism in a new way, carries us away with its difficult search for truth. The production of *At the Bottom* is in harmony with the theater and its director.

In the desire to support Efros at all costs, *Pravda* grasped the production's main theme: the cruel accounting of the characters with life. In the article "Argument about Man" (February 7, 1985), the venerable critic E. Surkov, known for his conservatism, unexpectedly shares some interesting details with us:

> The play was always performed with an intentional narrowing of the space on stage. Even where the action would break out into the courtyard under the open sky, it would be stifling and cramped. In Efros's production, the stage was open to its fullest depth and width. They even played in the auditorium. They played behind the monumental brick wall, which closed off the space on stage: in the apertures of the windows, on tiny platforms behind the windows. In the first half of the production, the action was, more often than not, built centrifugally: from the prison-like wall to the length of the stage, to its back and side.
>
> That was how the inner aspiration of the characters was realized in plasticity: from a flophouse, from the bottom up into space, freedom, into life. Anna is chained to the wall. She dies under it. Kostylev and Vasilisa don't move very far from the wall. All the others strain past the borders of their living space. And as far away from each other as possible—that's what's also important here. The ties between people are deliberately weakened in the production. Lines are often thrown across the whole stage, from one end to the other. Alienation and indifference rule here. Here, they do not look for paths to one another, as each one is locked in to his own misfortune and his own hope. Alone, he tries to throw the chains off of his fate.[26]

Indeed Surkov, being true to himself, dutifully concluded his review in the spirit of "historical optimism," but this only served to underline the production's duality.

So, *At the Bottom* as performed by the actors of the Taganka lived as if in two dimensions. In the first act there is expressiveness and the grotesque, a clownish carnival element characteristic of the Lyubimov school; in the second act prevails a "morning after" atmosphere, sharply changing the style to psychologizing the cruel prose of life and the tragic reflexes in the face of its perpetuality—a truly Effrosian beginning. Music, which plays a big, even overstated role in the production, abruptly underscores this gap. In the beginning the charming sounds of Mozart, Schubert, and Strauss predominate, but at the end, as the curtain falls, the performers

sing old Russian melodies while crowding together at the prison
wall.

Krivoy Zob (A. Grabbe) sweetly sings:

The sun rises and sets,
but it's dark in my jail,
days and nights are sentinels
guarding my window. . . .

Lyubimov's entire troupe joins in with tragic force:

I want to be free,
but I can't break my chains. . . .

This song sounds like a message to Lyubimov, who broke from
his students to his freedom. Efros proved his nobility in allowing
this despite his cautiousness. It was impossible for him not to see
that *At the Bottom* carried, aside from Gorky's theme, an ethical
protest by the theater against outer force over art. It seems to me
that Efros, together with Lyubimov's actors, consciously played *At
the Bottom* as a tragi-farce, conveying the bitter smile of the Taganka's
comedians over their own fate. It also commented on the very duality of art's role that the theater is forced to play against its will.

The history of Lyubimov's theater, having been allotted a part
in the wonderful beginning of Russian theater in the Soviet period,
symbolically concludes with *At the Bottom*. The Taganka under Efros or any other director is a different theater. Those who from the
start tried to curb this theater to make it resemble all of the other
obedient Soviet theaters considered it a better one now. The theater
world will, however, remember the Taganka of the 1960s, 1970s,
and 1980s as part of the history of the world stage, similar to the
way Meyerhold's theater is remembered.

Lyubimov and His Time: After the Taganka

1983

July. After a difficult season at the Taganka, at the height of the conflict with the authorities over *Boris Godunov*, Lyubimov unexpectedly receives permission to go to London to stage *Crime and Punishment* at the Lyric Theatre. Negotiations concerning this had been going on for five years previously. His wife Katalin and three-year-old son, Petya, leave with him for London.

Lyubimov sends a second letter to Andropov from the airport at Sheremetievo, stating the essence of the conflict between the Taganka and the Ministry of Culture and requesting that the ban on *Boris Godunov* be lifted. Further work by the theater, he says, is impossible otherwise.

> This was the unanimous decision of the theater collective: if they do not return the production *Boris Godunov, Alive, In Memory of Vysotsky*—that is, what we consider the best of what we have done—then we consider the continuation of our work to be senseless. [From Lyubimov's interview with *Kontinent*. No. 44, 1985.]

August. Lyubimov works intensely in London, ten hours daily. He selects the actors, whose professionalism, acknowledges Lyubimov, "is the highest in Europe." Rehearsals of *Crime and Punishment*, translated by N. Rzhevsky, are going well. D. Borovsky, who arrived with the Lyubimovs, finishes mounting the set, essentially repeating the Taganka set.

September 1. The world learns that a peaceful Korean airliner has been shot down by Soviet rockets. Passengers died, including women and children. Lyubimov watches the horrifying scenes on television, reads the Soviet press's false reports, and a moral protest grows in him.

> Before the première, the situation was very grave. Then the Korean plane was shot down. . . . It seems that we have experienced such horrible things for a long time already: all sorts of invasions, reprisals,

injustices. But this event is special: people are waiting for the plane to arrive, but no one comes; they've all been shot down and killed. . . . Unfortunately, Dostoevsky has turned out to be a prophet in *The Possessed*. . . . Time goes on, but the book becomes deeper and more frightening, as if it was just written. [From an interview with Yuri Lyubimov, *Index of Censorship*. No. 1, 1985.]

The opening of *Crime and Punishment* in London acquires a special meaning for Lyubimov.

September 5. Crime and Punishment premières at the Lyric Theatre in the London suburb of Hammersmith. Lyubimov gives a long interview to *Times* correspondent Brian Appleyard sharply criticizing the bureaucratic leadership of Soviet art and demanding that the bans on Taganka productions be lifted as a condition for his return. "I won't let them trample me anymore," he declares.

Filatov, an official of the Soviet Embassy in London, announces to Lyubimov in the presence of the British: "You have committed a crime and punishment will now follow." Lyubimov recalls the conversation: "I hit the roof—asked the interpreter to immediately translate these words to the British and left. He ran after me: 'We will find you anyway.' " The British showed the presumptuous Soviet diplomat the door.

Lyubimov asks for British protection against Soviet threats until his relations with the Soviet government improve. "I want to work in my own theater, but under the conditions created by them in the last few years, I cannot work," he declares.

Due to poor health, Lyubimov receives official approval by Soviet authorities to extend his stay in order to receive medical treatment.

October. Lyubimov and his family leave for Bologna where Lyubimov stages Wagner's opera *Tristan und Isolde*. The communist municipal authorities in Bologna reject a recommendation from Moscow that the disgraced director not be allowed to work in the Italian theater.

November 7. Rehearsals are going at full speed. "The deadlines here are very strict, as always," Lyubimov says in a telephone conversation. "The première is scheduled for December 1." In answer to a question regarding his health he says he is receiving medical treatment from local doctors: "The climate here also helps."

November 20. From Bologna, Katalin tells of news from Moscow;

possibly, the ban against *Boris Godunov* will be lifted: "In January they promise to resume rehearsals." Katalin asks that there be no political pronouncements in the émigré press concerning Lyubimov in order to ease his return to Moscow: "He suffers a great deal without the Taganka; every call from there makes him happy."

December 1. Tristan und Isolde premières. Reviews in the Italian press are unanimously enthusiastic.

1984

January. The actors of the Taganka Theater meet with P. N. Demichev at the Ministry of Culture in order to resolve the conflict with Lyubimov, and to secure his position as permanent director of the theater. "He's going to direct you from London?" the minister asks, though he assures the actors that no one plans to fire Lyubimov.

Waiting for events to develop, Lyubimov offers a summation of his situation, citing the example of V. Vysotsky:

> When he went to Paris and then around the world, he began to become torn internally. He understood that he's needed there, at home, but at home they were persecuting him. He sang about this in "Hunting for Wolves."
>
> Why does everything have to happen like this? What won't they do; when will they stop and think? Why do they always play hide and seek; do they really think that they're surrounded by blind kittens? It's all so painful and stupid! [From an interview with Lyubimov. *Strana i mir (Our country and the world)*. No. 1, 1984.]

On January 24 the *Evening Standard* presents its award for best theatrical production of the season to Lyubimov for *Crime and Punishment*. Former recipients of this award include Samuel Beckett, John Gielgud, Laurence Olivier, and Peter Brook. Lyubimov receives world recognition.

February. Yuri Andropov, on whom Lyubimov placed the hope of resolving the conflicts with the authorities, dies. K. U. Chernenko's advent to power dispels these illusions. On the day of Andropov's death, the Taganka Party-Office is ordered to look into the matter of Lyubimov's tenure in the party. The party members courageously get this matter off the day's agenda.

Lacking Andropov's support Lyubimov desperately attempts, through the Western press, to get Soviet authorities to understand that he does not want political asylum in the West, and that he wants to return to work in his homeland as soon as they guarantee conditions necessary for calm, creative work. His fate, however, is already decided. Reports from Moscow indicate that Demichev, the Minister of Culture, is looking for a director to replace Lyubimov.

March. At a general theater meeting on March 6, Shadrin, chairman of the Moscow Cultural Board, announces Lyubimov's removal as head director: "That's it. Lyubimov lost the game he was playing." A group of leading actors, including N. Gubenko, V. Zolotukhin, and V. Smekhov, come forward in protest.

Upon learning of his dismissal Lyubimov tells his friends over the telephone: "I have to thank them for not shooting me like Meyerhold."

On the next day A. Efros's appointment becomes known. Three other candidates—N. Gubenko, M. Zakharov, and V. Dunaev—refused to accept the position. With regard to this a malicious though fairly accurate joke is made up: "Efros, Anatoly Vasilievich, formerly a well-known director of the 1960s. Safeguarded by the government." With one blow the USSR Ministry of Culture headed by Demichev ruins two of the better Soviet directors, knocking their heads together and turning friends into enemies.

In the middle of March Lyubimov is expelled from the party under the laughable pretext of "failing to pay his member's dues." As a sign of protest some Taganka actors and designer David Borovsky leave the theater.

May. Beating back the Soviet authorities' blows Lyubimov plunges into his new work on the Western stage. Verdi's *Rigoletto* premières. He stages this in a stylized manner at the Teatro Comunale in Florence. N. Graf is the conductor and S. Lazaridis the set designer. His sharply contemporary interpretation of this famous opera causes stormy arguments among Italian music and theater lovers. Opinions are sharply divided. Also, the actor-singers are not united; some do not accept the work methods of the "communist" director, denied the label in his own country because of his dissentient manner. One of Lyubimov's Italian friends comments: "The country changes, the city changes, the theater changes, but the atmosphere around Lyubimov stays the same."[1]

July. By order of the Presidium of the Supreme Soviet of the USSR, signed by K. U. Chernenko, Yuri Petrovich Lyubimov is stripped of his Soviet citizenship "for actions that discredit the high status of a citizen of the USSR."

The chairman of the Soviet Embassy in Rome telephones Lyubimov, on vacation with his family in the Italian city of Viareggio, demanding that he return his Soviet foreign travel passport to the embassy. The shaken director asks: "Why should I return my passport, if I can't return to the Soviet Union anyway?"

Although the order was signed on July 11, Moscow reported it on July 27. In the opinion of many Western newspapers, Soviet authorities made the final decision to get rid of Lyubimov upon his participation in a Milan press conference with the well-known film director Andrey Tarkovsky; Tarkovsky announced his plans to stay and work in the West.

The most prominent newspapers of the free world commented with astonishment on the pathological stupidity of Soviet officials, who banished their best artists. On July 31 the *New York Times* reports Lyubimov's Bolognese press conference where the director repeats his assertion: "The cultural policy of the USSR is created by ignorant and incompetent bureaucrats." The prestige of the Soviet government and the interests of Russian culture are of little value to them.

August. Following his loss of Soviet citizenship Lyubimov receives numerous offers from European and American theaters. He and the Municipal Theater of Bologna enter into a two-year contract. The French Ministry of Culture offers him an experimental theater center from 1985 on in Bobigny, a northwestern working-class suburb of Paris. Intrigue by the French Communist Party, acting on orders from Moscow, forces Lyubimov to turn down this last offer.

October. Starting in the fall of 1984 Lyubimov begins a triumphant procession through European stages, realizing a series of dramatic and operatic productions in a neo-avant-garde "Taganka" style to which the European spectator is unaccustomed.

On October 12 Lyubimov and the Burgteatr troupe in Vienna present the German version of *Crime and Punishment*.

December. *Crime and Punishment* premières in Italian in Bologna. The production is shown in other Italian cities over two seasons.

1985

February 12. In the National Theater in Paris *The Possessed* premières, performed by British actors. The literary composition and staging is by Lyubimov, the English translation by Richard Crane, and the costume design by Stephanos Lazaridis. Well-known critic David Bogden writes in the *Times Literary Supplement:*

> A follower of Meyerhold, Lyubimov is today one of the leaders of expressionism in world theatrical art and his *Possessed*—a culmination of the director's twenty year searchings. . . . Like his friend Giorgio Strehler from the Piccolo-teatro in Milan, Lyubimov represents the so-called theater of the director and if someone doesn't like this movement in contemporary directing, he had better stay home with his nose in a book.

After thunderous success in Paris, *The Possessed* plays in Milan and then in London, becoming one of the main European theatrical events of the year. British actor Michael Feast was particularly successful in his brilliant performance of Verkhovensky.

May. Lyubimov's production of Bach's oratorio *Passion According to St. Matthew* premières at La Scala.

Summer. Lyubimov visits Israel to "pay homage to the Church of the Holy Sepulchre." He meets actors from Israel's Habima Theater, created by Vakhtangov in the 1920s.

> They received me as a close relative. For the first time, I felt as if I was in Moscow. Everyone speaks Russian and the actor's school is the same. Both I and the Taganka came out of the Vakhtangov Theater. To make a long story short, our meeting ended with my having agreed to go there next summer, on account of my being on holiday, to stage Babel's *Sunset*. [From Lyubimov's Boston lecture on February 24, 1986.]

November. Beethoven's opera *Fidelio* premières in Stuttgart with a new pessimistic solution for its finale, contrasting the general rejoicing of earlier productions. Lyubimov jokes:

> I became as if an "opera-pleni-potentiary" abroad. It seems to me that Beethoven also did not have a pretext for rejoicing: he has one hero—Fidelio freed in the finale—and all the other rebels are put in jail.

The journal *Kontinent (Continent)*, No. 44 publishes an extensive interview with Lyubimov. The correspondent asks: "Did the Taganka Theater serve as a type of showcase, called forth to create an impression of freedom in Soviet art?" Lyubimov replies:

From the sidelines, theatrical life seems pretty innocuous: even Zinoviev didn't understand and said that the Taganka Theater exists, it seems, with the permission of the KGB. How else could it be? If the KGB didn't permit it, no one would work—they would put the darlings in a Gulag or psychiatric hospital or somewhere else. It's those who live in the West who still haven't understood quite a lot of things about us—but those who've lived through our life are well acquainted with the rules of the game. There are those who just don't believe in miracles and there are those who know that they can happen. . . . After all they have different people there who, without question, need at least some prominent figures in art . . . in order to justify their own existence. . . . After I was given a theater—the spirit of the XX and XXII Congresses still dominated—it was already difficult to drive me back out. . . . In this case, evidently, they missed their chance. . . . It seems to me that the finale of the theater allows this argument to be decided. Those who governed us and those who, from the very beginning, didn't want our theater, simply took advantage of the moment and put an end to its existence. . . .

1986

January. Lyubimov makes his first trip to the United States. He chooses actors from the Arena Stage in Washington, D.C., for a production of *Crime and Punishment* to be staged the end of the year.

February. Lyubimov visits A. I. Solzhenitsyn in Vermont: "He's alive and well, works a great deal."

He meets with representatives of the academic and theater community at Harvard University, and visits the large Russian colony in Boston. The theme of his lecture: "From my personal experiences working in the East and the West."

Psychologically speaking, I don't see a big difference: how I worked there is how I work here. To put it another way, in answer to a question that is often asked me: for whom are you working here? *There* you had your own audience, here the audience is different, how can you establish contact with them? Be understood by them? Bring out their interest? I'll answer in a rather banal way: I simply think that the problems I consider important, which worry me, alarm me, the moral, spiritual problems that worried me *there* remain with me *here;* people will be found in the West who are preoccupied with them and interested in them. I was convinced of this, in part, by my work on *The Possessed* in England with very good actors. The main arguments arose with literate, educated people who said that the British, well, wouldn't understand it, that everything needs to be done differently, there's a different type of art here and different tastes. It's funny, but they put forth almost the same arguments as representatives of the USSR Ministry of Culture. But, luckily, here in the West, I am free in choosing my means, in proving that I am right and I have the right to "veto," the right to do what I want, if not with these, then with other actors and I can dictate my own conditions and do everything my own way. In this is the whole difference.

March. In Karlsruhe, West Germany, Lyubimov stages a new, contemporary opera by German composer Reiner Kunads based on Bulgakov's *Master and Margarita.*

April. Lyubimov's Zurich production of L. Janacek's opera *Jenufa* is a big success. Lyubimov goes to Paris to work on M. Musorgsky's unfinished opera, *Salammbo,* at the Grand Opera. The opera is orchestrated and conducted by Hungarian composer Zoltan Pesko.

June 16. Salammbo premières in Paris. It is designed by D. Borovsky; the main parts are performed by D. Veyzovich and S. Kopchak. Critical notices are highly restrained. Lyubimov is dissatisfied with the production and working conditions at the Grand Opera.

July–August. Lyubimov leaves for Israel to stage Babel's *Sunset* at the Habima Theater in Tel-Aviv. Among the actors are participants in the Habima Theater's first productions in the 1920s in Moscow, and young followers of Vakhtangov. The production subsequently received several international theater awards.

September. The Feast During the Plague, based on Pushkin's *Little Tragedies,* premières in Stockholm with Swedish actors from the Kunglig Dramatiska teatern under the direction of Ingmar Bergman. This production is shown in the United States in 1987 with great success.

October. The opera *Jenufa* premières at London's Covent Garden.

November. Lyubimov arrives in the United States to work on *Crime and Punishment* at the Arena Stage in Washington, D.C.

In mid-November, at the height of rehearsals, Lyubimov receives a copy of a letter from the Taganka actors' collective to M. S. Gorbachev, requesting his help in returning Lyubimov to the theater and his homeland.

December 22. Through the Soviet Embassy in Washington, Lyubimov telegrams M. S. Gorbachev expressing thanks for his attention to the actors' request.

The Western press reports Lyubimov's possible return to the Taganka.

1987

January. Crime and Punishment premières in Washington, D.C., on January 7. The American press gives it high praise, noting Lyubimov's innovative direction and the American actors' and spectators' difficulty in grasping the director's avant-garde esthetics.

Lyubimov arrives in Cambridge on the 11th to prepare *Master and Margarita* at the American Repertory Theatre.

A. Efros dies unexpectedly in Moscow on January 13.

Lyubimov interrupts his work in Cambridge at the end of January to leave for Bonn, West Germany, for a production of Tchaikovsky's *Eugene Onegin.*

February. The Taganka Theater goes on tour in Paris with *The Cherry Orchard, At the Bottom, War Doesn't Have a Lady's Face* and *The Misanthrope.*

March. At a press conference in Paris on March 10, after the theater's tour, the Taganka actors speak with uncertainty about Lyubimov's return. The correspondents ask how it was to work with Lyubimov and Efros and what distinguishes them as directors. Leading actress Alla Demidova answers:

> Imagine an actor and an armchair, to which he has to relate as if it was a horse and not an armchair. In such cases Stanislavsky said: "I see a horse and relate to it as such." Lyubimov would say: "I see that this is an armchair, but I'll relate to it as to a horse." And this is what Efros would say: "I see that it's an armchair, and I'll relate to it like an armchair, but deep inside I feel that I could ride it bareback."

Valery Zolotukhin, a leading actor, answers: "Efros concentrated on the inner life of the actor. He demanded a complete penetration of the character."

On March 17 Lyubimov arrives in Boston ill but works on *Master and Margarita*. Problems arise over rehearsal space and the readiness of the set.

On March 18 in the Parisian newspaper *Monde*, a "Declaration for the Press" signed by ten prominent Russian émigrés demands a rejection of Marxist-Leninist teachings by Soviet authorities as proof of M. S. Gorbachev's seriousness concerning "perestroyka" or reconstruction. The ten are V. Aksenov, V. Bukovsky, A. and O. Zinoviev, E. Kuznetsov, V. Maksimov, E. Neizvestny, Yu. Orlov, L. Plyushch, and Yu. Lyubimov.

Lyubimov announces on March 27 the American Repertory Theatre's unpreparedness for work on *Master and Margarita* and stops his work on the production. (For details see Lyubimov's interview with John Freedman in *The Boston Globe*, April 18, 1987, as well as the article "*Master and Margarita* in Boston" in *Novoye Russkoe Slovo (The New Russian Word)*, New York, April 30, 1987.)

April 30. Lyubimov and his family leave for Haifa, Israel, where he takes over the direction of a local theater and announces a production of Bulgakov's *Heart of a Dog*. Soon after he changes plans and moves to Jerusalem to live.

May. At the Taganka Theater a new permanent director is named—the old "Tagankovite," famous theater and film actor Nikolay Gubenko who played Boris Godunov in Lyubimov's final production. He announced to the press:

> Right now the theater is sick. It's understood that I do not have a right to take its recovery upon myself. . . . Right now the situation is paradoxical. The troupe asked me to come in, in order to lean on me in finding its former unity. And along with this, I feel that people think that all this will happen as if by itself. But it won't happen by itself, just as it won't "come" from me. All the more so—and I say this everywhere—I am not a stage director . . . practically speaking, the troupe has in me a debutant.

September. Lyubimov and his family become Israeli citizens, making it easier for them to obtain visas for their numerous trips abroad.

October–November. Lyubimov travels to Chicago for a production of A. Berg's opera *Lulu*. The premiere of *Lulu* at the Lyric Opera House on November 24th is a great success and gets extensive press coverage.

December. Lyubimov returns to Israel and begins to lecture on acting at Jerusalem University.

1988

January. New, semi-official contacts take place between Lyubimov and the Taganka Theater administration (permanent director, Nikolai Gubenko and director, Nikolai Duppak), concerning a trip to Moscow.

February 11. London, Associated Press: "While in the British capital, the former permanent director of the Taganka Theater in Moscow, Yuri Lyubimov, told the Associated Press news agency that 'he misses his theater, his friends and relatives.' During this conversation, he said that he looks upon the current changes in the Soviet Union with optimism. Lyubimov expressed the desire to visit Moscow in a personal visit without any pre-conditions: 'one has to spare one's nerves,' the director summed up."

March. The Taganka Theater leaves for Madrid for the Eighth Theater Festival with a production of Gorky's *Mother*, staged by Lyubimov in 1968. Simultaneously, the festival administration, at Angel Gutierrez's initiative, invites Lyubimov and his wife to come to Madrid.

March 17. Yuri Lyubimov arrives in Madrid for a meeting with the Taganka Theater collective, his pupils, who share the same views on art. "The meeting with Lyubimov was such, that no one could part," wrote V. Smekhov in the newspaper, *Moskovskie novosti* on April 3, 1988.

In Madrid, an agreement is reached in principle with the Taganka Theater administration to have Lyubimov visit Moscow in May in order to participate in the final rehearsals and opening of *Boris Godunov*, the banning of which, in December 1982, served as the final straw in the conflict between Lyubimov and the authorities, and culminated in the loss of Lyubimov's Soviet citizenship.

Late March. Lyubimov leaves for Stuttgart, West Germany to stage Wagner's opera, *Tannhäuser*, fulfilling a previous contract.

On March 30, 1988, the official Soviet press (the government newspaper *Izvestia*) publishes the first interview with Lyubimov after his exile, reporting his plans to visit Moscow. Yuri Lyubimov told the *Izvestia* reporter that he attentively follows the news about cultural life in the Soviet Union, reads journals and books and is inspired by Gorbachev's policy of *glasnost*. When the reporter asked if Lyubimov would put any conditions on his return, Lyubimov answered, "No. What conditions can I put? I repeat: it is not true that I didn't want to return to my homeland from London. Is it a condition when a person says, 'Bring the best creations of the theater back to life'? I did not have any political conditions and do not have any. I spoke only about working conditions: whether or not they would be left up to me; whether or not the banned productions would go back on stage. The question only concerned the creative side of my life."

April 5. David Remnik, the *Washington Post*'s Moscow correspondent, phoned Lyubimov in Stuttgart and obtained the details of the trip: the director would go to Moscow on a short visit as an Israeli citizen for a period of ten days. "I have to go, take a look, work a little in the theater," Lyubimov told Remnik over the phone from Stuttgart. "Just as before, I want to stage *Boris Godunov*. It is a great play that has never had an adequate stage incarnation."

May 7. Lyubimov's production of Wagner's opera, *Tannhäuser*, premiered in Stuttgart.

May. 8. On Sunday, on the eve of "Victory Day," Lyubimov arrives in Moscow after almost six years abroad. More than 100 people met Lyubimov at Sheremetievo Airport. On the next day he visited the graves of his parents and brother.

Officially, Lyubimov came to the USSR at the private invitation of Nikola Gubenko, the new artistic director of the Taganka Theater, and is staying at his apartment. He spends the rest of his time at the theater, directing rehearsals of *Boris Godunov* before the premiere. Nikolai Gubenko told the *Washington Post* correspondent, "The reforms in our country started twenty-five years ago in this theater, which Lyubimov founded. This theater gave birth to public opinion and the ideas of our intelligentsia. It always tried to tell the truth."

Late May. Lyubimov leaves Moscow for his family in Jerusalem. He promised to return to his theater next year to stage a production for the twenty-fifth anniversary of the Taganka Theater. The great Russian director's "Odyssey" continued.

Epilogue: Lyubimov and Efros

THEATERS, LIKE PEOPLE, ARE BORN, LIVE, AND DIE. UNDER Soviet conditions, however, theaters sometimes betray the laws of nature. Finding themselves in complete subordination to the government, they depend wholly on the authorities' whims. A theater may petrify but, through the authorities' goodwill, continue to drag on its placid existence like, for example, the lifeless Moscow Art Theatre of the last thirty or forty years.

The opposite also occurs. The dogmatic and orthodox Soviets do everything possible to shorten the life of a collective that displeases them—a theater still full of energy, creative plans, hopes, and youthful impulses. An example is Meyerhold's theater, closed down by government decree in 1937 as "harmful to the people." Its brilliant, world-famous director was arrested and allowed to rot in the basement of Lubyanka Prison.

A similar event happened fifty years later when the authorities dealt with the disobedient Taganka. True, times had changed for the better. Not brave enough to close the theater, they drove its director out of the country, turning next to a refined "re-education," morally corrupting from the inside the once amiable acting collective.

The three-year period after Lyubimov's expulsion was a heavy, moral ordeal for the Taganka. The whole theater world of the East and West followed with keen interest the duel between the small handful of actors and the mighty superpower. Who will gain the upper hand? Will the theater stand up for its position? Who will replace Lyubimov? Will the theater be able to work without him? After all, the theater is a theater of the author, a theater of the director!

179

It at first seemed that the once irreproachable Efros acted unethically in agreeing to replace Lyubimov. When he came to the theater some of the more radical members of the troupe said: "Let us die by ourselves!" It sounded loyal but wasn't very smart. Most actors, however, accepted the new director. Of course, no one wanted to die no matter how hard aggressive Russian émigré journalists tried to push them toward suicide. The Paris journal *Kontinent (Continent)*, edited by V. Maksimov, was especially malevolent. Not understanding the essence of the matter, or perhaps because of something else, it tried to exaggerate the conflict, crudely stirring Lyubimov against Efros and presenting Efros as a "Judas," and "strike-breaker," and even a "black dog." (See the interview with N. Gorbanevskaya in No. 44 of the journal.) As a result two great artists and friends turned into mortal enemies. All of this could not but create extreme tension around and within the theater.

Gradually however, Efros began work on new productions and the Taganka actors were convinced that the new director came not to destroy but to build. He preserved and continued, as much as he could, the best traditions of the Taganka founded by his predecessor and, being creative, brought something new and original to the theater. Alla Demidova wrote:

> Giving of ourselves completely, we worked like a "brigade of carpenters" (that was what Efros called us). And we succeeded in many things. . . . Along with this, we carefully preserved the old, basic repertoire, made a few new productions. . . . But along with this, it seemed to us that the Taganka had spent its nerve, its pointedness. It was said that we were losing our former spectator. . . . But it seems to me that the theater audience has changed in general.

Further on Demidova expresses a very important thought, illuminating the Taganka's "crisis" in the era of Gorbachev's "glasnost" from a new angle: The crisis exists in the whole Soviet theater system. The actress asks: "Who is this 'Taganka spectator' of today? After all, a need for social pointedness, which the former Taganka spectator satisfied in the theater, today a great deal of it can be satisfied by reading the newspapers." In other words, the old, publicistic Taganka is gone; new artistic ideas and leaders are needed. Efros, sharply feeling the times, headed toward this in his search for new moral and artistic foundations. He staged Molière's *The Misanthrope* with this goal; it was his last production.

When the personal passions seemed to quiet down and the theater entered into its tense, working rhythm, when life in Russia began to gradually change for the better, when new possibilities for creative searches opened up, the irreparable occurred at the Taganka Theater. There is a wise Biblical saying: "I want neither your honey nor your sting." It corresponds to the pithy, Russian poetic line: "More than all our sorrows, the master's anger and the master's love will pass by us."

In October 1986 General Secretary M. S. Gorbachev and his wife, Raisa Maksimovna, a doctor of philosophy, unexpectedly appeared at the première of the Taganka's *The Misanthrope*. These important guests, contrary to established custom, seated themselves not in the government box but in the orchestra among the ordinary spectators, as democracy demands. When the curtain fell they went backstage to congratulate the actors and director. Matter-of-factly, in the spirit of "democratization" and "glasnost," the Soviet leader and his wife expressed regret that some of the old Taganka productions, as staged by Lyubimov, had disappeared from the repertory, particularly *The House on the Embankment*. This sounded extremely tactless with regard to Efros, as if he were somehow to blame. And it started . . .

The theater troupe, reconciled with its new artistic director, evaluated this gesture as a signal for Lyubimov's possible reinstallment. The quieted passions stirred again with new force.

On October 28, 1986, the theater put together a collective petition addressed to the General Secretary. This unique document is here cited in full:

Dear Mikhail Sergeevich! The Taganka Theater collective turns to you with a great request—to do everything possible in order that Yuri Petrovich Lyubimov, our teacher, founder, and outstanding Soviet director would return to his homeland and to his theater.

Yuri Petrovich Lyubimov's activities and his whole life were geared toward the good of the people and Soviet art, he—through his productions—advanced that line of the Party and the government to which you, Mikhail Sergeevich, now call the people and the country.

We await our teacher and director. Again we convincingly ask you to do everything possible for Yuri Petrovich Lyubimov to return home, to his theater. With respect. . . .

The three-page letter includes 137 signatures. Almost all of the actors and crew signed, except for those that came to the theater with Efros. The split in the troupe was now definite. The last signature was that of A. Efros, who added the postscript: "I join in the request of Yu. Lyubimov's pupils, if he himself wants this. A. Efros." How much spiritual strength and wisdom it cost Efros to make this postscript only he knew.

From this moment on A. Efros's position in the theater became more than ambiguous; actually, it became unbearable. It would have probably made more sense for him to immediately apply for retirement. Possibly this would have saved his life. However, having been beaten by life more than once, and being devoted to theater, Efros kept silent and swallowed his hurt. True to his duties as artistic director, he continued to go to the theater, putting its fate before his personal injuries. Nothing changed his decision to go with the theater to the end, not the punctured tires on his car in front of the theater, not the insulting inscriptions, not the sidelong, mocking glances of those with whom he worked.

What about Lyubimov? After the famous letter his situation abroad proved to be no less delicate and dramatic than Efros's— maybe even worse. The letter came to him in the middle of November amidst his work on *Crime and Punishment* in Washington, D.C. Attending rehearsals at the Arena Stage Theater, which were proceeding with great enthusiasm, I saw his joyous excitement that his "Tagankovites" were proving their loyalty and gratitude to their teacher. It seemed to me that he thought about changing his fate once again. However, as the poet Yevtushenko once accurately observed concerning an idea in the Taganka production of *Galileo:* "He knew the world spun free, but he had a . . . family."

"Well, Yuri Petrovich, what next?" I asked Lyubimov frankly, as we sat in the rehearsal hall. "What did you answer them? What'd you decide?"

"I don't know yet," he answered pensively.

Everything is much more complicated right now than it seems. First of all, no one spoke to me officially about anything. Secondly, I have contracts abroad until 1991. Who'll pay for breach of contract? But the main thing is that I have a family, I have a young son, look how he speaks Italian, Hungarian, and now English in a rush. . . ."

Seven-year-old Petya, with his father's charming smile, really is extraordinary. Already under the spell of the theater, the endless moving from one country to another, and the nightly vigils of his father, whom he idolizes, Petya is precocious, in love with the stage like his father. Fearlessly he has appeared on stage and managed silent roles outstandingly. Even now, in *Crime and Punishment* at the Arena Stage, he appears in the finale in a long, white nightshirt and, with a powerful gesture, indicates the candle for repentance to the Washington Raskolnikov and leads him by the hand. Then, with pleasure, he comes out with the actors and bows freely to the audience, winning approving smiles and applause from the American spectators.

Pridefully watching his exceptional son, Lyubimov continued:

I answered my actors in a letter: well, my dear ones, thank you for the invitation, but you understand yourselves what it means to return to one's home . . . Start everything from scratch? Can we make it? After all, I'm not young anymore and you're not the same, let's, well, think things through, let's wait. . . . Why don't we first organize an exchange: I'll go with the Arena Stage to Moscow, and you bring your productions to Washington. We'll see how everything works out. Maybe I would go there, but with the condition that I will work there and abroad, with the right to travel freely.

Events then developed with catastrophic speed. At their own personal risk the actors of the Taganka telephoned Lyubimov's apartment in Washington. They spoke for hours and paid the bill out of their modest actor's pocket. Actress Tatiana Zhukova, in whose apartment the "Lyubimovites" gathered, was finally able to convince Lyubimov to support the initiative of the theater collective and meet them halfway by writing Gorbachev. On December 22 Lyubimov sent the following telegram through A. Potemkin, an official of the Soviet Embassy:

Dear Mikhail Sergeevich! I thank you for the kindness and attention to the request of my students, actors, friends, and fans of the theater concerning my return to my homeland to my home—the Taganka Theater. I would be happy if this served as a beginning for a discussion with the emigration. I believe in the serious intentions of your administration in eliminating the injustices of the previous administration. With respect, Yuri Lyubimov. Washington, December 22, 1986, 5:00 P.M.

On the basis of this vague telegram, put together more by a diplomat than an artist, the Western press, citing the Associated Press and the BBC, received news that Lyubimov would return to his homeland (*The London Times*, December 31, 1986). Almost simultaneously the administration of the Taganka Theater, as quoted by *Russkaya Mysl (Russian Thought)* in Paris, announced to the actors that after January 14 Efros would resign and Lyubimov take over direction of the theater.

On January 11, after the successful première of *Crime and Punishment*, Lyubimov and his family left Washington, D.C. for Cambridge to start work on *Master and Margarita* at the American Repertory Theatre.

We travelled in several cars. Lyubimov was in his own car, a Chrysler he had just bought, with his wife, Katalin, confidently sitting behind the wheel. She would not let her husband drive. On route Lyubimov spent a few hours in Philadelphia, where he met with local Soviet émigrés and ardent fans. In response to a question that persistently accompanied his encounters with such audiences—"Are you planning to return to the Soviet Union?"—Lyubimov answered, "I don't know . . . And you?" Laughter broke out and someone shouted: "We'll see how it goes with you. . . ."

January 14 came, the day when, as announced at the Taganka, the fates of Efros and Lyubimov would be decided. On this sunny, snowy day news arrived in Boston of Anatoly Efros's sudden death.

That day I kept an appointment with Lyubimov. Yuri Petrovich was pale. He quietly said:

> I didn't expect this and, believe me, wanted it least of all. My personal differences with Efros are one thing; what happened is another. I was informed over the telephone that he died in the Ministry of Culture where he was being "worked over." He fell over the table and passed away. I know from personal experience what a ministerial "working over" is. I came out of that building half-dead more than once myself. . . .

I left Lyubimov with a heavy, complex feeling. It seemed to me that now, with the post at the Taganka opening up in such a fateful way, Lyubimov would never want to occupy it. The question of his return became ever more problematic.

I saw that Lyubimov suffered. Matters dropped from his hands. In his cozy and spacious professor's apartment given him by the Harvard theater, something was amiss. Lyubimov turned down a widely publicized Harvard lecture and a creative seminar at the Harvard Russian Research Center for which he was being paid huge sums, even by American standards. In a few months (although it's true that it wasn't quite his fault), he stopped rehearsals of *Master and Margarita* at a local theater that had not fulfilled a slew of his conditions.

With a heavy heart Lyubimov left for Bonn in February to direct Tchaikovsky's *Eugene Onegin*. The Taganka Theater was on tour in Paris, just a two- or three-hour ride away. The actors insistently tried to get a meeting with him, but Lyubimov could not find the strength to explain himself face to face. He returned to America from Bonn on March 17.

He already knew that at a March 10 post-tour press conference of "Tagankovites" in Paris, the leading actors' opinion of his return had split. Alla Demidova said: "Of course we would like him to return, insofar as our careers started with him." Valery Zolotukhin, performing with Demidova at the Odeon in Chekhov's *The Cherry Orchard*, expressed himself, according to the Associated Press, even more specifically, announcing that he was not sure that all of the actors wanted Lyubimov to return. "I personally feel," he declared, "that Lyubimov conducted himself less than honestly and correctly in relation to the theater." "That means you don't want him to come back?" asked Demidova. "I don't know," answered Zolotukhin, "it's a complex question. We hear so many rumors around that it's hard for us to judge."

In a few days Lyubimov ended the whole tragic story concerning his return. On March 18 the Paris newspaper *Monde* published a "Declaration for the Press" by ten prominent members of the Russian emigration, accusing the Gorbachev regime and idealistically demanding that "perestroyka" or "reconstruction" begin with the Soviet system by turning down the "prevailing ideology." Lyubimov signed the declaration. It said, "then and only then can an honest dialogue arise with the authorities, and not dubious negotiations at the back door." Contrary to the hopes of the declaration's authors and possibly against their consent, the text was published in the Soviet press to prove their extreme disloyalty toward their homeland.

The position of Lyubimov's opponents and friends, awaiting his return, was expressed by the chief editor of *Moskovskie Novosti (Moscow News)*, Egor Yakovlev: "[Lyubimov] has personally cut himself off on the eve of his seventieth anniversary. He was presented with a chance to return, and he did not avail himself of the possibility. . . ."

We do not know the details as to why Lyubimov put his signature on this letter, going back on his rule of non-participation in political emigration games. Was he provoked at this difficult moment in his life? Some light is shed by the famous sculptor Ernst Neizvestny, who also signed; he reported that V. Bukovsky and V. Maksimov composed the text of the declaration, and the others agreed to it by telephone. "I thought one thing then," wrote Neizvestny to Egor Yakovlev, "now I look at the problems differently." (*Russkaya Mysl*, September 4, 1987.)

Lyubimov made no statement about the matter. On April 30 he flew to Israel with his family, planning to base himself there for a long time. On September 30, his seventieth birthday, he continued to live in Jerusalem close to the Church of the Holy Sepulchre, before which all the world's vanity is nonsense.

With the strength of Providence, two of the greatest artists of the Soviet theater in the second half of the twentieth century—Lyubimov and Efros—proved to be tightly bound together. Each of them respected the other's art and talent to the very end. As individuals, they had two completely different natures. Much has already been said about Lyubimov's rebellious character. Now I feel a duty to, if briefly, tell about Efros as I knew him in Moscow.

I saw almost all of his best productions on Chekhov Street and on Malaya Bronnaya. He had the habit of standing at the entrance to the wardrobe watching how people entered the theater. It seemed that he knew each spectator by sight. After every production he hid himself in the shadows and watched those same faces with a soft smile, trying to discern how they had changed after two and a half hours of theater. Had he achieved his goal?

He was very sensitive to the opinions of others. He started one of his books with an agonizing admission of a sleepless night after an unsuccessful première: "A ridiculous production, I came out to bow ridiculously, the alienated faces of people I know. It's painful to think that you will be cursed and laughed at in so many places today. In the morning, and early in the morning, work is already scheduled, and one has to come *with ideas, again with ideas* [my emphasis.]"

I became better acquainted with Efros not long before my departure from Moscow. In the summer of 1981, while living in the writers' village of Peredelkino, I frequented the summer home that, year in and year out, his closely-knit family rented. It was a modest house with a garden in the front, strawberries, and a crooked birch tree. Its bent, snow white trunk caused one to reflect on truth and distortion in art as well as life.

In the evenings Anatoly Vasilievich, as everyone called him, arrived at the summer house with an absentminded smile, tired, and wrung out. He listened more than he spoke. He was reserved in general. He always concentrated on private thoughts.

No, he did not complain about circumstances or time, or about his grown-up student-actors with whom he lost touch over the years. However, I always felt that he had a Sisyphus complex—he kept rolling a boulder up a mountain, barely reaching the top before the rock rolls down again.

Efros felt lost in the face of injustice, the misunderstanding of his pure intentions. At such times melancholy would seize him. I remember with sadness how he told a story of his actors, who loved him in their own way. Once, when they were touring, they demanded an accounting from him. Why does he stage these plays and not others, and give certain parts to some and not to others. "This happens with children," said Efros, "when they grow up and start looking at themselves from above. I didn't know how to talk to them. After all, I'm just another director for them."

Right then Efros, with his eyes lighting up, remembered his work in a theater in Minneapolis, and the congenial and trustful atmosphere that arose between him and the American troupe that had invited him to stage Gogol's *Marriage* and Bulgakov's *Molière*.

As strange as it may seem, it was precisely there, in a foreign land that I felt myself in charge of the situation, and no one, not even once, asked me a catch question, no one demanded an accounting of my actions. No one! There were different difficulties there, ones that had to do with the matter at hand, and they were easy and pleasant to overcome.

As I later found out in the United States, he had kept quiet about the offer made him in Minneapolis to stay at the theater as artistic director; Efros, not considering it for long, declined.

He stoically withstood the many injustices and injuries that occurred in his life. This was his human weakness—vulnerability before life's turmoil and before himself. He apparently understood this and tried to express in his productions his bitter reflections on human nature, the utter conflict resulting from the fullness and excitability of feelings. This is the reason why Efros's student Olga Yakovleva, a trembling, restless bird with a nervous cry, became the best actress in his theater.

Articles and probably books will be written about the work and tragic fate of Anatoly Efros. His final and fateful undertaking, which was hard to understand or anticipate, will find its own explanation. This sincere and shy man, irreproachably devoted to art, succumbed to the administration's promises and lures, deciding (I believe from worthy and pure motives) to take upon himself the direction of the Taganka.

Analyzing Othello Efros once wrote:

It seems to me that the essence of Othello is in his weakness, in his feeling of being foreign, a kind of inferiority in comparison to *those others* [emphasized by Efros]. Yes, he is trustful of *the bad*, because he feels himself to be *a stranger*. In this is his vulnerability and weakness. It is precisely the absence of harmony in his soul that broke the ground for the misfortunes that occur in the play.

Didn't the sensitive artist draw the spiritual make-up of Othello from himself?

Efros was extremely vulnerable. He was sickly, twice suffering serious heart attacks. The first time the ignorant cultural bureaucrats disgracefully drove him out of the Lenkomsomol Theater that he had revived from ruins, making it the most popular Moscow theater of the 1960s. Again, in the 1970s, when he overcame the insult, he began work as an assistant director at the Malaya Bronnaya (in the building once housing the Jewish Theater), turning it from a mediocre theater to the pride of Moscow. Spectators broke down the doors to see Efros's wonderful productions of Dostoevsky, Chekhov, Shakespeare, and Gogol, but the posters' bold type announced the name of another, mediocre director—the official artistic director. According to hypocritical Soviet standards Efros was only a humble assistant.

I don't want to cast aspersions on the kind, bright Dunaev. He agreed to serve as a cover for the outcast Efros and in so doing made possible productions of national classics; this deserves gratitude. But consider: how does a master feel, knowing he is number one in his field, but forced to remain an apprentice until he grows old! What goes on in his soul?

"He simply fell on the street and died on his way to the theater," said G. A. Tovstonogov, a director famous for his conformity. In New York in May 1987 he thus explained the cause of Efros's death in response to my direct question. It does not seem to occur to those who think like this that Efros's death is one of the many tragedies that befall those honest Soviet artists who need to be a bit different and as a result are unforgivably trusting of evil. This tragic trust destroyed a great artist of the Russian stage.

Efros's death clouded the widely publicized campaign concerning the democratization of the Soviet theater. It serves as an evil omen; other unexpected and untimely losses followed: Andrey Mironov, Anatoly Papanov, Ignat Dvoretsky . . . Only superficially do they seem coincidental; they are, however, connected to the cunning maneuvers of the cultural bureaucrats. I believe that people and circumstances predetermined and precipitated Efros's death. Highly talented and easily wounded, he was completely unsuited for political battle and intrigue.

The history of the Taganka Theater is one of the most heroic and one of the saddest chapters in the history of the Russian stage. Returning to the Taganka's lesson one sees that the theater did not end when Lyubimov left it; it went on to London to tell how the Soviet government does not give the artist freedom to work and how there is no road back to their homeland for those actors who leave the country. And the Taganka didn't end, in my opinion, when another director came in from a different school of theater, but equal to Lyubimov in talent and in his devotion to the Russian stage.

In my opinion the Taganka Theater ended because both Lyubimov and Efros ultimately lost the hope of being understood by their fellow countrymen, crippled both spiritually and morally by years of Soviet rule. The Taganka Theater ended when Lyubimov, Efros, and their followers realized that people will ever misunderstand the selfless and noble labors, the unavoidable mistakes, the joys and sufferings, and the personal sacrifices that are born of love for great Russian theatrical art. History will understand and forgive them for this.

Repertoire of the Taganka Theater (1964–84)

1964.   April 23. *The Good Woman of Setzuan*, B. Brecht. Translation: Yu. Yuzovsky and E. Ionov. Translation of poems: B. Slutsky. Designer: B. Blank. Music: B. Khmelnitsky and A. Vasiliev. Production by Yu. Lyubimov. Actors: Z. Slavina, B. Khmelnitsky, V. Zolotukhin, R. Dzhabrailov, V. Vysotsky, and others. (The production runs to this day.)

1964.   October 14. *A Hero of Our Times*, based on the work by M. Lermontov. Adapted by N. Erdman and Yu. Lyubimov. Designer: V. Dorrer. Music: M. Tariverdiev. Production by Yu. Lyubimov. Lead role: N. Gubenko. (The production lasted less than a season.)

1965.   February 2. *Anti-Worlds*, poetry by A. Voznesensky. Designer: E. Stenberg. Music: B. Khmelnitsky, A. Vasiliev, and V. Vysotsky. Director: P. Fomenko. Production by Yu. Lyubimov.

1965.   April 2. *Ten Days That Shook the World*, based on the work by John Reed. Adapted-Composed by Yu. Lyubimov, I. Dobronravov, I. Dobrovolsky, and S. Kachtelyan. Designer: I. Tarasov. Music: N. Karetnikov. Choreographer: N. Avaliani. Texts of songs by Brecht, Blok, Tyutchev, Vysotsky, and others. Production Manager: A. E. Poray-Koshits. Lighting: K. I. Panshin. Engineer-Radio-operator: V. M. Titov. Actors: Entire company. Producer-Director: Yu. Lyubimov. (The production runs to this day.)

1965.   November 4. *The Fallen and the Living*, D. Samoylov, B. Gribanov, and Yu. Lyubimov. Poetry by V. Mayakovsky, N. Aseev, M. Svetlov, A. Tvardovsky, M. Kylchitsky, P. Kogan, V. Bagritsky, S. Gudzenko, and others. Music from the works of D. Shostakovich. Director: P. Fomenko. Production by Yu. Lyubimov.

1966.   May 17. *Life of Galileo*, B. Brecht. Translation: Lev Kopelev. Designer: E. Stenberg. Music from the works of D. Shostakovich,

B. Khmelnitsky, and A. Vasiliev. Production by Yu. Lyubimov. Lead role: V. Vysotsky.

1967. (The exact date of the première unestablished.) *The Investigation*, Peter Weiss. Translation: Lev. Ginzburg. Director: P. Fomenko. Lead role: N. Gubenko. (The production ran for one season then closed by censors.)

1967. May 16. *Listen!*, Mayakovsky. Designer: Enar Stenberg. Composer: Edison Denisov. Directors: Boris Glagolin and Valery Raevsky. Production by Yu. Lyubimov. Actors: F. Antipov, I. Bortnik, I. Dykhovichny, R. Dzhabrailov, T. Zhukova, V. Zolotukhin, M. Politseymako, Z. Slavina, V. Smekhov, A. Sabinin, Yu. Smirnov, B. Khmelnitsky, V. Shapovalov, N. Shatskaya, and others.

1967. November 17. *Pugachev*, based on the work by S. Yesenin. Interludes by N. Erdman. Designer: Yu. Vasiliev. Music: I. Butsko. Director: V. Raevsky. Producer: Yu. Lyubimov. Lead roles: N. Gubenko and V. Vysotsky. (The production ran for several consecutive seasons.)

1968. (The exact date of the première unestablished.) *From the Life of Fyodor Kuzkin (Alive!)*), based on the stories of B. Mozhaev. Adapted by Yu. Lyubimov. Designer: David Borovsky. Music: E. Denisov. Producer-Director: Yu. Lyubimov. Lead role: V. Zolotukhin. (The production was banned under personal instructions of E. A. Furtseva and P. Demichev, both Ministers of Culture of the USSR.)

1968. November 14. *Tartuffe*, Molière. Translation: M. Donsky. Arrangement: M. Anikst. Production by Yu. Lyubimov. Lead roles: F. Antipov, A. Demidova, V. Smekhov, V. Sobolev, Z. Slavina, and others. (The production runs to this day.)

1969. May 23. *Mother*, based on the work by Gorky. Composed by Yu. Lyubimov and B. Glagolin. Designer: David Borovsky. Composer: Yu. Butsko. Lighting: O. Gordeev. Radio: N. Florov. Arrangement: V. Klyuev and V. Kondratov. Producer: Yu. Lyubimov. Director: Boris Glagolin. Lead roles: Entire company.

1969. December 4. *Rush Hour*, Jerry Stawinsky. Adapted by V. Smekhov. Designer: D. Borovsky. Lighting: K. Panshin. Production by Yu. Lyubimov. Lead roles: V. Smekhov, I. Kuznetsova, and G. Roninson. (The production runs to this day.)

1970. December 18. *What Is to Be Done?*, based on the work by N. Chernyshevsky. Composition and production by Yu. Lyubimov. Designer: D. Borovsky.

1971. January 6. *The Dawns Are Quiet Here . . .* , B. Vasiliev. Adapted and directed by Yu. Lyubimov and B. Glagolin. Designer: D. Borovsky.

1971. November 29. *Hamlet*, Shakespeare. Translation: B. Pasternak. Designer: D. Borovsky. Music: Yu. Butsko. Production Manager: A. Poray-Koshits. Lighting: K. Panshin. Production by Yu. Lyubimov. Lead roles: V. Vysotsky, A. Demidova, V. Smekhov, B. Khmelnitsky, and others. (The last performance was on July 13, 1980.)

1972. December 18. *Under the Skin of the Statue of Liberty*, based on the poetry of E. Evtushenko. Composed by Yu. Lyubimov, B. Glagolin, A. Vasiliev, V. Smekhov, and L. Filatov.

1973. April 2. *Comrade, Believe . . .* based on the work by Pushkin. Composed by Borovsky. Music: G. Pyatigorsky. Production by Yu. Lyubimov.

1974. April. Benefit Performance, based on the plays of A. Ostrovsky: *The Marriage of Balzaminov, The Storm*, and *Guilty Without Guilt*. Composed by B. Glagolin and A. Vilkin. Designer: D. Borovsky. Music: N. Sidelnikov. Production by Yu. Lyubimov. (The production was not included in the repertoire.)

1974. April 16. *Wooden Horses*, Fyodor Abramov. Designer: D. Borovsky. Composer: N. Sidelnikov. Directors: A. Vilkin and B. Glagolin. Production by Yu. Lyubimov. Lead roles: A. Demidova, Z. Slavina, T. Zhukova, and L. Bortnik. (The production runs to this day.)

1975. June 30. *The Cherry Orchard*, A. P. Chekhov. Designer: Valery Levental. Music: G. Pyatigorsky. Assistant Director: E. Kucher. Director-Producer: Anatoly Efros. Lead roles: A. Demidova, V. Vysotsky, T. Zhukova, V. Zolotukhin, and others. (The production runs to this day.)

1975. July. *Fasten Your Seatbelts*. Composed by G. Baklanov and Yu. Lyubimov. Designer: D. Borovsky. Music: L. Nono. Production by Yu. Lyubimov. (The production was not kept in the repertoire.)

1976. April 21. *Work is Work*, a pantomime with the songs of Bulat Okudzhava. Instructor in eurythmics: I. V. Burov. Actors: Aida Chernova and Yu. Medvedev. Guitar: Dmitry Mezhevich.

1976. June. *The Exchange*. Yu. Trifonov. Adapted by Yu. Trifonov and Yu. Lyubimov. Designer: D. Borovsky. Music: E. Denisov. Assistant to the Director: E. Kucher. Producer: Yu. Lyubimov. Lead roles: L. Filatov, A. Vilkin, and I. Ulianov.

1977. April 6. *Master and Margarita*, M. Bulgakov. Composed by V. Diachin and Yu. Lyubimov. Designers: M. Anikst, S. Barkhin,

D. Borovsky, Yu. Vasiliev, and E. Stenberg. Composer: E. Denisov. Choreographer: V. Manokhin. Director: A. Vilkin. Production by Yu. Lyubimov. Lead roles: D. Shcherbakov, N. Shatskaya, A. Trofimov, V. Smekhov, I. Dykhovichny, Z. Slavina, A. Sabinin, M. Lebedev, G. Roninson, and others.

1977.   October 6. *Sotnikov*, V. Bykov. Adapted by V. Bykov and Yu. Lyubimov. Designer: D. Borovsky. Director: B. Glagolin. Production by Yu. Lyubimov. (The production was not included in the repertoire for unknown reasons.)

1978.   March 8. *In Search of Genre*. Composed by Yu. Lyubimov, V. Vysotsky, V. Zolotukhin, L. Filatov, and D. Mezhevich. Designer: D. Borovsky. Lead role: V. Vysotsky. Production by Yu. Lyubimov. (The production was not included in the repertoire for unknown reasons.)

1978.   May. *The Official Register*, from the works of N. V. Gogol. Composed by Yu. Lyubimov. Designer: Eduard Kochergin. Composer: Alfred Shnitke. Conductor: Gennady Rozhdestvensky. Director: B. Glagolin. Production by Yu. Lyubimov. Actors: I. Andreev, F. Antipov, I. Bortnik, A. Grabbe, A. Davydov, A. Zaytsev, V. Smekhov, Yu. Smirnov, and others.

1979.   February 12. *Crime and Punishment*, based on the work by Dostoevsky. Composed by Yuri Karyakin. Designer: D. Borovsky. Composer: E. Denisov. Director: Yu. Pogrebnichko. Production by Yu. Lyubimov. Lead roles: A. Trofimov, V. Vysotsky, R. Dzhabrailov, Z. Slavina, and others.

1979.   February 20. *Turandot or The Congress of Whitewashers*, B. Brecht. Translation: L. Fradkin. Designer: D. Borovsky. Music: A. Shnitke. Director: E. Kucher. Production by Yu. Lyubimov.

1979.   (The exact date of the première is unknown.) *Cross-Roads*. (The production was announced for the 1979–80 season, but did not appear on stage. The compiler does not have other facts at his disposal.)

1980.   June 12. *The House on the Embankment*. Yu. Trifonov. Adapted by Yu. Trifonov and Yu. Lyubimov. Designer: D. Borovsky. Composer: E. Denisov. Director: B. Glagolin. Production by Yu. Lyubimov. Lead roles: V. Smekhov, I. Bortnik, F. Antipov, R. Dzhabrailov, G. Vlasov, L. Steinreich, and A. Sabinin. (The production was a huge success. It was closed in 1984 by the censors and was restored in 1987.)

1980.   December 24. *A Little Orchestra of Hope*, three one-act plays by A. Volodin, S. Zlotnikov, and L. Petrushevsky. Designer: D. Borovsky. Director: S. Artsibashev. Production by Yu. Lyubimov. (The productions runs to this day.)

1981.   July 27–28. *In Memory of Vysotsky*. Composed by Yu. Lyubimov with the entire company. Designer: D. Borovsky. Producer: Yu. Lyubimov. Actors: All leading actors. (The production was prohibited.)

1981.   October. *The Three Sisters*, A. P. Chekhov. Designer: Yu. Kononenko. Composer: E. Denisov. Director: I. Pogrebnichko. Production by Yu. Lyubimov.

1982.   Early December. *Boris Godunov*, A. Pushkin. Designer and Producer: Yu. Lyubimov. Choirmaster and composer: D. Pokrovsky. Actors: All leading actors. (The production was banned by the authorities.)

1984.   Late December. *At the Bottom*, M. Gorky. Designer: Yu. Vasiliev. Director: B. Glagolin. Production by A. Efros. Actors: I. Bortnik, V. Zolotukhin, Z. Slavina, O. Yakovleva, M. Politseymako, T. Zhukova, A. Trofimov, R. Dzhabrailov, N. Sayko, Yu. Smirnov, V. Semenov, and others.

Notes

The Taganka in Soviet Life

1. *Pravda*, May 29, 1977.

2. A. N. Radishchev "Puteshestvie iz Peterburga v Moskvu." ("Journey from Petersburg to Moscow.") In *Russkaya proza XVIII veka (Russian Prose XVIII Century)*, Vol. 2, (Moscow-Leningrad: Gos Izdat Khudozhestvennoy Literatury, 1950), p. 79.

3. False Demetrius: Early seventeenth-century imposter claiming to be the murdered son of Ivan the Terrible. (Translator's note.)

4. Iron Felix: Felix Edmundovich Dzerzhinsky (1877–1926), head of the Cheka, the secret police and a forerunner of the KGB. (Translator's note.)

5. Zhdanovism: after Zhdanov, Andrey Aleksandrovich (1896–1948), powerful Soviet official who set political standards for the arts. (Translator's note.)

6. Yuri Lyubimov, "Discussion," *Teatr*, No. 4 (1965), p. 59.

7. Yuri Trifonov, *Dom na naberezhnoy. (The House on the Embankment.)* (Ann Arbor: Ardis, 1983), p. 90.

8. He was a member of the Communist children's organization, Pioneers. (Translator's note.)

9. *Bogatyr* at the crossroads: In Russian fairy tales the folk hero or *bogatyr*, when at the crossroads, faces several choices, knowing each will lead to his doom. (Translator's note.)

10. Nikolai Lukyanovich Duppak: Manager of the Taganka. (Translator's Note.)

11. Yuri Lyubimov, *Stsenicheskaya adaptatsiya "Mastera i Margarity" M. Bulgakova. (Stage Adaptation of M. Bulgakov's "Master and Margarita.")* (London: Overseas Publications, 1985), p. 10

12. Ibid., pp. 10–11.

Lyubimov and His Time: Before the Taganka

1. P. A. Markov. *O teatre. (On Theatre.)* Vol. 4. (Moscow: Iskusstvo, 1977), p. 568.

196

2. Boris Pasternak. *Stikhotvoreniya i poemy. (Poems and Verse.)* (Moscow-Leningrad: Gos Izdal Khudozhestvennoy Literatury, 1965), p. 463.

3. *Corvée:* In feudal law, the regular work vassals owed their lord. (Translator's note.)

4. Lyubimov (Youri Liobimov) with the collaboration of Marc Dondey, *Le Feu sacre.* (Paris: Fayard, 1985).

5. *Kulaks:* Richer peasants who used hired labor and opposed the Soviet regime's policy of collectivization. (Translator's note.)

6. Yuri Olesha. "Rech na I Vsesoyuznom siezde sovetskikh pisateley." ("Speech Before the First Constituent Congress of Soviet Writers.") In *Yu. Olesha. Selected Stories.* (Letchworth-Herts, England: Bradda Books, Ltd., 1974), pp. 41–42.

7. Trifonov and Lyubimov, "Discussion." *Teatr*, No. 9 (1977), pp. 52–53.

8. "Zhizn i tvorchestvo K. S. Stanislavskogo." ("The Life and Creative Work of K. S. Stanislavsky.) *Chronicle*, Vol. 4, (Moscow: VTO, 1976), p. 440.

9. "Postanovlenie o likvidatsii teatra im. Vs. Meyerholda." ("Resolution on the Dissolution of the Meyerhold Theatre.) *Teatr*, No. 1 (1938), p. 5.

10. "Stanislavskogo." *Chronicle*, Vol. 4, 508–09.

11. Refers to the war between Finland and the Soviet Union during World War II. (Translator's note.)

12. NKVD: People's Commissariat for Internal Affairs, at this time supervising both the police and the secret police. (Translator's note.)

13. Markov. *O teatre*, Vol. 4, p. 569.

14. S. Volkov. "Razgovor c Yuriem Lyubimovym. ("A Conversation with Yuri Lyubimov.") *Sem dney*, (New York) No. 17 (1984), pp. 7–12.

15. *Pravda*, January 28, 1949.

16. *Sovetskie khudozhestvennye filmy. Annotirovanny katalog (Annotated Catalogue of Soviet films)*, (Moscow); Iskusstvo, 1961), Vol. 2, p. 424.

17. Volkov. "Razgovor c Yuriem Lyubimovym," p. 10.

18. Markov. *O teatre*, Vol. 4, p. 569.

19. "The Crosses Yuri Lyubimov Bears," *Times.* September 5, 1983.

20. From my conversation with Lyubimov on March 24, 1986 at Harvard.

21. "Intervyu c Yu. Lyubimovym N. Gorbanesvskoy." ("N. Gorbanevskaya's Interview with Yu. Lyubimov.") *Kontinent*, No. 44 (1985), p. 415.

22. Ibid.

The Stage and the Audience

1. Dubna at Kurchatov's: Dubna is the Institute of Nuclear Research near Moscow; I. Kurchatov is an academician and the director of works on atomic science and technology.

2. V. Aksenov. "Teatralnaya veshalka." ("Theatrical Cloakroom.") *Panorama*. January 20, 1984.

3. *Kolkhoznitsa:* A female member of a collective farm. (Translator's note.)

4. "Intervyu c Yu. Lyubimovym korrespondenta BBC Z. Zinnika." ("Z. Zinnika's BBC Interview with Yu. Lyubimov.") *Sem dney* (New York), No. 3 (1983), p. 15.

5. "Po svidetelstvu V. Yenyutinoy." ("As Witnessed by V. Yenyutino.") In *Vera Yenyutina. Roli i zhisn. (Vera Yenyutina. Life and Roles.")* (Monterey: self-published, 1985), p. 102.

6. Quotes from this meeting taken from Maksudova, "Dve vstrechi N. S. Khrushcheva s predstavitelyami tvorcheskoy intelligentsii." ("Two Meetings Between N. S. Khrushchev and Representatives of the Artistic Intelligentsia.") (December 1962 and March 1963). *USSR: Vnutrennie protivorechiya* (New York), No. 6 (1982), pp. 80–206.

7. A. Anikst. "Zrelishche neobichayneyshee." ("An Extraordinary Spectacle.") *Teatr,* No. 7 (1965), p. 29.

8. V. Aksenov. "Teatralnaya veshalka." ("Theatrical Cloakroom") *Panorama,* January 20, 1984.

9. L. A. Okun. "Ozornye chudesa." ("Mischievous Miracles.") *Strana i mir* (Munich), No. 12 (1984), pp. 69–74.

10. *Skomorokh:* a wandering minstrel-clown. (Translator's note.)

11. "O zhizni i tvorchestve L. V. Varpakhovskogo." ("On the Life and Creative Work of L. V. Varpakhovsky.") In *L. Varpakhovsky. Nablyudeniya, analiz, opyt.* (Moscow: VTO, 1978.)

12. Bulat Okudzhava. "My rano povzrosleli." ("We Grew Up Fast.") Vengersky ezhenedelnik *Ilet ish irodalom (Élet és îrodalom),* December 9, 1983. See also: Alexander Gershkovich, "Neobychnoe intervyu Bulata Okudzhavy." *Obozrenie* (Paris), No. 8 (1984), pp. 23–25.

13. Quotes from this production taken from: Fyodor Abramov. *Derevyannye koni. (Wooden Horses.)* Leningradi Lenizdat, 1979.

14. *Sazhen:* A Russian measure roughly equivalent to seven and one-half feet. (Translator's note.)

15. "Tochki nad 'i.' " *Literaturnaya gazeta.* March 8, 1978.

16. K. Rudnitsky. "Priklyuchenie idey (Dostoevsky na noskovskoy stsene konets 70-kh—nachala 80-kh gg.) ["The Adventures of an Idea (Dostoevsky on the Moscow stage in the late 1970s to early 1980s.")] In *Dostoevsky i teatr, sbornik statey. (Dostoevsky and the Theater: A Collection of Essays.)* (Leningrad: Iskusstvo, 1983.)

17. A. P. Chekhov. *Tri Sestry. (The Three Sisters.)* In *Polnoe sobranie sochineny i pisem (Collected Works and Letters),* Vol. 11. Moscow: OGIZ (1948), p. 303.

Vladimir Vysotsky: Actor and Poet

1. Alla Demidova. "Vysotsky—Hamlet." *Yunost,* No. 6, 1982. Also see her article "Roli i gody." ("Years and Roles.") *Literaturnoe obozrenie,* No. 1, (1983), pp. 89–93.

2. For more information on Vysotsky's fate after his death see the following of my publications: "Poslednyaya rol Vladimira Vysotskogo." ("Vladimir Vysotsky's

Last Role.") *Obozrenie* (Paris), No. 2 (1982); "Posle Vysotskogo." *Novoe Russkoe Slovo* (New York), August 1, 1984; "Den rozhdeniya svobodnogo iskusstva." ("The Birth of Unrestricted Art.") *Russkaya Mysl* (Paris), February 7, 1985; "My ne umrem muchitelnoyu zhiznyu." ("We Will Not Die by Tortured Life.") *Novoe Russkoe Slovo* (New York), July 25, 1985.

3. I will attempt to reconstruct this unusual production from my own impressions supplemented by tape recordings, slides, and the eyewitness accounts of ardent fans such as Samuel Rakhlin, well-known Danish film reporter and author of the filmscript for *Vladimir Vysotsky* (1981); Alma Law, professor at the City University of New York, prolific translator of plays, well-known popularizer of Soviet theatre in the United States, and author of a series of articles on the Taganka Theater; and Dr. Nicholas Rzhevsky, author of "Adapting Drama to the Stage: Liubimov's Boris Godunov." *Slavic and East European Arts*, Special Issue, Vol. 3, No. 1., (Winter-Spring 1985), p. 171.

4. Quotes from this chapter taken from: Vladimir Vysotsky, *Pesni i stikhi* (Vladimir Vysotsky. *Songs and Poems.*) In two volumes. (New York: Literaturnoe zarubezhe, 1981). Boris Berest, editor; Arkady Lvov, compiler; R. Rublev, consultant.

5. Quotes in this chapter from a tape of the Taganka Theater production kindly given me by S. Rakhlin.

6. "Bath" refers to a Russian bath, or sauna. (Translator's note.)

7. In the production, Stalin's name was drowned out by Zolotukhin's voice to avoid censorship, even though everyone in the auditorium could easily figure out whose profile from the "times of the personality cult" had turned blue on the singer's breast. It goes without saying that this song was not included in the Soviet collection of Vysotsky's poems *Nerv (Nerve)*, compiled by R. Rozhdestvensky.

8. N. Krymova. "O Vysotskom." ("On Vysotsky.") *Avrora* (Leningrad), No. 7, (1983), p. 100.

9. V. Vysotsky. *Pesni i stikhi, (Songs and Poems.)* Vol. 1, p. 88.

10. Eldar Ryazonov. "Stenographic Report of Speech at the Plenary Session of the Film-Makers Union of the USSR, December 2, 1980," in *Motion Pictures in the USSR, 1972–1982*, by Val. S. Golovsky as told to John E. Rimberg, with the assistance of Steven Hill. (Ann Arbor: Ardis, 1985), p. 251.

11. St. Kunaev. "Chto tebe poyut." *Nash sovremennik*, No. 7, (1984), pp. 179–80.

12. Yuri Trifonov. "Slovo proshchaniya." In V. Vysotsky, *Pesni i stikhi*, Vol. 2 (1981), p. 251.

The End of the Taganka

1. V. E. Meyerhold. *Stati, pisma, rechi, besedy. Chast vtoraya. (Articles, Letters, Speeches, Discussions. Part Two.)* (Moscow: Iskusstvo, 1968), p. 571.

2. Lyubov Rudneva. "Poiski i otkrytiya." ("Searches and Discovery.") In *Tvorcheskoe nasledie V. E. Meyerholda. (The Creative Heritage of V. E. Meyerhold.)* Moscow: Iskusstvo, VTO, 1978, p. 408.

3. A. S. Pushkin. *Polnoe sobranie sochineny v desyati tomakh. (Collected Works in Ten Volumes)*, Vol. 5. Leningrad: Nauka, 1978, pp. 195–96.

4. From my personal archive.

5. From my conversation with Lyubimov at Harvard on March 24, 1986.

6. *Art Under Bulldozers (The Blue Book)*, edited by Alexander Gleser. (London: Overseas Publications Interchange, 1976), p. 1.

7. *Sakharovskie slushaniya. Chetvertaya sessiya. (The Sakharov Hearings. Session Four.)* New York: Lissabon Overseas Publications Interchange, 1983, as quoted in Semen Reznik, *Novoe Russkoe Slovo*, February 8, 1986.

8. Lyubimov cited this conversation in an interview with M. Fillimor, *Strana i mir*, No. 1, (February 17, 1984), p. 131.

9. Yuri Zubkov. *Vremya i teatr*. (Moscow: Znanie, 1971), p. 104.

10. Algis Zhyuraytis. "V zashchitu 'Pikovoy damy.' " ("In Defense of 'The Queen of Spades.' ") *Pravda*. March 11, 1978.

11. History acknowledges the article's unscrupulousness in its exclusion in *Letopis gazetnikh statey*, where all newspaper publications are usually taken into account. Cf. *Letopis*, No. 17 (1978).

12. *Unita*. April 6, 1975.

13. K. U. Chernenko. "Aktualnye voprosy ideologicheskoy, massovo-politicheskoy raboty v partii." ("Pressing Questions on Ideological and Mass Political Work in the Party.") *Pravda*. June 15, 1983.

14. Ibid.

15. Ibid.

16. "The Cross Yuri Lyubimov Bears." *Times* (London), (September 5, 1983), p. 13.

17. Ibid.

18. M. Fillimor, *Strana i mir*, No. 1 (February 17, 1984), p. 131.

19. A. Efros. "Pismo v redaktsiyu." ("Letter to the Editor.") *Kontinent* (Paris), No. 46 (1985), pp. 336–69.

20. A. Efros. "O nashem dele." ("Concerning Our Cause.") (March 28, 1984), p. 8.

21. Ibid.

22. A. Vosnesensky. "Proraby dukha." ("Managers of the Spiritual Works.") *Literaturnaya gazeta*, March 7, 1984.

23. Ibid.

24. G. Mikhailov. "Ostrovok nadezhdy." ("A Little Island of Hope.") *Vechernaya Moskva*, January 5, 1985.

25. Marianna Stroeva. "Esli k pravde svyatoy . . . " ("If the Path toward the Sacred Truth . . . ") *Literaturnaya gazeta*, January 30, 1985, p. 8.

26. E. Surkov. "Spor o cheloveke." ("A Dispute about Man.") *Pravda*, February 7, 1985.

Lyubimov and His Time: After the Taganka

1. A. Law. "The Trouble with Lyubimov." *American Theatre* (April 1985), p. 6.

Suggested Reading

Batchelder, Vernita Mallard. "The Theatre Theory and Theatre Practice of Jurij Ljubimov: 1964–1971." Diss. U of Georgia, 1978.

Burns, John F. "Leading Soviet Director is Said to Be Ousted." *New York Times*, 7 March 1984: C 17.

Clemens, Walter. "Taganka: The Scene for Moscow's Avant-Garde Drama." *Boston University Journal* vol. xvii No. 1, 1969.

Cullen, Robert B. and McGuigan, Cathleen. "Director Without a Country." *Newsweek* Jan. 19, 1987: 60.

Law, Alma. "The Trouble with Lyubimov." *American Theatre* Apr. 1985: 6–11.

Lyubimov, Yuri. "Words and Images from the Modern Scene." *Culture*, vol. v, no. 1, 1978. The UNESCO Press.

Miller, Arthur, *The Theatre Essays*. New York: Viking Press, 1971.

Ratcliffe, Michael. "The Black Wall." Observer Review 24 Feb. 1985: 25.

Temko, Ned. "Soviet Press Cracks Down on Theatres." *Christian Science Monitor* 11 Feb. 1983.

"The Crosses Yuri Lyubimov Bears." *London Times* 5 Sept. 1983: 13.

Trilling, Ossia. "Whither the Russian Theatre?" *Survey* Autumn 1971, vol. 17, no. 4, (81)

Vinocur, John. "A Soviet Exile Reflects on His Lot." *New York Times* 11 Nov. 1984: C1.

Volkov, Solomon. "At the Scene of Lyubimov's 'Crime'." *American Theatre* Apr. 1987: 12–18.

Zaitsev, Mark. "Soviet Theatre Censorship." *The Drama Review* 19.2 (1975)

Appendix: Words and Images from the Modern Scene

The Algebra of Harmony: A Meditation on Theatre Aesthetics

It is a sin for me to complain of my lot as an actor—since I was successful. But the fact remains that I took up producing because I was dissatisfied. As an actor, I often made the producer's life intolerable: as soon as we set to work, I already had a vision of how the spectacle was going to turn out. And the result of this foreknowledge of the end-product was, naturally, to exclude all possibility of spontaneity—besides irritating the producer, of course—and it gave rise to conflicts. Strangely enough—or perhaps naturally—we usually argued not about my part, and not about the actor's psychological approach to it, but about plastic and spatial problems of stage production.

Amongst us, there is still a tendency to regard bold plastic so-lutions with suspicion: we are accustomed to strive for verisimilitude and everyday reality. Yet the important thing in art is not to re-produce reality, but to give an artistic image of it. Despite this, there is a strange but very widespread tendency to underestimate the importance of form in the creation of imagery. The psychological mood of the actor cannot be conveyed clearly and convincingly to the audience unless it is expressed in precise dramatic form. Lacking this, the actor ends by obscuring rather than clarifying the emotional experience of the character he is portraying, so that the spectator needs, as it were, an X-ray apparatus in order to discern what is going on.

Throughout my acting life, the theater has always been a source of irritation to me, and it still is. But I think this is a healthy feeling. It is impossible not to be irritated by all the coarsely daubed back drops, all the stage props—goblets, beards and wigs; all the décor, designed to imitate "real" life—bushes and clouds, hammocks and lawns. . . . Not to be irritated by the general belief that it is essential for the actor to use make-up, paint and powder his face, though this is invariably senseless and even—in the case of men—downright repulsive. For what can be better for the spectator than to see the actor's face, reflecting his changes of mood; to see him pale, or blush. . . .

I was inspired in my work as a producer by an active dislike of what I usually saw in the theater. The emergence of new trends in art is always the result of rejection of existing aesthetic canons. This is a complex process: all the experience accumulated through-out the centuries is assimilated, but the stimulus is provided by rejection of the past. In my case, the main point was the rejection of the exclusive monopoly of the psychological realistic school in the theater, the protest against the tendency to concentrate on one type of theatrical production only, to the exclusion of all the others.

We were very much hampered by our narrow academic inter-pretation of the Stanislavsky system, which in fact offers very wide possibilities, as shown by the repertory of the Moscow Art Theater in Stanislavsky's time: it included Maeterlinck's *Blue Bird*, Hamsun's *At the Gate of the Kingdom*, works by Dostoevsky, Chekov, Gorky, Tolstoy. . . . An extremely wide selection! And every author re-quires a different type of production, a different theatrical style. Stanislavsky himself, when founding his method, incorporated all the finest artistic achievements of the past. For his theory, he drew on the work of Pushkin, Gogol—outstanding personalities and art-ists; but at the same time added something new of his own. And every true artist does the same, for it is not possible, in art, to mark time. Every new artist brings with him a new approach, a new individual style.

I trained in the Vakhtangov theater, but I was always interested in new methods. For two years, I attended the seminar of Mikhail Nikolaivich Kedrov, then director of the Art Theater, an outstand-ing actor and producer and a great expert on the Stanislavsky sys-tem. He held a seminar every Friday, from four to six, which was attended by actors, producers and critics of a great variety of schools of thought. These included Lydia Sukharevska and Nikolai Gritsenko, Mikhail Zharov and Nikolai Annenkov—I name such very different personalities on purpose, to indicate that the Kedrov seminar attracted very wide-spread interest. Some people stopped attending, declaring that they were too old to change their ways, that the result of studying the new methods was to incapacitate them, leaving them rather in the position of the centipede always wondering which foot to use. For the possibilities it offered were endless.

I very much admired two of Kedrov's productions—*Long-Distance Reconnaissance* by Kron and Tolstoy's *Fruits of Enlightenment*, both reflecting his enthusiasm for Stanislavsky's latest experiments in method. I do not think I had ever before seen psychological portraits so vividly conveyed to the audience.

But as soon as Kedrov came to believe that this method could be universally applied to all dramatic structures, his productions, in my opinion, ceased to be convincing. Such was the case, for instance, when he put on Shakespeare's *A Winter's Tale*.

It is my conviction that poetic drama is governed by completely different laws. It was for this reason that the Moscow Art Theater always found Shakespeare a hard nut to crack, and the list of its triumphs does not include any of the works of the great English writer. Pushkin, similarly, defies presentation based on psychological analysis: *Boris Godunov* is constructed on entirely different principles.

Our Vakhtangov Theater Studio made a valuable contribution to the development of the contemporary theater, and the seed from which it developed was a fruitful one. It is a traditional form of theater drawing its inspiration from carnival festivities and fair booths; and it still continues to bear fruit, so important was it as a theatrical phenomenon. Of course, even it has occasional lapses—resorting to gimmicks and vaudeville methods—but then every original trend in art is always accompanied by inferior imitations.

After Kedrov's seminars and as a result of ten years of acting, I had a great many ideas of my own about our difficult profession; I wanted not only to talk about certain theories which seemed to me to be interesting, but also to try them out in practice. So I became an instructor in the B. V. Shchukin Studio attached to my old theater, the Vakhtangov.

It was with great pleasure that I took up my duties and I decided that it would be most interesting, both for me and for the students, to work on Brecht, who presents the actors with a number of serious problems. His works require sharp, sober and precise delivery of the dialogue and rigorous artistic presentation extending the range of acting techniques leading to the development of actors and producer alike. The production of Brecht calls for a knowledge of both music and the arts—for a high cultural standard, in fact. Most important of all, with Brecht more than any other author, actors must be able to communicate directly with the audience and to adopt a precise ideological approach. It was in view of this that I asked permission to arrange for students to present their graduation performance during their third year. I thought it would be easier for young actors to go into the professional theater if they had already done very difficult work as students, and this timetable gave them the fourth year in which to perfect their art by, as it were, trying it out on the spectator. I know from my own experience that young actors take time to acclimatize themselves to the theater, and are of very little use at the beginning.

As was customary in the Vakhtangov Theater Studio, I drew up a program for the production of several scenes, lasting about forty minutes each, which I submitted to the head of the department. It was approved, and toward the end of the third year I began to work on the production. It was then that the first mishaps occurred. Opinions in the department were divided: some people thought that the excessive rationalism of Brecht was incompatible with the essentially emotional character of the Russian theater; at the same time, many people liked the production. There were lengthy disputes but in the end we were fortunately given permission to present the spectacle in the student theater.

The upshot of all our ordeals was that I was appointed director of the Theater of Drama and Comedy. I wrote to the Department of Culture saying that I would agree to become director of the theater on condition that I could take the young actors from the Studio with me, and that my production could be the first to be presented in my new theater. The whole of the existing repertoire was taken off, and the theater was entirely reorganized—re-created from scratch, in fact.

Looking back over the first ten years of my work in the new theater, I see that it falls into three main stages.

The first stage was marked by the continuation of the Brecht-Vakhtangov line, with the production of *The Good Woman of Setzuan*, *Ten Days that Shook the World*, (based on the book by John Reed),

Mother and *What to Do?* All of these plays reflect the Brechtian conception of the theater, as I understand it, inspired by folk tradition, carnivals, and life in the market square. Although I consider our prose and poetry more interesting than our dramatic works, Brecht's influence accounts for our frequent use of prose works in the theater. Also, prose, of course, gives me more opportunities for creating stage settings on a number of planes.

The second stage began when Andrei Voznesensky and I set out to adapt his poems to the theater. We planned a special performance, which we called "The poet and the theater." Voznesensky read his poems, and they were enacted on the stage. I wanted to bring the poet into our theater, although he was in no sense theatrical, and did not even like the theater. He simply used to say: "Here are some poems for you. Make what you like of them." We made a poetry spectacle, which was later called *Antiworlds*. It is still being put on. It was the first of our series of poetry spectacles, to be followed by others: *The Dead and the Living* (verses written by wartime poets), *Listen* (about the poet Mayakovsky), *Pugachev* (based on Yesenin's poem), and another presentation of works by Voznesensky, *Look Out!*.

This last spectacle, *Look Out!* is worth describing in greater detail. It was an experiment based on the principle of open production; it consisted of fragments, without any real subject. Before the performance, I warned the audience that what they were about to see was not really a performance, but a public rehearsal, and that they must regard it as such. Naturally, our performance was in fact prepared beforehand, and it was only on exceptional occassions that I interrupted it in order to explain to the actors and the audience if a mistake had been made. We adopted this form of presentation in order to associate the audience with the creative preparatory work of the actors, and show them more clearly the purpose of our experiments. This seems to me to be a perfectly legitimate way of proceeding; nobody is surprised, for instance, when artists show their sketches and drawings, or writers publish their diaries, notebooks and rough drafts. During the performance, the house lights were left on in the theater, and I gave directions as in a public rehearsal, sometimes even making the actors repeat the verses several times, explaining their mistakes.

Similar poetry readings are still being staged, the latest one being one devoted to the work of Aleksander Sergeivich Pushkin, called *Comrade Believe!*

The third kind of show we put on comprised presentations of the classics. These included, first and foremost, works of Molière, Shakespeare and Ostrovsky, plus ones of Gorky, Chernyshevsky and Brecht.

Why is it that, during the ten years of our theater's existence, our repertoire continued to consist mainly of these plays? On what principle was the selection made? It is difficult to answer this question in a few words, but I think the main factor is that I feel an overriding urge to deal in the theater with human problems which seem vital to me personally. These themes vary, but they are all of direct concern to me at the time. After all, I myself change, and life forces me to devote my attention to different phenomena as they arise. And although I am aware that this is a truism, I cannot avoid emphasizing once more that the art of the theater is essentially topical. It is vitally important that the themes I select should make a direct appeal to today's audience, since a play, unlike a book or a painting, requires immediate understanding. A book can still be understood in a hundred years; the theater lives only today. History remains but a collection of tales and legends. But if the subject we present to the spectator is really amongst the most vital of our time, and the problems we regard as ours personally are regarded by vast numbers of peoples as "their own," it is evident that the choice of subject has been correct.

Unfortunately, it is most often in the classics that such vital subjects are to be found—indeed, it is the very fact that they deal with eternal problems and contain undying images and characters that makes them classics.

The Taganka Theater has often been criticized on the ground that the production style we use has the effect of squeezing out orthodox drama, due to the overriding influence of the producer or even—some maintain—his overweening presumption and desire to stamp his imprint on everything. If it is true that in the modern theater the author is squeezed out by the producer, I think it is usually from necessity. And the reason why we give productions of prose works or poetry is not that we wish to use them as a vehicle for the producer; it is simply because of the poverty of our drama, with its tendency to use outmoded forms and avoid pressing topical problems.

When your enthusiasm is fired by an important theme and you are already beginning to imagine how it can be presented, you try to work out methods for achieving the desired effect with the means available in the theater. Since prose works, being freer in form, offer more possibilities for staging, they are, of course, more likely to appeal to a producer of my type than works written for the theater.

All the same, the squeezing out of the author is not a deliberate policy, only an emergency measure; if there appeared another playwright of the stature of Brecht, things would return to normal again. There would be a new trend in the theater, a new artistic manner, as always happens when there is an outstanding dramatist. Such was the case with Shakespeare, Molière, Chekhov. . . . But when no such dramatist exists, the producer has willy nilly to take over part of the writer's role and find means of staging non-theatrical material.

Dramatists have always had very close links with the theater. Shakespeare was an actor, Molière the director of a company, Brecht a producer, Chekhov wrote plays with individual actors in mind. Dramatists who are not directly connected with the theater tend to be very upset if their text is cut in any way, or adapted for the stage. But Brecht, for instance, when producing, made radical changes in the works of other dramatists—Shakespeare's *Coriolanus*, for instance, and works of Gozzi and others. Then there is of course another, more important reason why literary works have to be adapted for presentation in the theater: the time factor; because of the time that has elapsed since the writing of the work it is essential to make certain changes, cuts and changes of emphasis, even when staging a classical work of unquestionable quality.

Take, for instance, the case of *Hamlet*. There are many points that are not clear, perhaps because the text has been distorted with the passage of time. In the space of four centuries, many additions have been made, both to the text and to the tradition of the acting of it, so that the text as we know it is buried under so many layers of criticism and interpretation that it is difficult to make out the original form. In addition, the translator plays an extremely important role, since translation is always a matter of interpretation.

A play like *Hamlet* is a universal storehouse, a treasure-house to which everyone makes his own contribution. It is not just a play, but an image of perfection, an unattainable ideal. That is why every artist dreams of staging *Hamlet*.

The Germans, I think, say that time is an honest man. Time judges everything, and it forces me to change my attitude to an old play, and to the ways of presenting it in the theater. How does it do this?

In the first place, as time passes, our scientific and technical progress brings changes in the pace of life, knowledge of new phenomena and understanding of the vicissitudes of history. We have learned to adapt ourselves to receiving a great deal more information than in the past, and are able to digest it much faster. Thus practically all productions consist of one or two parts, very rarely three. This is no mere coincidence: the spectators themselves live at a certain pace, their lives are so tense and complicated that they find long five-act productions fatiguing. Drawn-out scenes or long monologues and dialogues tire us—me, at any rate. Information nowadays is so diverse that the spectator is accustomed to grasping it like lightning; a hint suffices. I know from my own experience. I get bored in the theater when I have to sit through long explanations of the action, detailed analysis of characters I have already grasped.

The fact that we now live at a faster pace has obliged us to change the conception of time on the stage, and to seek new forms of expression in the theater.

So we have, very reluctantly, to discard the old aesthetic canons which predominated in the theater for over fifty years. In the case of Chekhov's plays, for instance, the whole of the action may take place in the dining-room or the drawing-room; Chekhov's dramatic formula can be summed up in his famous statement that "while people are dining, simply dining, their fate is being decided." Looking further back, it will be remembered that Shakespeare's plays encompassed whole nations and continents, presenting battles and spanning centuries, and in order to fit in all this material some of them were divided up into as many as thirty-five to forty episodes. This is almost on the montage principle, which was to be so brilliantly exploited, in our time, by Meyerhold in the theatre and Eisenstein in the cinema. So the old structures are being revived, but enriched, nowadays, by the experience of the other arts, in particular the cinema.

All this has a very direct influence on theatrical production, which matures in the depths of the unconscious and continues to torment until eventually assuming specific form, rhythm and shape.

As a rule, I only begin to speak about a production I am planning when I have the whole thing mapped out—not completely, perhaps, but at least the general lines must be clear in my mind.

My plan may mature in a number of ways.

I had long dreamed of staging *Pugachev*, but until I had conceived a means for staging it—solving the spatial problem, at least for the decor—I could not include this poem in the repertoire. I realized, of course, that the methods of the realist theater could not be applied, and that I must create a poetic mood for this production, corresponding to that of Yesenin's poem. At the time when Yesenin wrote *Pugachev*, he was fascinated by imagism, and the mood of this poem—ornamental, powerful—calls for a specific scenic style. We were assisted in our research, fortunately, by the existence of a recording made of the poet reading this poem. Yesenin read his poems magnificently, and this rendering of Khlopusha's monologue is astounding; it provided, as it were, a key, and set the tone for our production.

But any production is inevitably influenced by the style not only of the work, but also of the theater in which it is staged. For the theater is like a living organism, with its own ways of behavior, its own thoughts and laws. When choosing works and material to stage, you have to bear in mind what is suitable for that particular theater, and what is not. One of the productions of the Taganka Theater was devoted to the Ostrovsky jubilee and the show we staged was, in my opinion, what was required of this type of theater. We took three Ostrovsky plays—*The Storm*, *The Marriage of Balzaminov* and *Enough Simplicity in Every Wise Man*—and mixed them up, like a layer-cake. As you know, Ostrovsky's characters crop up in one play after another. For instance, actors appear in *The Dowerless Girl*, again in *The Forest* and again in *Talents and Admirers*, as do also merchants and government officials.

The production was staged in the style of a benefit performance, juggling with historical fact and making the actors play their parts before the dramatist. It was entitled "The Benefit Performance." But, in the course of working on the production, I realized that it was not possible simply to make a mechanical mixture of several different plays, for it became clear that the emotional and intellectual level of the themes used by the author varies form one play to another. In *The Storm*, for instance, the theme of Dykoi and Kabaniha, which is a vulgar one, fits in perfectly with that of Misha Balzaminov. And the desire of Misha Balzaminov to make a career, to be "up to the mark," strangely enough, matches the careerism of Glumov—each in its own way, of course, with a different shade of emphasis. And the stupid, petty tyranny of General Krutiskoy links up with the theme of Dykoi. This blending of themes re-creates Ostrovsky's world, with its problems and its characters. Such was the character of "The Benefit Performance." The actors play their parts, and Ostrovsky sits there on a chair in the center and makes his comments. Some he praises, to others he says "you've got the tone wrong" or "you're over-acting."

I work in very close contact with the composer and the artist on the maquette and, as soon as I meet the actors, I show them the maquette, even sometimes, at strategic moments, "over-playing" my intentions, in order to make clear to the actors the style and manner of the production I am planning. It is essential that the maquette should give a graphic representation of the production. There may, when I first meet the actors, be certain gaps in my production plan, and there has to be a lot of experimenting before all these gaps can be filled in. But these problems cannot be solved sitting round the table—at this stage, actors are in danger of over-theorizing. It often becomes evident that the play contains its own logical scheme, but it is cold and theoretical and not calculated to fire the enthusiasm of the actors.

It makes me sad to see that the producer, with his theorizing about methodology, tends to paralyze the actor, sap his initiative and make him inert. The producer's approach should always be based on the personality of the actor: some will want an analysis of the play before starting work, others a description of the period and details about the author, or a demonstration of what the producer has in mind. I frequently give such a demonstration. I know that drama schools reject this method, or question it; in my opinion, though, there is nothing against demonstrating ideas, so long as no attempt is made to impose them. On the contrary, a demonstration, provided it is skillful and tactful, fires the actor's imagination. But it is essential that the producer should be convinced of this theory. I sometimes help with the analysis and point to the analogies that should be brought to light by examination of the inner significance of certain roles. When I have doubts, I try scenes out again and again. Actors often protest that I am forcing the pace. Soviet actors are too much accustomed to being spoon-fed, afraid to stand on their own feet, with the result that they have to be pushed.

The actor should want to express his own ideas. Active though the producer may be, it is still the duty of the actor to make his own contribution; not simply remain passive, but help to develop the producer's plan. At the same time, though, it is essential to keep in mind the production as a whole, and the way in which every individual part fits into it. The producer can work out details with the actors, and analyze specific scenes. I myself am overjoyed when an actor suggests his own interpretation of certain scenes or roles, and readily accepts it; but for an actor to turn my whole conception of the play upside down—that cannot be. The theater is a collective art, but to imagine that, in the process of staging a production, the actors can work on an equal footing with the producer is naive. Acting and producing are two different professions: the producer plans and composes the production, the actor is an executant. This in no sense belittles him. Ulanova also was an executant; her choreographer worked out her every movement, but she was able to invest the whole with her own unique understanding and enchantment.

I am writing this in the summer. The theater is deserted, all the actors having gone off on holiday. But all of us, wherever we may be, are thinking just now of Pushkin, whose 175th anniversary is being celebrated throughout the country.

Tvardovsky once remarked that, whereas we are familiar with Pushkin from childhood, we do not come to understand him until much later. I would even add that the process is never completed. It is a long time, now, since my production of *Comrade, Believe*; it represented a certain level of understanding of Pushkin's work, but even after finishing the production, I went on turning the poem over in my mind.

And thinking about Pushkin's dramas and dramatic art: the years have gone by, conceptions have changed, new ideas have emerged, we have seen the work of Stanislavsky and Vakhtangov, Meyerhold and Brecht. What is there in common between these people, all so very different, and Pushkin? A great deal, and in particular: the conception of the people's theater.

We sometimes tend to toss great names around too lightly. We even tend to forget that Stanislavsky conceived the Moscow Art Theater as a people's theater, to be "artistically accessible, a protest against the pompous humbug of the academic tsarist theater." Do we always remember, when picking apart Brecht's theory of the epic theater, what its main purpose was—to speak bluntly and directly about the contemporary world, i.e., about the people?

Marina Tsvetaeva, speaking about the alleged incompability between Mayakovsky and Pushkin, wrote that great minds meet.
Pushkin, Stanislavsky, and Brecht are all landmarks along the road
to the development of the people's theater, the theater of festivities
and carnivals, dating back to Aeschylus and Aristophanes. This
tradition still bears fruit to this day. Indeed, all the dramatic October
happenings, with their vast artistic repercussions, represent a continuation of this tradition.

And as regards the conventions of dramatic art, here again, we
have Pushkin to teach and guide us. "How on earth can we talk of
verisimilitude," he wrote, "when the hall is divided into two parts,
one of which contains a couple of thousand people, virtually invisible
to those who are on the stage!. . . "

It is true that there is no portrait of Pushkin in the foyer of the
Taganka Theater, but his aesthetic principles are very dear to us.
He is our ally.

Both I and my comrades in the theater felt this very clearly when
we were preparing our production on Pushkin. We wanted to encompass the whole of Pushkin's world, which is unique, with all
its magnificent facets, at once harmonious and contradictory. But
this was only one side of the problem. I had always been convinced
that no actor, however talented he was, and made up for the part,
side-whiskers and all, could ever manage to convey the unfathomable
depth and boundless variety of the poet, what the Pushkin specialists
call the "universality" of his genius. We decided to adopt a modern
approach to Pushkin. We made a study of the circumstances of the
poet's life, but deliberately refrained from any attempt to recon-
stitute them. The actors playing the part of Pushkin (there were
five of them) looked at the poet, to use Gogol's words, "through
contemporary spectacles," and tried to present him in the form in
which he lives in our minds and hearts.

Our aim was to make the spirit of Pushkin, the Pushkin we all
love in our own special intimate, personal way, live for a few moments in the theater.

I am against idols, if only because it is difficult to comprehend
the life of a man such as Pushkin from a kneeling position! None-
theless—to paraphrase Tvardovsky's words—I will say that, if
forced to select a poet to worship, my choice would fall on Pushkin.

His name is still to this day synonymous with harmony—the
supreme synthesis of art. But it is important to remember that the
ease and spontaneity of Pushkin's harmony was not lightly achieved.

It came to him not from the mountain peaks, nor yet from the Arcadian vales, but at the cost of toil and suffering. The harmony of Pushkin is that of a civic-thinking and -feeling person.

Poetry is eternal. The art of production (as we understand it) is relatively recent, less than a hundred years old. But, in the course of its existence, it has undergone considerable changes, and has been enriched by the experiences of outstanding personalities in various fields of art. Starting as mere supervision, it came to encompass action analysis, counterpoint and polychromatic montage. Yet it continues to be an art. It cannot be dissected like a corpse, any more than harmony can be verified by algebra. Meantime the harmony of the contemporary theater has become far more complex; the simple elements have developed into more intricate, almost algebraic structures. But they will bear no fruit unless the artist's hand is impelled by the rhythmic pulse of life.

A Note on Actors and the Acting Profession

I am surprised, in discussions on the subject of theatrical production, by the arbitrary views that are sometimes expressed about the relations between the actor and the producer. Some people seem to think it their duty to defend the poor actor against the dictatorship of the producer. Critics writing about the young Moscow Art Theater complained bitterly about the tyranny of the producer restricting the freedom of artistic creativity, declaring that it was no mere chance that this theater had no oustanding figures. But we know now that they were in fact legion!

The actor is an executive artist; it would be a mistake to think that this description is derogatory. Would it be belittling Galina Ulanova to say that every movement she made was designed by a skilled choreographer? She was a consummate professional precisely because she had the ability to master these movements and use them as a vehicle for the expression of her own personality, soul and spirit, her experience of life and creative urge. And theatrical productions—of this I am increasingly convinced—must be staged like a ballet, with the same attention to plastic and spatial problems. For there are occasions when the turn of a head can change the whole tableau.

Many good productions are spoiled by the fact that the actors have not been taught the importance of the spatial dimension. The producer will design tableaux intended to convey the essence of the psychological situation and the meaning of the work as a whole. But you have only to move a couple of feet to one side, and the whole effect will be destroyed, just as it is in a modern painting if the position of even one figure is changed. Professor Alpatov, for instance, demonstrated that the composition in the pictures of Velasquez is based on a precise geometrical structure, which must be observed in every detail.

But comparisons such as these with the ballet or painting are not welcomed by those actors who fail to appreciate the true professionalism of the dancer, the painter or the musician. The trouble is that it is easy, in the theater, to cover up professional shortcomings. When a singer fails to reach top B, or a ballerina is unable to perform thirty-two fouettés, it is obvious that their technique is at fault and, therefore, that they are insufficiently qualified. Why is it that such a lamentably amateurish attitude exists only on the theater? An actor who, metaphorically speaking, is unable to perform 32 fouettés or reach the top note, will often try to justify himself at length by saying that he does not need to, and that all this has been thought up by the producer. The very same actor, who has been rushing desperately around offering his services to cinema and television studios, ready to take up any pose and do anything asked of him, only to fit in with the three meters of film he is allocated, and submit meekly when half his footage is cut out in the editing, will complain, when he comes to the theater, that the demands of the producer stifle his creativity.

In point of fact, it is the other way around: an actor cannot be creative without the controlling hand of the producer. I myself was for many years an actor in the Art Theater, and know very well how egocentric and vain actors can be. I saw so many of them, though talented, turn into repetitious stilted puppets, pitiful imitations of themselves! There is a poem by A. Voznesensky which contains the following line: "The urge to murder is akin to the urge to create." It might be said that the urge to self-destruction is innate in many actors.

The actor who concentrates exclusively on himself begins to eat himself away, just as poison eats away the stomach. The only solution is to break the circle of the actor's individualism and amateurish self-sufficiency, and to place him in a broader context. This is exactly what the producer exists for: to indicate all the ways in which man is connected with the world around him and do away with the arbitrary individualism of the actor; the art of production was established when it became clear that a stage performance is not merely the sum of the images created by the performers, but something of more universal significance. However, no living drama has ever come into existence except through the work of someone with his own individual aesthetic principles. This was true of the drama of Sophocles, of Shakespeare, and of Stanislavsky.

The theater cannot exist without a highly organized overall artistic structure. The argument adduced by N. Tolchenova in Volume 6 of the journal *Teatr*, to the effect that "something which is diverse can never become monolithic" is, in my opinion, extremely naive. Moreover, life itself, at every turn, is "diverse," a combination of the tragic and the comic. And we see the same thing, surely, in the theater of the Renaissance and the Middle Ages, the work of Shakespeare and Pushkin. As Marx wrote, one of the special features of English tragedy—so offensive to French sensibilities that Voltaire even dubbed Shakespeare a "drunken savage"—is the fantastic mixture of the exalted and the base, the terrifying and the comic, of heroism and buffoonery. Drama is constructed of struggle and contradiction. The dialectic of the theater consists in the ability to compress all the diversity of life into synthesized images. This is yet another reason why the work of the producer is necessary in order to give a performance unity.

Another accusation still levelled against producers is that, in their search for technical niceties, they tend to forget all the true spiritual values of life; it is true, of course, that producers are of all kinds— they differ as much as actors do. But in art, there exists nothing without form; form is the only means for the expression of truth in art. For me, the feeling of the theater is inseparable from the feeling of life. I became a producer precisely because, acting in "naturalist" plays about everyday life, I was unable to lie. My career as an actor was fairly successful, until one day I began to ask myself: what am I, a grown man, doing here, smearing my face with make-up and painting my lips? And I was in despair. I was ashamed to find myself in the midst of a lot of door-mats representing grass, dusty papier-mâché "bushes," and backdrops daubed with land-scapes. But the real sky, I thought, is a thousand times better than the sky shown in the theater, real grass immeasurably better than floor-cloths, and the trees shown on the backdrops bear no resemblance to real trees, about whose sticky spring leaves Dostoevsky wrote. In fact, though, it was not a question of make-up and stage properties; it had become evident to me that what was needed was metaphors, not imitations and images, and not copies either. In other words, to proclaim the truth, in the theater, we must be able to invent. Man does not engage in mimicry, like a monkey; he approaches the world not as a copyist, but as a man of action, a transformer and a creater.

"Verisimilitude is still regarded as the main factor in the creation of dramatic art. But what if it is demonstrated that the very essence of dramatic art excludes verisimilitude?" asked Pushkin, adding that there is a more important factor—audacity, "the audacity of invention, conception of the overall plan impregnated with creative thought, the audacity of Shakespeare, Dante, Pushkin in *Boris Godunov*, Goethe in *Faust*, Molière in *Tartuffe*."

Indeed, the genius of Shakespeare's works lies in the fact that they are at once intensely poetic and exceptionally realistic. Realistic, thanks not to external verisimilitude, but to the use of metaphors reflecting, in concentrated form, the essence of life. Thus, when presenting *Hamlet*, I decided that there must be no elaborate décor, such as to split the play up into different scenes; the dynamism of the action must be preserved. So, with the artist D. Borovski, we opted for the curtain, which constitutes the only "setting" for the performance. This traditional stage prop is, for us, metaphorical—it can serve to indicate the theatrical character of the performance; for the king, it represents the official, ceremonial curtain; it may be the curtain behind which plotting goes on. . . . In the scene of the revolt of Laertes, sounds of shouts and the clash of arms come from behind the curtain, and the audience is left to imagine for itself the crowd that is not shown on the stage.

I do not understand how any producer can set to work without first explaining to actors how he intends to proceed, any more than a painter could be unable to say how he intended to produce a picture—in oils, water-color, or Indian ink. The actor also has to know what technique he is to use, what the purpose of the production is, and what problems he is to help the audience to solve. The producer's plan, far from hampering the actor, helps him to find the only true and correct mood. Can it be said, for instance, in the play *Dawns Are Quiet Here* that the production stifles the actors? On the contrary—I would even go so far as to say that all the artistic and technical problems are solved in such a way that the work of the actors is thrown into sharp relief, which leaves them freer to establish direct contact with their audience.

The producer's plan must, of course, take account of the personality of every actor and the nature of the theater. The execution of the plan is by no means a mechanical process—the gap between theory and practice is immense. Rehearsing is a creative process, in the course of which the original plan becomes modified, and much that appeared in the abstract to be ideal is subsequently discarded. The producer's imagination is creative only in so far as it produces circumstances conducive to the success of the actor's work. It is for this reason that I readily accept—and I think it would be stupid not to—any actor's suggestions which are calculated to facilitate the true representation of the general ideas contained in the production in question. It is of course impossible to think of everything beforehand, but I do consider it essential to inform the actors, from the outset, what general ideas the work contains, and on what aesthetic principles the production is to be based. The actors need to know in which style each particular spectacle is to produced—for after all, Ostrovsky and Esenin cannot be played in the same way. In working on Esenin's *Pugachev*, for instance, recordings of the poet's voice and also all the metaphors with which his verse is so extraordinarily rich helped us to find the right overall emotional atmosphere for the production. But the artistic style in which to present the play did not become clear until the stage setting had been designed, with a step slope on which it was impossible to stand upright leading to the executioner's block. This made it impossible to use a realistic style.

My deal has been, if possible, to work out all the details of staging before starting to rehearse. For *Hamlet*, a heavy curtain of woven wool was laboriously manufactured, and light fabric was to be used for the stage décor—but this failed to set the right mood for the actors. In the case of *Mother* likewise, the real work on the production could not begin until the general ideological and artistic principles had been decided on: the contrast between Tsarist Russia and its old repressive machinery—the militia—on the one hand, and on the other the force of the people opposed to oppression, between the state machine and the cowering crowd which subsequently, in an outburst of fury, turns on its oppressors and drives them off.

As soon as the actors playing the parts of Pavel, Nilovna and Nakhodka found themselves facing a concrete opponent, they grasped the true significance of the struggle; it then became possible to compose the precise psychological portrait of each character. The necessity for composing such a portrait had long since been demonstrated by the Art Theater. For instance, such of Kedrov's productions as *The Fruits of Enlightenment* and *Long-Distance Reconnaissance* contained subtle psychological portraits. Kedrov was at that time applying Stanislavsky's last discovery, generally known as the "method of physical actions." But when Kedrov attempted to produce Shakespeare by this same method, the result was, in my opinion, not a success; no method has absolute value.

All the good productions I can remember have been constructed with the utmost precision. It cannot be said, surely, that the extremely careful composition of the roles in the *Blue Bird* or *The Ardent Heart* prevented the outstanding actors to give a brilliant performance? This is so obvious that I hesitate even to mention it.

In a general way, I see no point in comparing the Art Theater acting tradition with that of other theaters. It would be dishonest to ignore the history of the Art Theater and the work of Stanislavsky; but only the mediocre can take his theories as absolute dogma. To do so is to destroy the living essence of Stanislavsky, which was based on development and constant renewal. Stanislavsky maintained that an actor needs to learn his trade afresh every five years. Why has this been forgotten?

The repertoire of the Moscow Art Theater in the early days consisted of the works of Chekhov, Gorky, Tolstoy, Ibsen, Maeterlinck, Shakespeare, Andreev . . . a remarkably broad and colorful range. What are the reasons for the choice of such very diverse authors? The main one was the search for vehicles for the application of new styles and different artistic techniques. On very many occasions, it will be remembered, Stanislavsky was too miserable and upset even to come to the theater. And why did he found the Studio? It was in order to stimulate the actors' professional activities and spur them to strive to renew their methods. There are some critis who, while calling themselves ardent enthusiasts of dramatic art, in fact encourage it to become fossilized, thus running counter to the directives of the party and the state. After remarking that "there exists in our country considerable numbers of works uninteresting in regard to subject and unremarkable in regard to form," L. I. Brezhnev,

219

in his address to the XXIVth congress of the party, proclaimed that: "We are in favor of encouraging artistic research, giving free rein to individuality, fostering talent and making room for a variety of styles and forms evolved on the basis of the method of socialist realism."

Those who profess to take up the defense of down-trodden actors are in fact, in many instances, profoundly indifferent to their fate. And very many talented young people are transformed, in a few years, into mediocre hacks. Why? Simply because producers neither make sufficient demands on them nor insist that they perfect their professional skill. To imagine that actors can work without a producer to guide them is like saying, "Let us go into the forest and look for something there." In order even to look for mushrooms, we have first to know that some kinds grow on tree stumps, others on grass. We also have to know where the North is, the South, the East and the West; otherwise we may lose the way. The producer is the man who has a compass, indicating the meaning and style of work. There is absolutely no question in the producer's guidance turning the actor into a puppet: its purpose is simply to prevent the actor from going astray, and to enable him to seek in the right direction.

We are living in a stormy period, marked by sweeping changes and innumerable historical events. Incidentally, I am becoming increasingly aware of an unexpected theater problem—that of the intermission. An hour of the performance has already passed, and then comes the interval. If there were a television set in the foyer, the spectators would be able to see the latest news about the latest space flight, or events of world-shaking importance. How, after this, can he be expected to believe in the importance and reality of the work being presented on stage? In the light of this, attempts to differentiate between the actor and the producer appear absurd and unimportant. It is essential not to split up the living theater, whose unity derives from the fact that its various components all have different functions, each of them vitally important. The main concern is not this. We must set ourselves even higher goals, ensure the constant renewal of professional skills, avoid dwelling on the past, and throw open the theatre to the winds of change, so that it may give a true and vivid reflection of the profundity and complexity of the problems of the contemporary world.

(Translated from Russian by Aline B. Werth.)

Index

Abalkin, N., 57
Abramov, F., 20, 84, 157
Akhmadulina (poet), 51, 56
Akhmatova, Anna, 53
Akimov (director), 6, 158
Aksenov, Vasily, 51, 52, 53, 58, 130, 150
Aleksandrov (composer), 12
Alexander I, Czar, 139
Alive, 30, 67, 84, 167
American Repertory Theater, xv, 175, 176, 184
Andreev, Boris, 44
Andropov, Yuri, 33, 114, 137, 146, 147, 150, 152–53, 167, 169
Anikst, Aleksandr, 57
Antipov, Fyodor, 115, 117, 120, 121–22
Anti-Worlds, 67
Appleyard, Brian, 153, 168
Arbuzov, A., 45
Arena Stage, xv, 173, 174, 175, 182, 183
"Argument about Man," 162
Ascent, 119
Associated Press, 177, 184, 185
At the Bottom, 155, 158–63, 175

Babel's *Sunset*, 172, 174
Bagritsky, Eduard, 72
Bagritsky, Vsevolod, 72, 73
Ballad of a Soldier, 119
Barrault, Jean-Louis, 19
Batalov, Alexsey, 119
BBC, 153, 184
Beckett, Samuel, 74, 169
Beethoven, Ludwig von, 172
Benackova, Gabriela, xv
Benefit Performance, 20
Bensenev, 37
Berg, Alan, xii, 176
Bergman, Ingmar, 174

Beriya, Lavrenty, 41
Birman, 37
Black Snow: A Theatrical Novel, 151
Blue Bird, 36
Boell, Heinrich, 19
Bogden, David, 172
Bolshoy Theater, 41, 93, 149
Bondarchuk, Sergey, 119
Boris Godunov, xvi, 5, 62, 137–44, 177
    banning of, xvi, 39, 67, 105, 137–38, 143–44, 151, 152, 167, 169, 177
    costumes in, 141
    Taganka rehearsal for, 140–43, 178
Borovsky, David, xi, 8, 75, 79–80, 94, 154, 167, 170, 174
Bortnik, Ivan, 117, 119, 141, 160, 161
Boston Globe, The, 176
Boyadzhiev, G., 47, 57
Brecht, Bertolt, 6, 19, 46, 47, 80, 147, 148
Brezhnev, Leonid, 48, 130, 137, 146, 147, 148
Brook, Peter, xiv, 169
Brustein, Robert, xv
Bukovsky, V., 176, 186
Bulgakov, Mikhail, xiii, 3, 24, 28, 93, 151, 174, 176, 187
Burian, Yuri, 46

Caine XVIII, 47
Castro, Fidel, 19
Chekhov, Mikhail, 37, 158, 185, 189
    The Three Sisters, 100, 101, 103, 104
Chernenko, K. U., 151–52, 169, 171
Chernyshevsky, Nikolai, 5
Cherry Orchard, The, 175, 185
Chicago Lyric Opera, xiii

221

Chukhray, 54
Comandarm 2, 40
Compassion for Life, 38
Comrade, Believe, 6, 20, 67, 139
Covent Garden, xv, 174
Crane, Richard, 172
Crime and Punishment, xiv–xv, 21,
    67, 80, 92–99, 110, 111, 171
    comparison of Budapest and Mos-
        cow productions of, 95–99
    London production of, 152, 153,
        167–68, 169
    U.S. production of, 173, 174,
        175, 182, 183, 184
"Crosses Yuri Lyubimov Bears,
    The," 153
Cyrano de Bergerac, 42

Dawns Are Quiet Here, The, 23,
    79–83, 141
Death of Tarelkin, 40
Demichev, Pyotr, 3, 114, 151, 153,
    169, 170
Demidova, Alla, 18, 46, 109, 115,
    119, 125, 175, 180, 185
Devil, The, 94
Diaghelev, Sergei, 156
Diky, 6, 37, 39
Dr. Zhivago, 45
Does a Person Really Need a Lot? 46
Dostoevsky, Fyodor, 45, 92, 95,
    153, 168, 189
Dunaev, V., 155, 170, 189
Dunaevsky, Isaac, 12, 39, 44
Duncan, Isadora, 37
Duppak, Nikolay Lukyanovich, 101,
    177
Durenmatt, F., 74
Duvale, Jacques, 38
Dvoretsky, Ignat, 189
Dykhovichny, I., 28
Dzhabrailov, R., 18, 115, 121–22

Efros, Anatoly, 47, 155–63, 170,
    175, 180–81, 182, 186–90
Egor Bulychev, 44
Ehrenburg, Ilia, 53, 54, 56

Eisenstein, Sergei, xii, 41, 158
Erdman, Nikolay Robertovich, xi,
    xiii, 28, 41, 45, 47, 56
Esenin, Sergei, see Yesenin, Sergei
Esslin, Martin, xvi
Eternally Living, 45
Eugene Onegin, 175, 185
Exchange, The, 30

Fadeev, A., 42
Fallen and the Living, The, 67–73, 127
Farada, S., 26
Feast, Michael, 172
Feast During the Plague, 174
Fedin, K., 44
Fidelio, 172
Filatov (actor), 115
Filatov, Pavel, 153, 168
First Studio of the Moscow Art
    Theatre, 37
Fomenko, P., 74
Fonda, Henry, 20
Forest, The, 6
Freedman, John, 176
French Communist Party, 171
Friends of the Theater, 147
From the Life of Fyodor Kuzkin, 20
Furtseva, Ekaterina, 3, 52–53
Fyodor Kuzkin, 146

Gabrilovich (playwright), 40
Gagarin, Yuri, 19, 46
Galich, A., 45, 46, 56
Galileo, see Life of Galileo
Gielgud, John, 169
Glezer, A., 145
Gogol, Nikolai, xiii, 6, 187, 189
Good Woman of Setzuan, The, 6, 19,
    20, 46, 47, 56, 67, 127
Gorbachev, Mikhail, 175, 176, 178,
    180, 181, 183, 185
Gorbachev, Raisa, 181
Gorbanevskaya, N., 180
Gorky, Maksim, 44, 177
    At the Bottom, 155, 156, 158, 159,
        160, 161
Grabbe, A., 163

Graf, N., 170
Grand Opera, Paris, 149, 174
Grossman, Vasily, 51
Grotowski, Jerzy, xiii
Gubenko, Nikolay, 18, 115, 117,
    119, 141–42, 143, 154, 155,
    170
  as Taganka director, 176, 177, 178
Gudzenko (poet), 68
"Guitar Is What I Have, A," 117
Gutierrez, Angel, 177

Habima Theater, 172, 174
Hamlet, 6, 25, 30, 67, 79–80, 109,
    115, 116, 118, 122, 124–25,
    127–29, 141, 146
Harvard University, 173, 185
Heart of a Dog, 176
Hochhuth, Rolf, 74
House on the Embankment, The (Tri-
    fonov), xiii, 181
  performances of, xiii, 5, 22, 23,
    43, 80, 120, 142–43, 146, 150
  rehearsal of, 8–17
How Steel Hardens, 6, 40, 158
Humanité, 93
"Hunting for Wolves," 150, 169

Idiot, The, 45
"I don't like . . .", 128
Index of Censorship, 168
*In Memory of Vysotsky, see Poet Vladi-
    mir Vysotsky, The*
Innokentievna, Elizaveta, 19
Inspector General, The, 6, 40, 158
Investigation, The, 74
Ionesco, Eugene, 74
Irkutsk Story, The, 45
Italian Central Committee, 149–50
Ivan the Terrible, 158
Ivashev, V., 119
Izvestia, 159, 177–78

Janáček, Leos, xv, 174
Jenufa, 174
Jerusalem University, 177
Julian Beck theater, xiii

Kachalov (actor), 36
Kalokagatii, 29
Kapitsa, P. L., 147
Keepers of the Keys, The, 75
Kern (actor), 95
KGB, 173
Khmelnitsky, B., 18, 46, 68, 115,
    120
Khrushchev, Nikita, 44, 45, 46, 48,
    51, 53–54, 55, 151
Khutsiev, 54
King Lear, 143
Kirill Izvekov, 44
Kogan, Pavel, 68, 69, 70, 71, 72
Kohout, Pavel, 75
Kontinent, 155, 167, 173, 180
Kopchak, S., 174
Kornilova, E., 90
Kremlin Chimes, The, 64
Krymova, N., 127
Kuban Cossacks, 43–44
Kulchitsky, Mikhail, 68, 70, 71, 72,
    73
Kunads, Reiner, 174
Kundera, Milan, 75
Kunglig Dramatiska teatern, 174
Kunyaev, Stanislav, 130–31
Kurosawa, 19
Kuznetsova, I., 68, 76, 81

Ladynina, M., 44
La Scala, 149, 172
Latinovich, Zoltan, 21
Law, Alma, xv
Lazaridis, Stephanos, 170, 172
Lebedev, M., 26
Lenin, V. I., 35, 39, 145, 147
Lenin Komsomol Theater, 47
Lenkomsomol Theater, 158, 188
Life of Fyodor Kuzkin (Alive), The, 3,
    67
Life of Galileo, The, 6, 110, 127,
    147–48
Lilliom, 94
Listen! 30, 67
Literaturnaya Gazeta, 93, 155–57,
    160–61

Little Tragedies, 174
Livanov, Boris, 52–53
Living Theater, Judith Malina's, xiii
London *Evening Standard*, 169
London *Times*, 153, 168, 184
London *Times Literary Supplement*, 172
Lower Depths, The, see At the Bottom
Lulu, xii–xiii, 176
Luzhsky (actor), 36
Lyric Opera House, 176
Lyric Theater, 153, 167, 168
Lyubimov, David (brother), 34, 35, 36, 178
Lyubimov, Katalin (wife), 92, 167, 168–69, 177, 184
Lyubimov, Natalia (sister), 34, 36
Lyubimov, Petya (son), 21–22, 92, 167, 183
Lyubimov, Yuri Petrovich:
  as an actor, 33, 37, 38, 41–47
  after the Taganka Theater, 167–86
  The Algebra of Harmony, 202–14
  as *auteur* director, xiv, 20
  before the Taganka Theater, 33–47
  as Communist Party member, 45
  confrontations with actors and audience, xv, 16–17
  a conversation with, 18–23
  description of, 18
  as a father, 21–22, 92, 183
  House on the Embankment rehearsal and, 8–17
  Israeli citizenship, 176
  leaves Taganka Theater, 105, 152–54
  loses Soviet citizenship, 171, 177
  A Note on Actors and the Acting Profession, 214–20
  return to Moscow, 177, 178, 181–86
  on role of the actor, xii
  selection of works by, xiii, xiv
  Soviet government and, xv–xvi, 3–4, 47, 67, 92–93, 148–54,
    167, 168, 169–71, 175, 177–78, 183–84, 185
  transfer to Taganka Theater, 47
  see also specific works directed by Lyubimov
Lyubov Yarovaya, 64, 65

Maeterlinck, Maurice, 36
Maksimov, V., 176, 180, 186
Malaya Bronnaya, 188–89
Maltsev, Elizar, 54
Maly Theatre, 39, 65
"Managers of the Spiritual Works," 156–57
Mandata, The, 45
Man with a Rifle, 39
Marinsky Theatre, 138
Markov, P. A., 33, 44
Marriage, 187
Massoviet Theater, 39
Master and the Margarita, The, (Bulgakov), xiii, xv, 3–4, 22, 24
  Lyubimov's comments on production of, 30
  opera based on, 174
  performances of, xiii, xv, 3–4, 22, 24–30, 93, 141, 146, 158, 175, 176, 184
Mayakovsky, 6
Mayakovsky, Vladimir, xiii, 30, 55, 67
Mayorov, Kolya, 68, 69, 70, 71, 72
Meany, George, 145
Metropole, 130
Meyerhold, Vsevolod, xii, xiii, xvi, 5, 6, 18, 19, 39–41, 45, 46, 64, 79, 158, 172
  Boris Godunov production, 39, 138
  Soviet government and, 39–40, 179
  Stanislavsky and, 40–41, 58
Meyerhold Theater, 39–40, 138, 163, 179
Mikhailova, G., 158–59
Mikhoels, 6
Miller, Arthur, xvi, 19, 74
Mironov, Andrey, 189

Misanthrope, The, 175, 181
Molière, 30, 147, 148, 181
Molière, 187
Molnar, Ferents, 94
Monde, 176, 185
Morozov, Savva, 156
Moscow Art Theatre, 36, 39, 100, 138, 156, 158, 179
Moskovskie Novosti, 177, 186
Moskvin (actor), 36
Mother, 6, 23, 177
Mozart and Salieri, 45
Mozhaev, Boris, 3, 20, 30, 67
Mrozek, 74
Much Ado About Nothing, 41, 42
Municipal Theater of Bologna, 171
Musorgsky, M., 174
Myagkova, I., 159
"My Hamlet," 128–29

Namestnick (Deputy), 74
Napolitano, Giorgio, 149–50
Nash Sovremennik, 130–31
National Theater, Paris, 172
Neizvestny, Ernst, 51, 157, 176, 186
Nekrasov, 157
Nemirovich-Danchenko, V.I., 40, 138
New Economic Policy (NEP), 24, 35
New York Times, 171
NKVD Ensemble of Song and Dance, 41
Nono, L., 149
Novoye Russkoe Slovo, 176
Novy Mir, 46, 51

October Revolution, 18, 33, 35, 147
Odeon theater, 185
Okhlopkov, 6
Okudzhava, Bard Bulat, xiii, 56, 80, 116
Okun, Leonid Aleksandrovich, 65–66
Olesh, Yuri, 37
Olivier, Laurence, 19, 169

One Day in the Life of Ivan Denisovich (Solzhenitsyn), 46
One Life, 40
Open Theater, Joseph Chaikin's, xiii
Ostrovsky, N., 6, 20, 40, 158
Othello, 188

Papanov, Anatoly, 189
Passion According to St. Matthew, 172
Pasternak, Boris, 33, 37, 45, 124
Pesko, Zoltan, 174
Plotnikov, Boris, 119
Poet Vladimir Vysotsky, The, 67, 114–26, 140, 147, 152, 154, 167
Pogodin, N., 39
Pekrovsky, Dmitry, 140
Politseymako, M., 81, 104, 160
Portnov, Lev Matveevich, 147
Possessed, The, 151, 168, 172
Potemkin, A., 183
Pravda, 3–4, 27, 29, 42–43, 47, 92–93, 148–49, 158, 162
Princess Turandot, 39, 56
Prokofiev, S., 138
Pugachev (Yesenin), 5, 6, 67, 110, 127
Pushkin, Aleksander, 20, 45, 174
  Boris Godunov, xvi, 5, 39, 62, 67, 105, 137–44
Pyriev, I., 43

Queen of Spades, The, 149

Rabin, O., 145
Radomyslensky, 38–39
Rappoport, I., 45
Reed, John, xiii, 5, 58, 147
Remizova, A., 45
Remnik, David, 178
Richelieu, Cardinal, 148
Rigoletto, xv, 170
Robinson Crusoe, 42
Romeo and Juliet, 45
Roninson, G., 18, 76
Rostropovich, Mstislav, 157
Rozhdestvensky, Robert, 130, 132

Rozov, V., 45, 155
Rudnitsky, K., 68–69, 96–99
Rush Hour, 75–78
Russkaya Mysl, 184
Ryazanov, Eldar, 129
Rzhevsky, Dr. Nicholas, 151, 167

Sabinin, Aleksandr, 9–10, 18, 26, 76
*Sacred Fire, The (Le feu sacre: Souvenirs
    d'une vie de theatre)* (Lyubi-
    mov), xii
Sailor's Silence, 45
Saint Exupéry, Antoine de, 33
Sakharov, Andrey Dmitrievich, 146
Salammbo, 174
Samoylov, D., 68, 69, 72, 73
Savchenko, A., 76
Sayko, N., 81
Second Moscow Art Theatre, 37–39
Shchukin, Boris, 39, 40
Sellars, Peter, xvi
Semenov, V., 161
Shadrin, Vladimir, 154, 170
Shakespeare, William, xii, 41, 124,
    128, 189
Shapovalov (actor), 18, 27–28, 81,
    119
Shatskaya, N., 18, 29, 81
Shcherbakov, D., 18, 76
Shchukin Theatre Institute, 6, 46
Shepitko, Larisa, 119
Shestakov, V., 138
Shnitke, A., 149
Sholokhov, Mikhail, 54
Shostakovich, D. D., 41
Shukshin, Vasily, 119, 129, 157
Sidorenko, T., 77
Simonov, E., 45
Simonov, Konstantin, 30, 47, 56
Simonov, Ruben, 39, 42
Skomororokh, 138–39
Slavina, Z., 18, 27, 28, 46, 160
Slutsky, Boris, 71–72
Smekhov, Veniamin, 11, 15, 18, 26,
    76, 115, 119, 125, 154, 170,
    177
Smirnov, Yuri, 26, 28, 46

Solzhenitsyn, Aleksandr. 46, 51,
    157, 173
Songs and Poems (Vysotsky), 132
Sovetskaya Kultura, 47
Soviet Union, government of,
    47–48, 51–56, 74, 114
    art patrons in, 156–57
    banning of *Boris Godunov*, xvi, 39,
        67, 105, 137–38, 143–44,
        151, 152, 167, 169, 177
    Lyubimov and, *see* Lyubimov,
        Yuri Petrovich
    Meyerhold Theater and, 39–40,
        179
    moral opposition of theater to,
        5–6
    role of art and, 145–46
    second Moscow Art Theatre and,
        38–39
    Taganka and, *see* Taganka Theater
Sovremennik theater-studio, 45,
    156
Stalin, Joseph, 22, 33, 37, 44–45,
    46, 150, 151
Stanislavsky, K. S., xvi, 5, 36, 37,
    38–39, 46, 158
    acting system of, 46, 111, 175
    Meyerhold and, 40–41, 58
Stawinsky, Jerzy, 75
Stolper, A., 42
Strehler, Giorgio, 172
Stroeva, Marianna, 160–61
Such Love, 75
Suicide, The, 40, 45
Sunset, 172, 174
Surkov, E., 162
Suslov, Mikhail, 48, 53, 55, 148

Tabakov, O., 19, 45
Taganka Theater, 175, 177–78
    actors of, *see names of individuals*
    Efros and, *see* Efros, Anatoly
    end of, 139–63, 189–90
    Gubenko named as director of,
        176
    Lyubimov assigned to, 47
    Lyubimov leaves, 105, 152–54

Lyubimov's return visit to, 178, 181–86

new building for, 23, 101–102

origins of, 6

repertoire of, chronology of, 191–95

Soviet government and, xv, 3–4, 20, 23, 30, 105, 137–38, 146–54, 156, 167, 169, 170, 175, 179, 180, 181–82

works performed at, *see individual works*

Tairov, Alexander, 6

Tannhauser, 177, 178

Tarkovsky, Audrey, 119, 157, 171

Tartuffe, 6, 30, 67, 146, 147, 148

Tchaikovsky, Pëtr Ilich, 149, 175, 185

Teatr, 57

Teatralnaya Zhisn, 147

Teatro Comunale, xv, 170

Ten Days That Shook the World (Reed), xiii, 5, 6, 22, 47, 57–66, 67, 110, 127, 147

"The atro-prison-like étude," 130

Third Sister, The, 75

Thirteenth Chairman, The, 23

Three siters, The, 67, 100–105

Tovstonogov, Grigory, 54, 189

Trifonov, Yuri, xiii, 5, 20, 30, 38, 51, 56, 150, 157

rehearsal of *The House on the Embankment* and, 8, 10

Vysotsky obituary, 133

Tretiakov, P. M., 156, 157

Tristan and Isolde, 168, 169

Trofimov, A., 95, 97, 98

Tselikovskaya, L., 45

Turandot, or the Congress of Whitewashers, 20, 148

Tvardovsky, Andrey, 46, 51

Twelve Angry Men, 20

Under the Warm Sun of Love, 149

Union of Soviet Cinematographers, 129

Utyosov, Leonid, 13, 14

Vaktangov, Evgeny, 37, 46, 56, 172, 174

Vaktangov Theater, 6, 20, 33, 172

Lyubimov with, 39, 42, 45, 46

Valkyrie, 41

Vechernaya Moskva, 158–59

Verdi, Giuseppe, 170

Veyzovich, D., 174

Vigszinhaz Theater, 21, 93–94

Viktorovich, Leonid, 79

Vilar, John, 46

Vladi, Marina, 92, 131–32

Vlasova (actress), 15

Volkov, Fyodor, 35

Volodya (poet), 130

Voznesensky, Andrei, xiii, 51, 53, 54–55, 56, 67, 156–57

Vyazemsky, P., 138

Vysotsky, Vladimir, xi, 18, 68, 73, 92, 109–33, 146, 150, 169

collections of works of, 132

death of, 109–10, 112–13, 114, 116, 137, 150–51, 157

evaluated as a poet, 130–131, 133

as Hamlet, 127–28

last role of, 111–12

"My Hamlet," 128–29

The Poet Vladimir Vysotsky, 67, 114–26, 140, 147, 152, 154

Wagner, Richard, 41, 168, 177, 178

Waiting for Godot, 74

War Doesn't Have a Lady's Face, 175

Washington Post, 178

Weigel, Helene, 19

Weiss, Peter, 74

What Is to Be Done (Cheryshevsky), 5, 6, 23, 67

"White-Hot Bath," 122–24

Wilson, Robert, xiii, xiv

Window to the Country, A, 40

Woe From Wit, 36, 40, 54

Wooden Horses, 23, 84–91

Work Is Work, 18

Yakovlev, Egor, 186

Yakovleva, Olga, 188

Yanshin, Mikhail, 52
Yarov, N., 42
Yefremov, O., 19, 45, 51, 56
Yelanskaya (actress), 100
Yesenin, Sergei, xiii, 5, 67
Yevstigneev, E., 45
Yevtushenko, Yevgeny, xiii, 51, 53, 54, 56, 182
Yezhov, 150
Young Communist League, 36
Young Guard, The, 42

Zakharov, M., 155, 170
Zakhava, V., 42, 44

Zavadsky, Yuri, 56
Zhdanov, 53
Zhukova, Tatiana, 18, 46, 81, 86, 115, 160, 183
Zhyuraytis (conductor), 93, 149
Zolotukhin, Valery, 14, 15–17, 18, 61, 69, 115, 117–18, 119, 122–24, 154, 160, 170, 175, 185
Zoshchenko, Mikhail, 53
Zubkov, Yuri, 57, 147